ALL·OUT AVENGERS

TEACHABLE MOMENTS

EARTH'S MIGHTIEST HEROES! UNITED TO FIGHT THE FOES NO SINGLE SUPER HERO COULD WITHSTAND! STRAP IN FOR ACTION!

AVENGERS CREATED BY STAN LEE & JACK KIRBY

ALL-OUT AVENGERS: TEACHABLE MOMENTS. Contains material originally published in magazine form as ALL-OUT AVENGERS (2022) #1-5 and FREE COMIC BOOK DAY 2022: SPIDER-MAN/VENOM #1. First printing 2023. ISBN 978-1-302-94701-9. Published by MARVEL WORLDWIDE, INC., a subsidiary of MARVEL ENTERTAINMENT, LLC. OFFICE OF PUBLICATION: 1290 Avenue of the Americas, New York, NY 10104. © 2023 MARVEL No similarity between any of the names, characters, persons, and/or institutions in this book with those of any living or dead person or institution is intended, and any such similarity which may exist is purely coincidental. **Printed in the U.S.A.** KEVIN FEIGE, Chief Creative Officer; DAN BUCKLEY, President, Marvel Entertainment; DAVID BOGART, Associate Publisher & SVP of Talent Affairs; TOM BREVOORT, VP, Executive Editor; NICK LOWE, Executive Editor, VP of Content, Digital Publishing; DAVID GABRIEL, VP of Print & Digital Publishing; SVEN LARSEN, VP of Licensed Publishing; MARK ANNUNZIATO, VP of Planning & Forecasting; JEFF YOUNGQUIST, VP of Production & Special Projects; ALEX MORALES, Director of Publishing Operations; DAN EDINGTON, Director of Editorial Operations; RICKEY PURDIN, Director of Talent Relations; JENNIFER GRÜNWALD, Director of Production & Special Projects; SUSAN CRESPI, Production Manager; STAN LEE, Chairman Emeritus. For information regarding advertising in Marvel Comics or on Marvel.com, please contact Vit DeBellis, Custom Solutions & Integrated Advertising Manager, at vdebellis@marvel.com. For Marvel subscription inquiries, please call 888-511-5480. **Manufactured between 2/10/2023 and 3/14/2023 by SEAWAY PRINTING, GREEN BAY, WI, USA.**

10 9 8 7 6 5 4 3 2 1

JENNIFER GRÜNWALD
COLLECTION EDITOR

DANIEL KIRCHHOFFER
ASSISTANT EDITOR

MAIA LOY
ASSISTANT MANAGING EDITOR

LISA MONTALBANO
ASSOCIATE MANAGER, TALENT RELATION

JEFF YOUNGQUIST
VP PRODUCTION & SPECIAL PROJECTS

JAY BOWEN
BOOK DESIGNER

DAVID GABRIEL
SVP PRINT, SALES & MARKETING

C.B. CEBULSKI
EDITOR IN CHIEF

TEACHABLE MOMENTS

DEREK LANDY
WRITER

JAY LEISTEN
INKER

GREG LAND
PENCILER

FRANK D'ARMATA
COLORIST

VC's CORY PETIT
LETTERER

MARTIN BIRO
ASSISTANT EDITOR

GREG LAND & FRANK D'ARMATA
COVER ART

ANNALISE BISSA
ASSOCIATE EDITOR

TOM BREVOORT
EDITOR

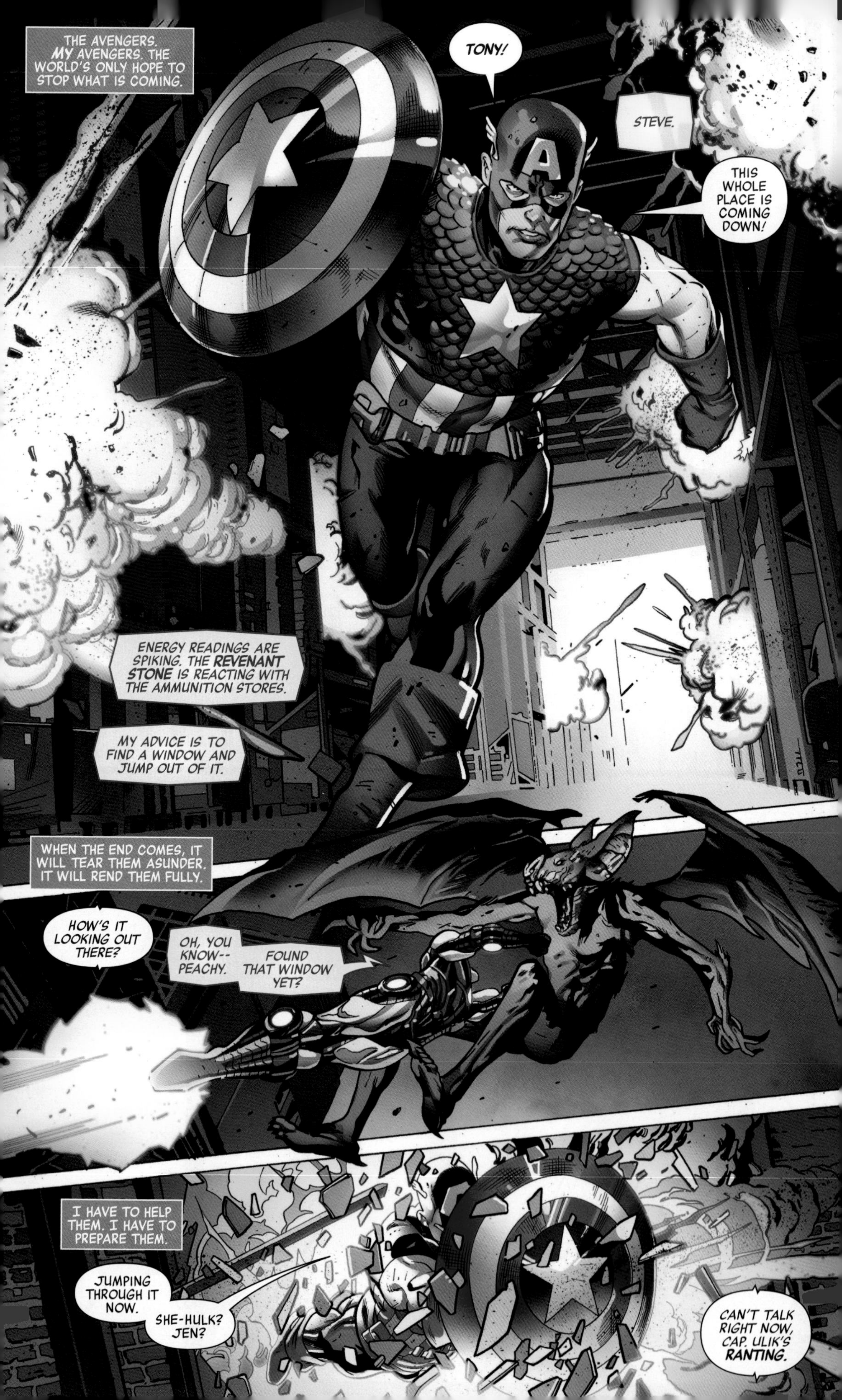

THE AVENGERS. MY AVENGERS. THE WORLD'S ONLY HOPE TO STOP WHAT IS COMING.
TONY!
STEVE.
THIS WHOLE PLACE IS COMING DOWN!
ENERGY READINGS ARE SPIKING. THE REVENANT STONE IS REACTING WITH THE AMMUNITION STORES.
MY ADVICE IS TO FIND A WINDOW AND JUMP OUT OF IT.
WHEN THE END COMES, IT WILL TEAR THEM ASUNDER. IT WILL REND THEM FULLY.
HOW'S IT LOOKING OUT THERE?
OH, YOU KNOW-- PEACHY.
FOUND THAT WINDOW YET?
I HAVE TO HELP THEM. I HAVE TO PREPARE THEM.
JUMPING THROUGH IT NOW.
SHE-HULK? JEN?
CAN'T TALK RIGHT NOW, CAP. ULIK'S RANTING.

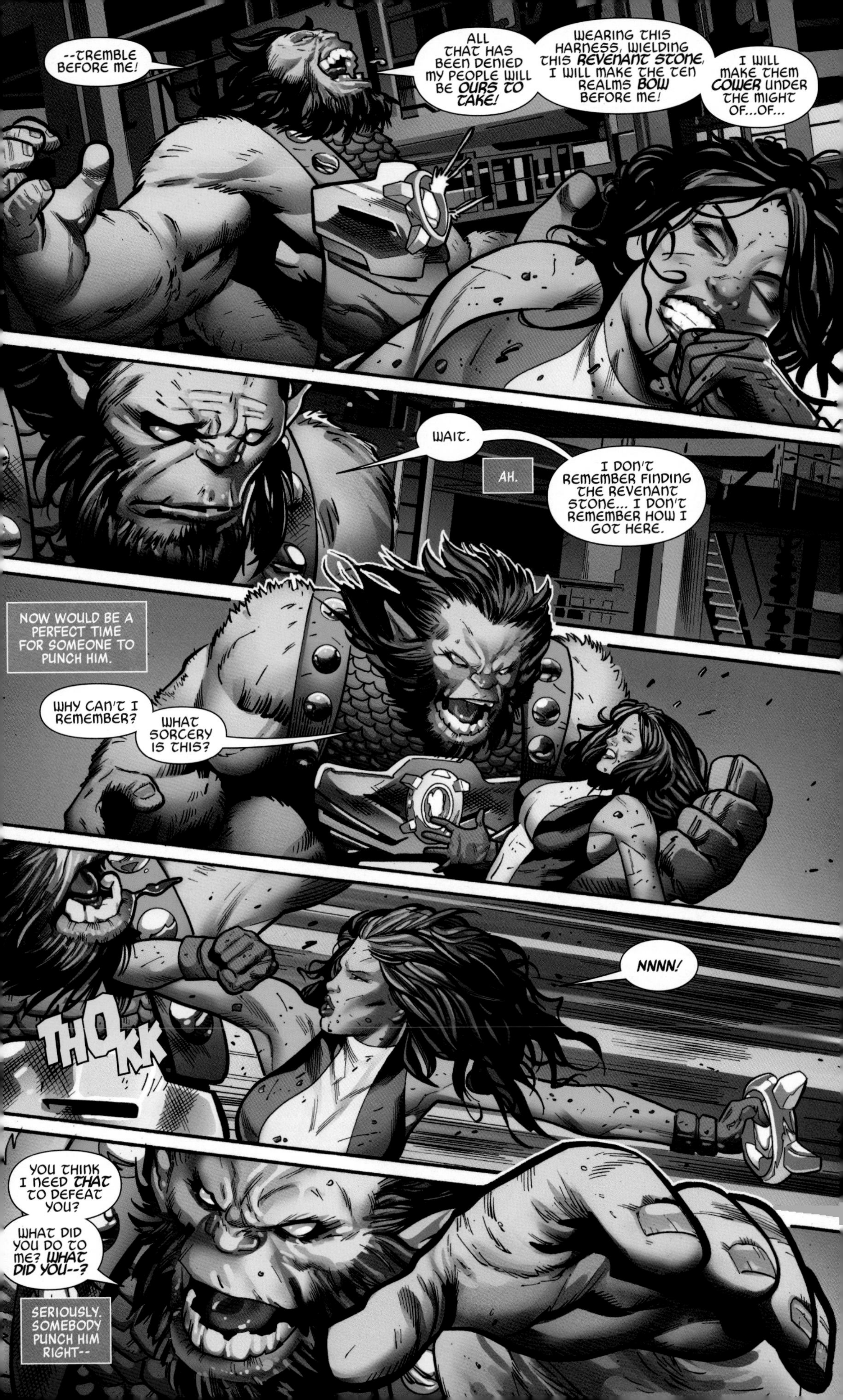

--TREMBLE BEFORE ME!
ALL THAT HAS BEEN DENIED MY PEOPLE WILL BE OURS TO TAKE!
WEARING THIS HARNESS, WIELDING THIS REVENANT STONE, I WILL MAKE THE TEN REALMS BOW BEFORE ME!
I WILL MAKE THEM COWER UNDER THE MIGHT OF...OF...
WAIT.
AH.
I DON'T REMEMBER FINDING THE REVENANT STONE... I DON'T REMEMBER HOW I GOT HERE.
NOW WOULD BE A PERFECT TIME FOR SOMEONE TO PUNCH HIM.
WHY CAN'T I REMEMBER?
WHAT SORCERY IS THIS?
NNNN!
THOKK
YOU THINK I NEED THAT TO DEFEAT YOU?
WHAT DID YOU DO TO ME? WHAT DID YOU--?
SERIOUSLY. SOMEBODY PUNCH HIM RIGHT--

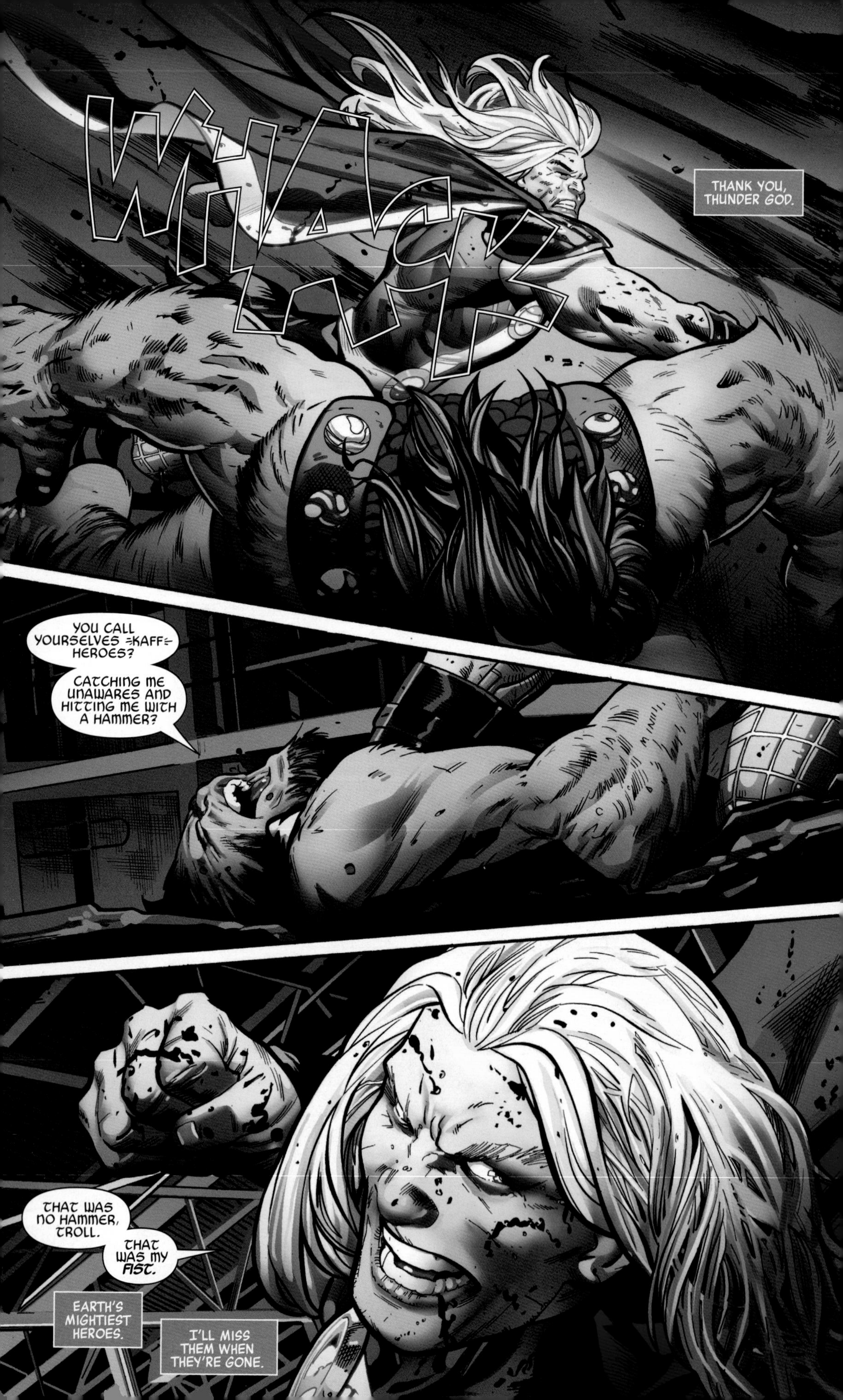
WHACK
THANK YOU, THUNDER GOD.
YOU CALL YOURSELVES =KAFF= HEROES?
CATCHING ME UNAWARES AND HITTING ME WITH A HAMMER?
THAT WAS NO HAMMER, TROLL.
THAT WAS MY FIST.
EARTH'S MIGHTIEST HEROES.
I'LL MISS THEM WHEN THEY'RE GONE.

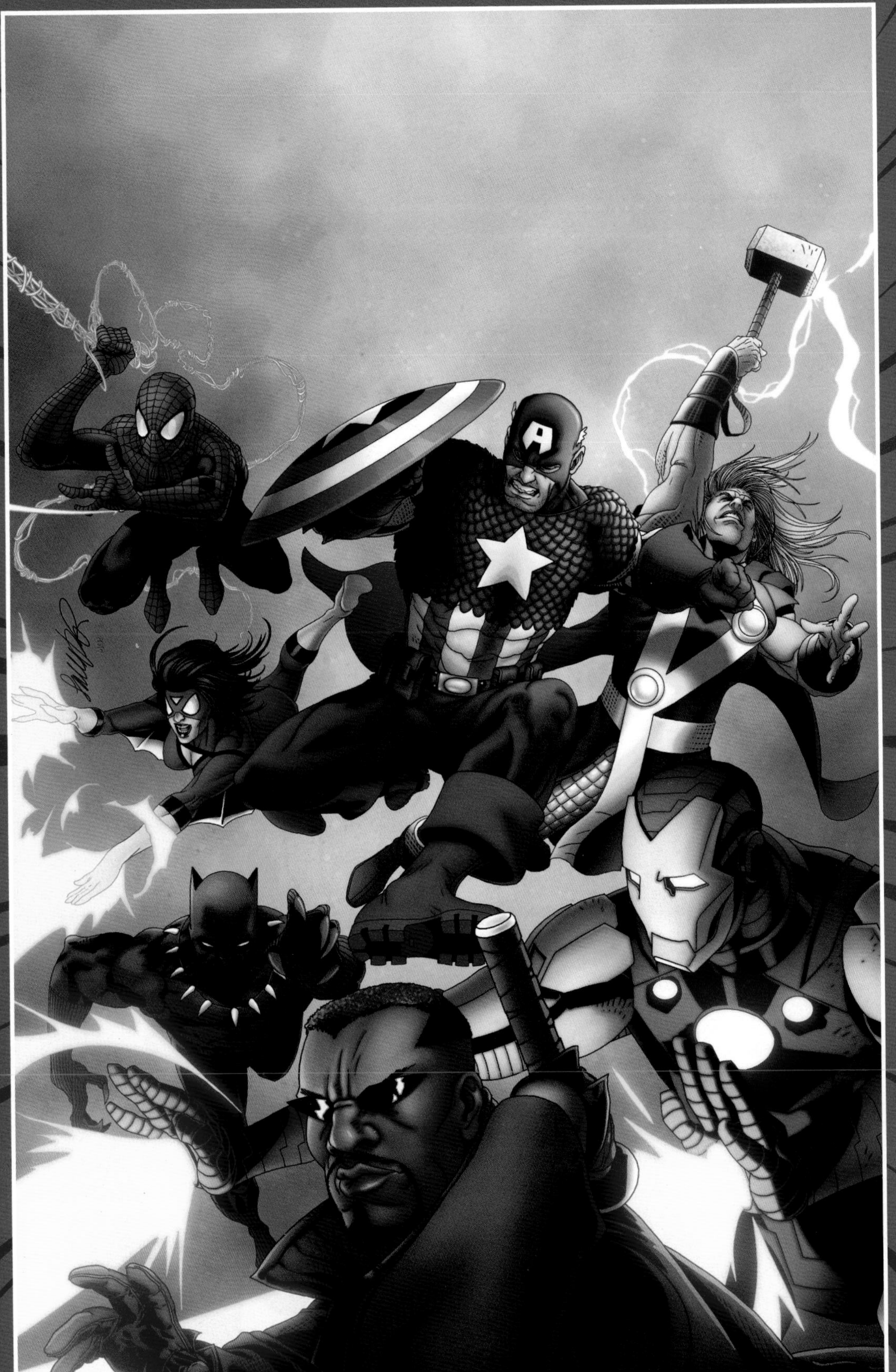

SALVADOR LARROCA & MORRY HOLLOWELL
#1 VARIANT

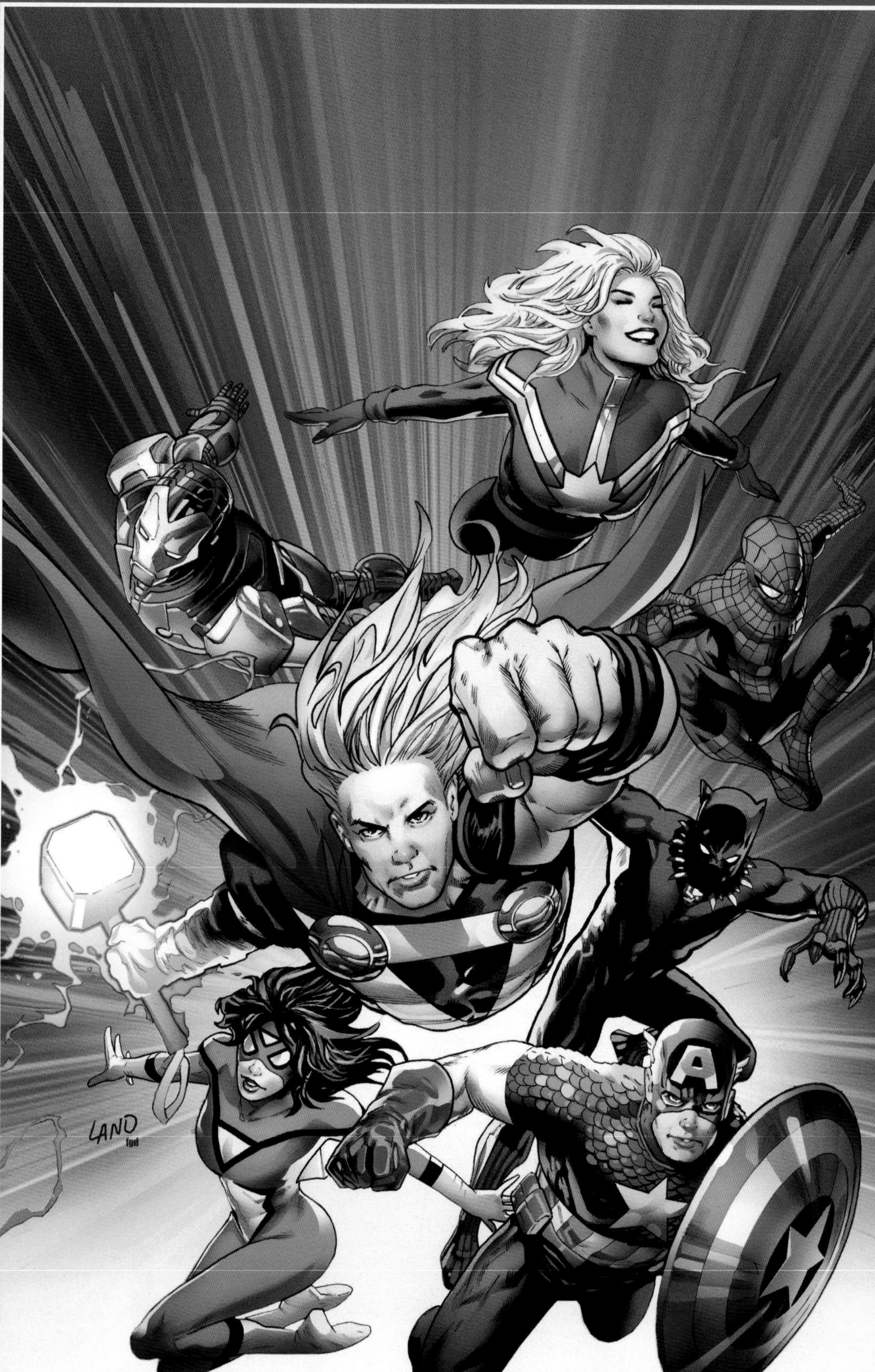
LAND

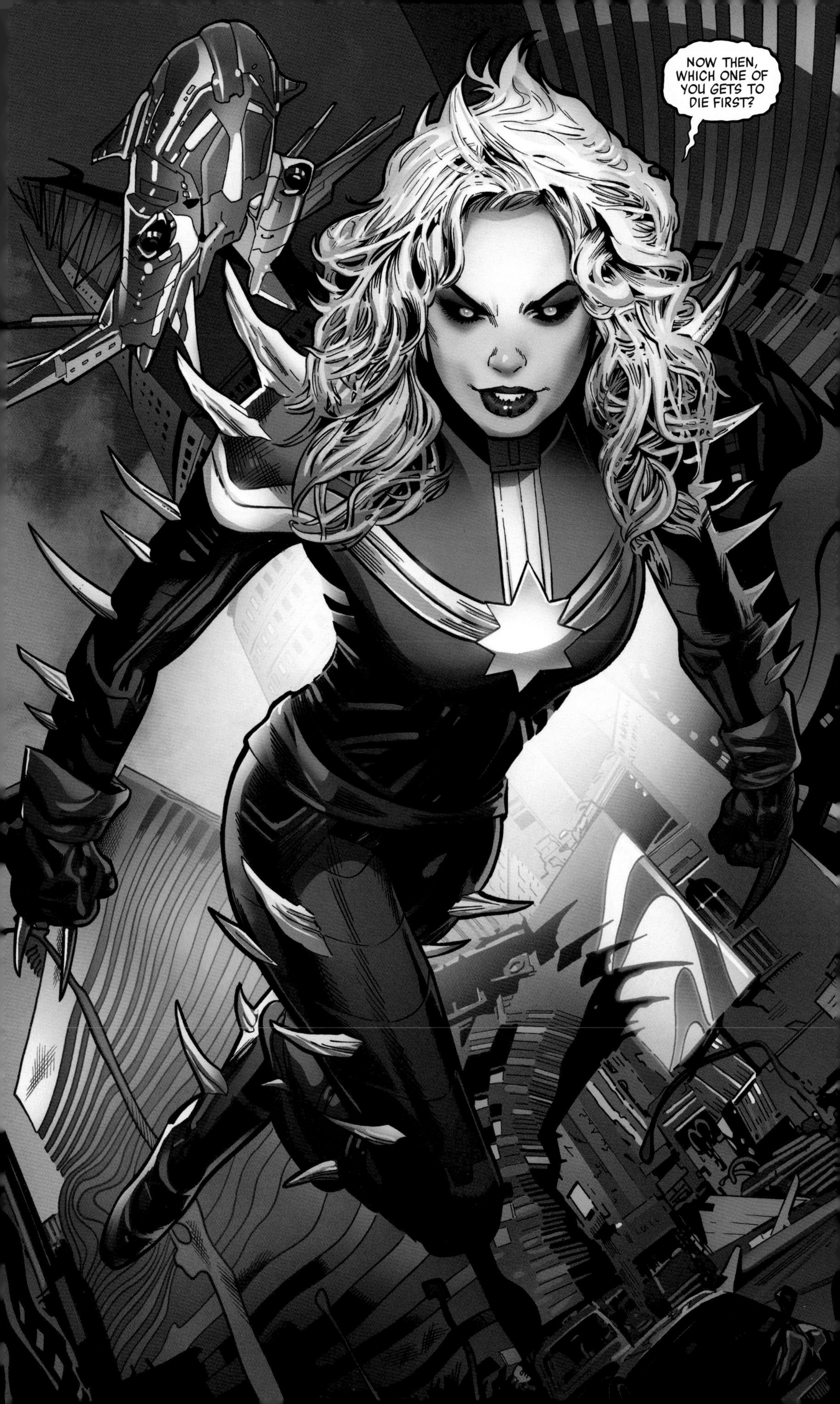
NOW THEN, WHICH ONE OF YOU GETS TO DIE FIRST?

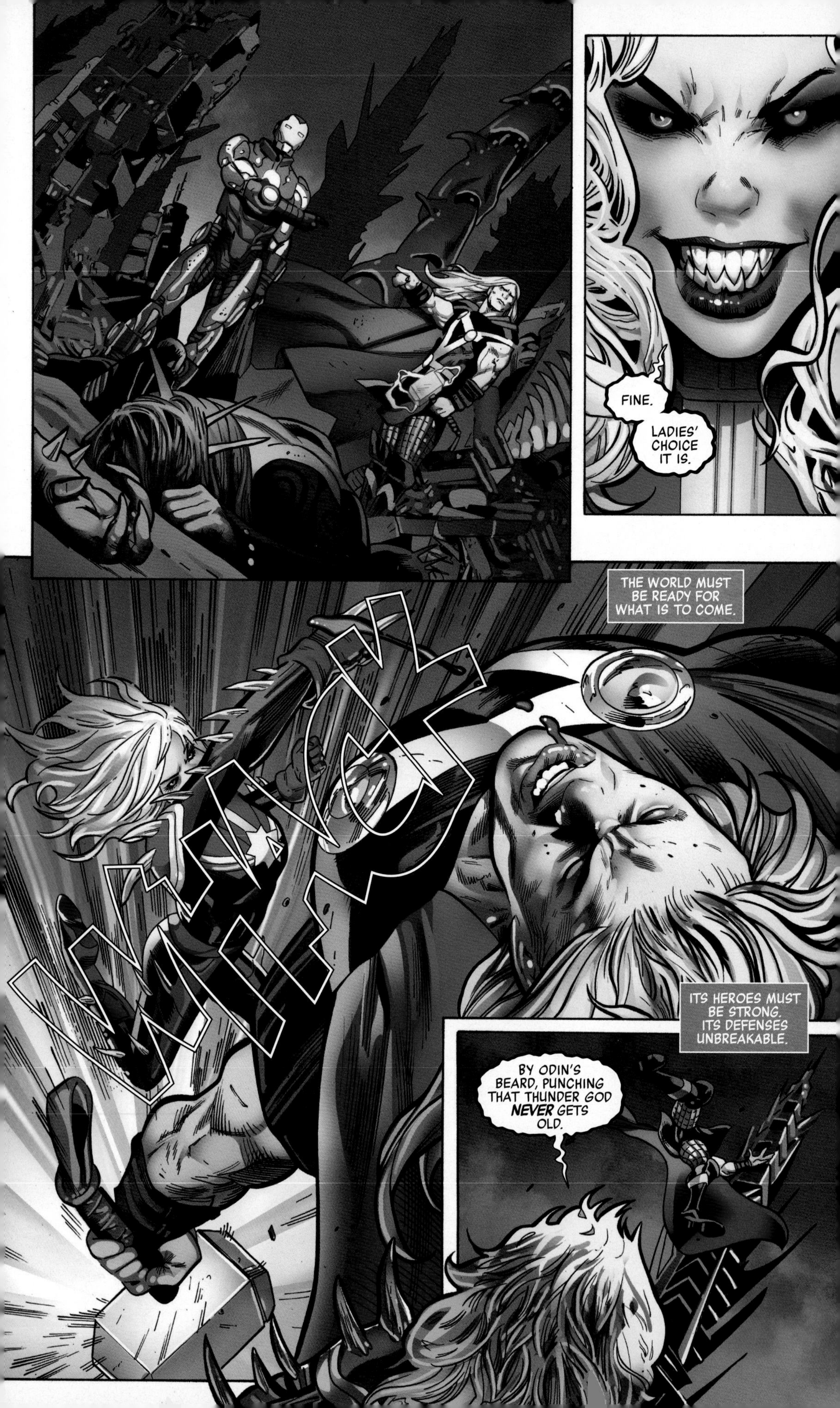
FINE.
LADIES' CHOICE IT IS.
THE WORLD MUST BE READY FOR WHAT IS TO COME.
ITS HEROES MUST BE STRONG. ITS DEFENSES UNBREAKABLE.
BY ODIN'S BEARD, PUNCHING THAT THUNDER GOD NEVER GETS OLD.

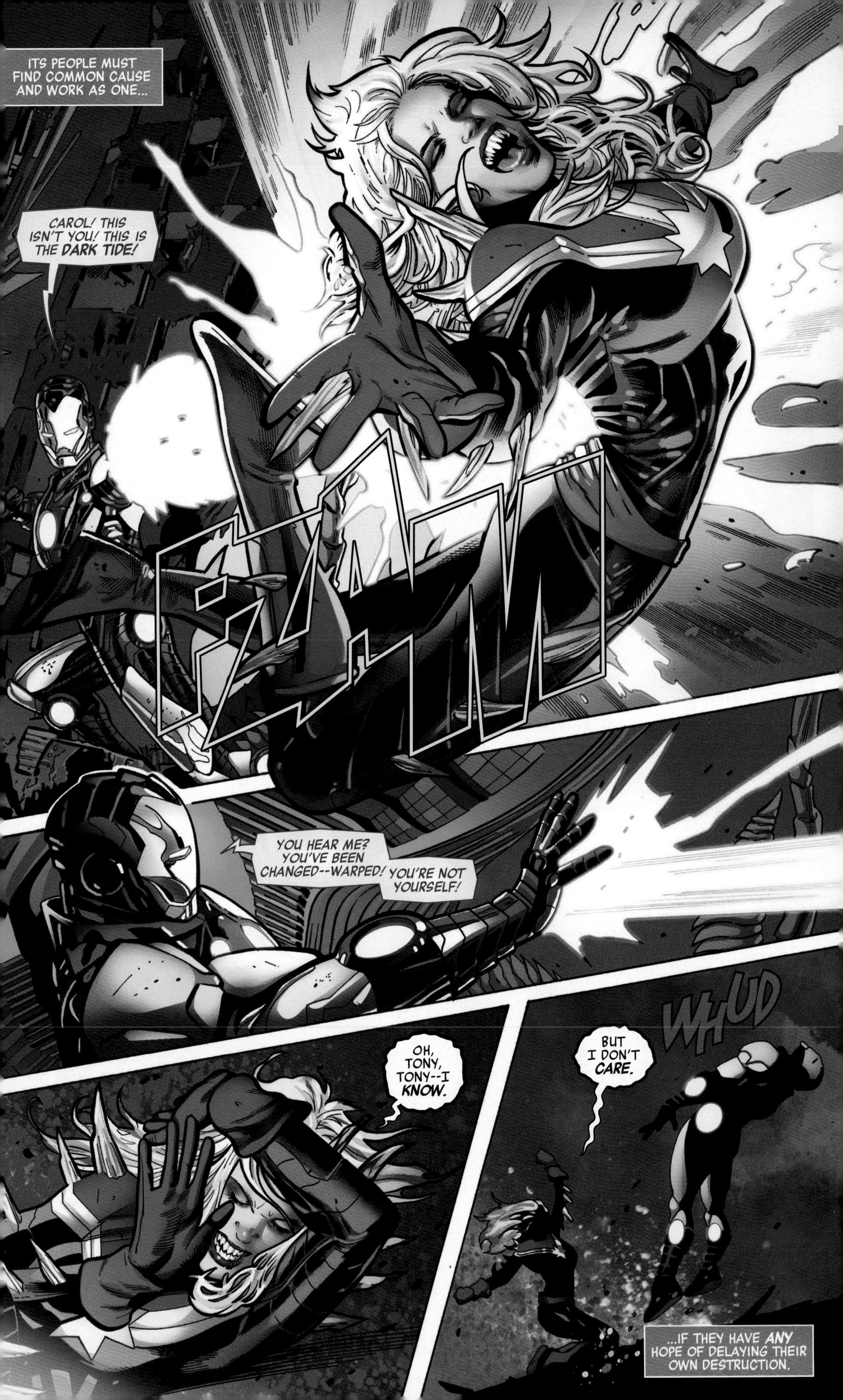
ITS PEOPLE MUST FIND COMMON CAUSE AND WORK AS ONE...
CAROL! THIS ISN'T YOU! THIS IS THE DARK TIDE!
ZAAM
YOU HEAR ME? YOU'VE BEEN CHANGED--WARPED! YOU'RE NOT YOURSELF!
OH, TONY, TONY--I KNOW.
BUT I DON'T CARE.
WHUD
...IF THEY HAVE ANY HOPE OF DELAYING THEIR OWN DESTRUCTION.

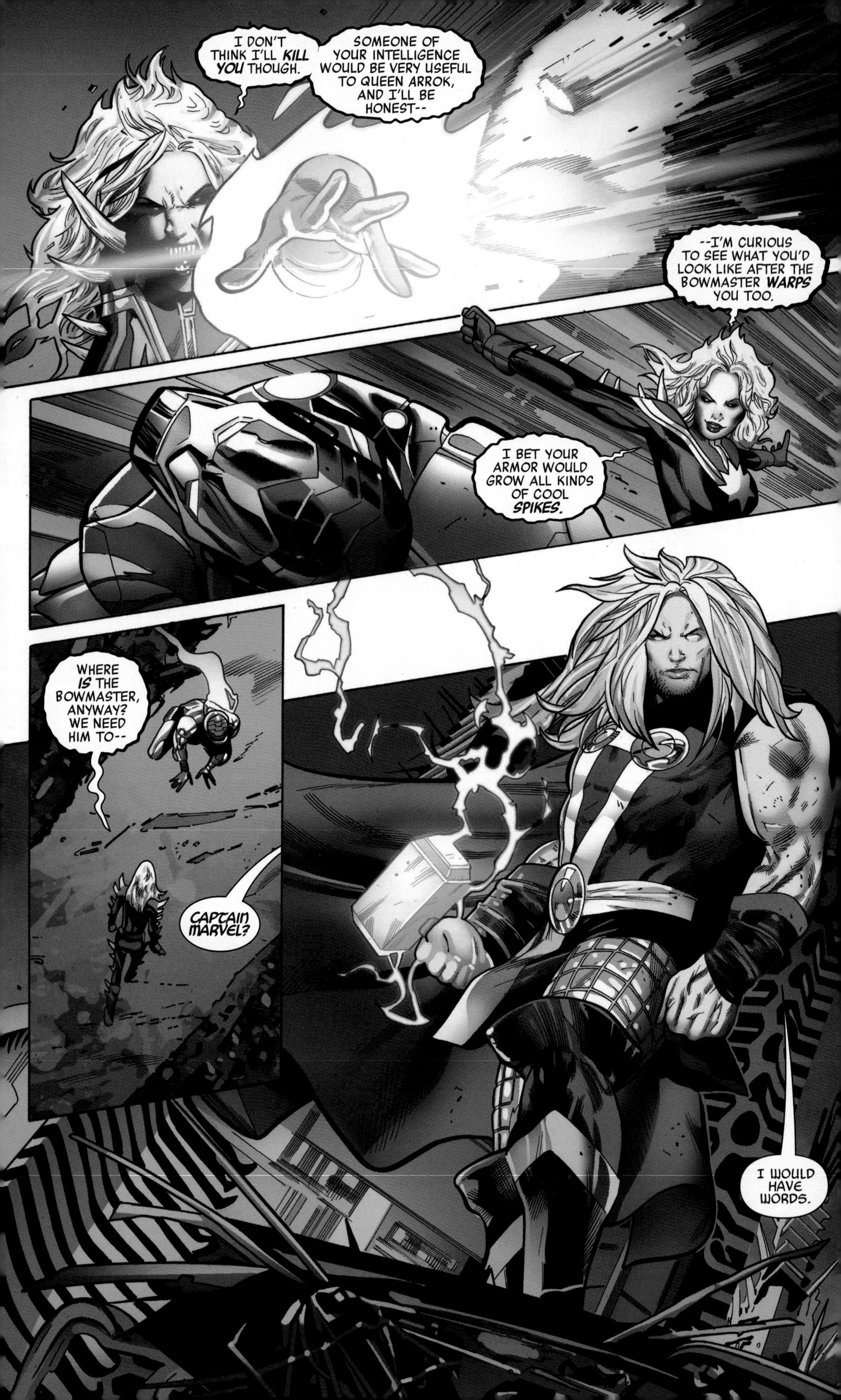
I DON'T THINK I'LL KILL YOU THOUGH.
SOMEONE OF YOUR INTELLIGENCE WOULD BE VERY USEFUL TO QUEEN ARROK, AND I'LL BE HONEST--
--I'M CURIOUS TO SEE WHAT YOU'D LOOK LIKE AFTER THE BOWMASTER WARPS YOU TOO.
I BET YOUR ARMOR WOULD GROW ALL KINDS OF COOL SPIKES.
WHERE IS THE BOWMASTER, ANYWAY? WE NEED HIM TO--
CAPTAIN MARVEL?
I WOULD HAVE WORDS.

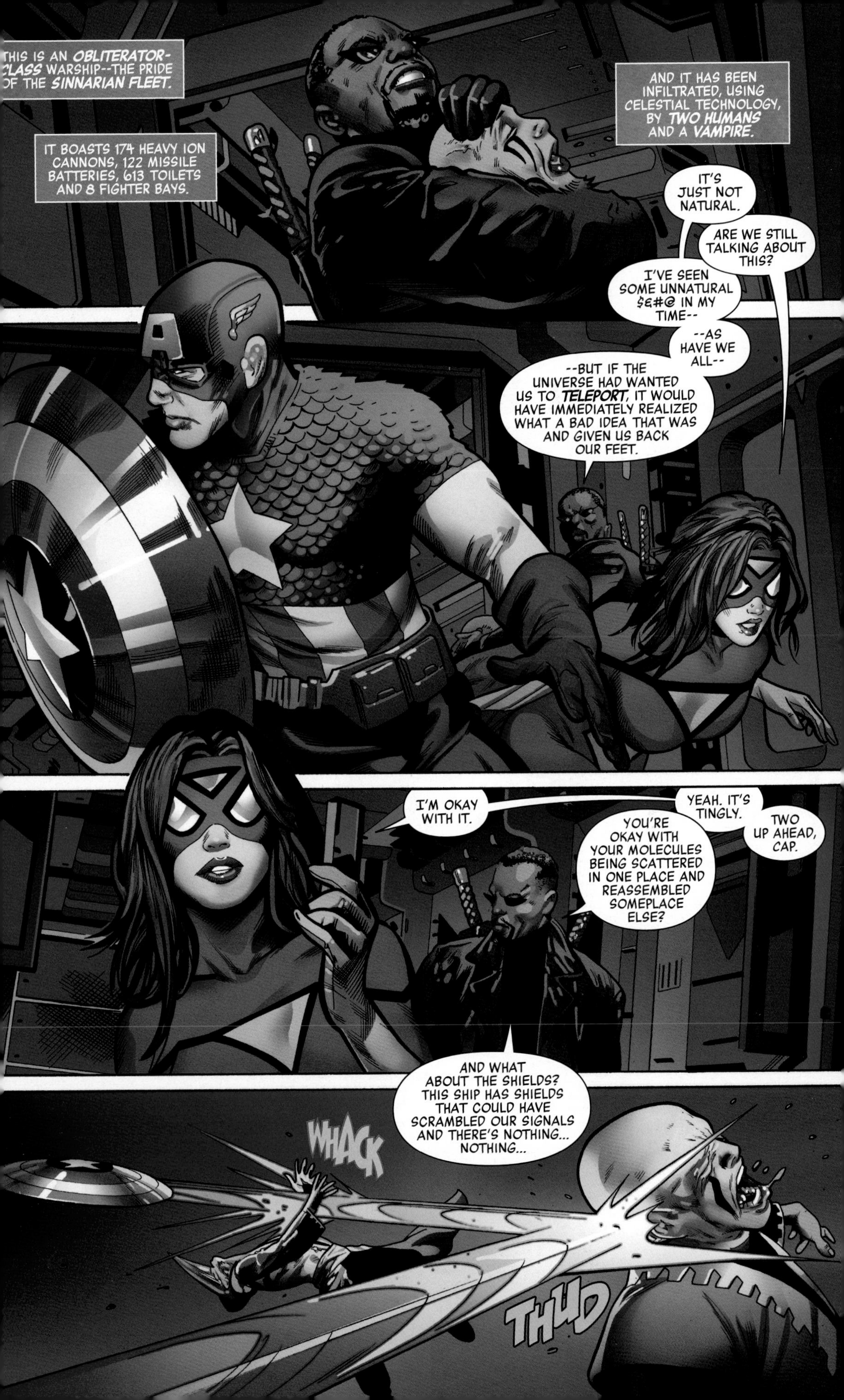
THIS IS AN OBLITERATOR-CLASS WARSHIP--THE PRIDE OF THE SINNARIAN FLEET.
IT BOASTS 174 HEAVY ION CANNONS, 122 MISSILE BATTERIES, 613 TOILETS AND 8 FIGHTER BAYS.
AND IT HAS BEEN INFILTRATED, USING CELESTIAL TECHNOLOGY, BY TWO HUMANS AND A VAMPIRE.
IT'S JUST NOT NATURAL.
ARE WE STILL TALKING ABOUT THIS?
I'VE SEEN SOME UNNATURAL $&#@ IN MY TIME--
--AS HAVE WE ALL--
--BUT IF THE UNIVERSE HAD WANTED US TO TELEPORT, IT WOULD HAVE IMMEDIATELY REALIZED WHAT A BAD IDEA THAT WAS AND GIVEN US BACK OUR FEET.
I'M OKAY WITH IT.
YEAH. IT'S TINGLY.
YOU'RE OKAY WITH YOUR MOLECULES BEING SCATTERED IN ONE PLACE AND REASSEMBLED SOMEPLACE ELSE?
TWO UP AHEAD, CAP.
AND WHAT ABOUT THE SHIELDS? THIS SHIP HAS SHIELDS THAT COULD HAVE SCRAMBLED OUR SIGNALS AND THERE'S NOTHING... NOTHING...
WHACK
THUD

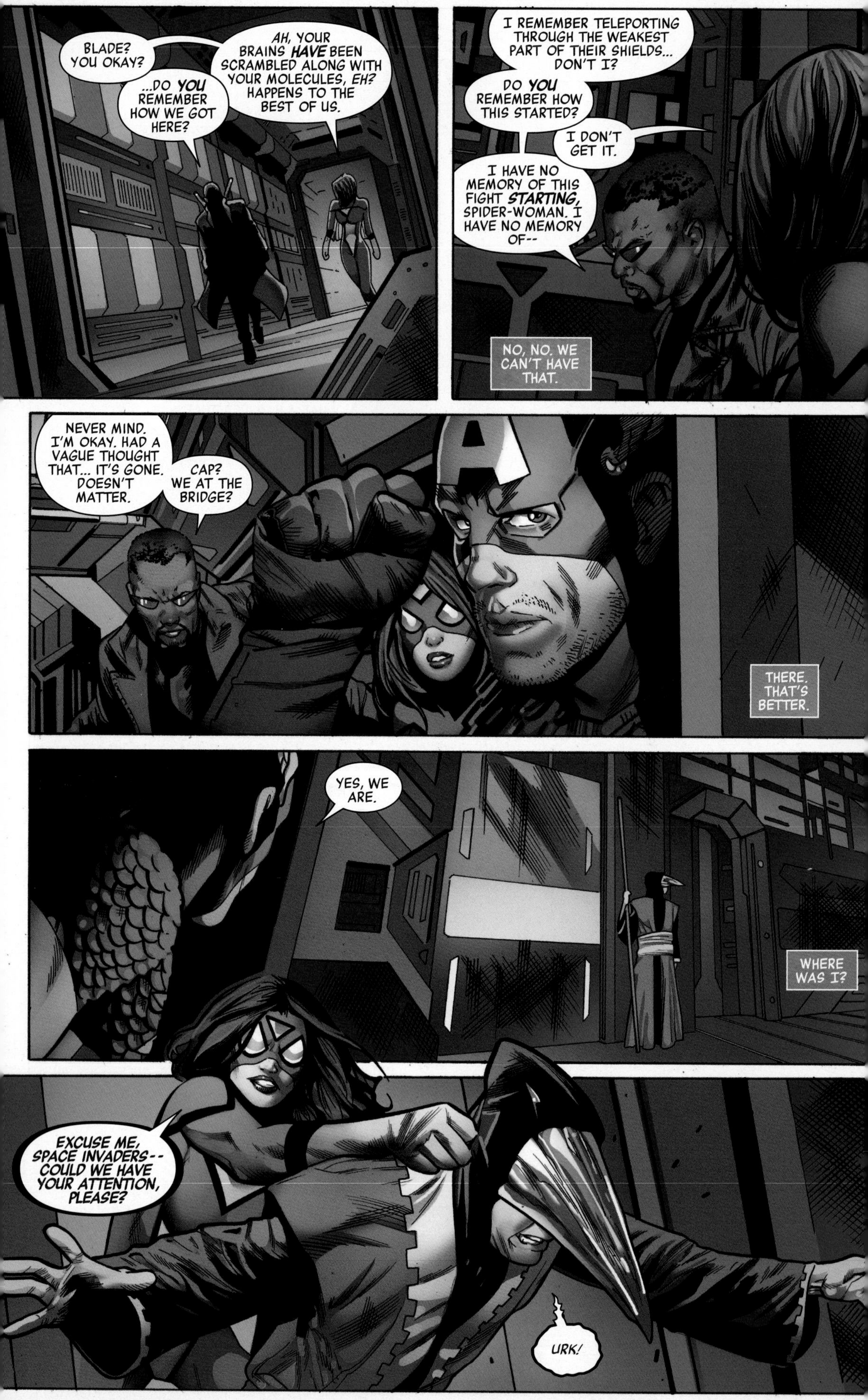

BLADE? YOU OKAY?
...DO YOU REMEMBER HOW WE GOT HERE?
AH, YOUR BRAINS HAVE BEEN SCRAMBLED ALONG WITH YOUR MOLECULES, EH? HAPPENS TO THE BEST OF US.
I REMEMBER TELEPORTING THROUGH THE WEAKEST PART OF THEIR SHIELDS... DON'T I?
DO YOU REMEMBER HOW THIS STARTED?
I DON'T GET IT.
I HAVE NO MEMORY OF THIS FIGHT STARTING, SPIDER-WOMAN. I HAVE NO MEMORY OF--
NO, NO. WE CAN'T HAVE THAT.
NEVER MIND. I'M OKAY. HAD A VAGUE THOUGHT THAT... IT'S GONE. DOESN'T MATTER.
CAP? WE AT THE BRIDGE?
THERE. THAT'S BETTER.
YES, WE ARE.
WHERE WAS I?
EXCUSE ME, SPACE INVADERS-- COULD WE HAVE YOUR ATTENTION, PLEASE?
URK!

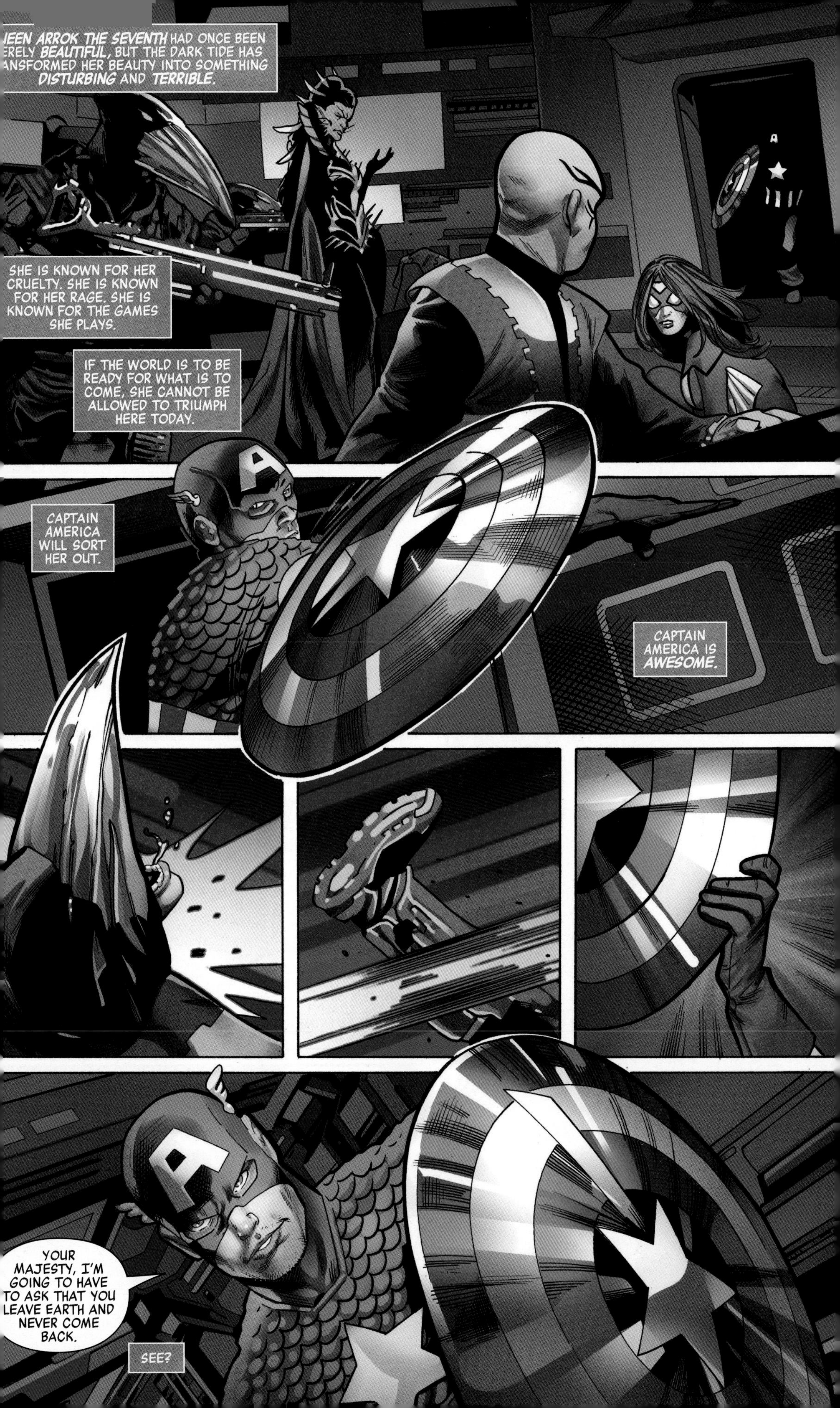

UEEN ARROK THE SEVENTH HAD ONCE BEEN ERELY BEAUTIFUL, BUT THE DARK TIDE HAS ANSFORMED HER BEAUTY INTO SOMETHING DISTURBING AND TERRIBLE.
SHE IS KNOWN FOR HER CRUELTY. SHE IS KNOWN FOR HER RAGE. SHE IS KNOWN FOR THE GAMES SHE PLAYS.
IF THE WORLD IS TO BE READY FOR WHAT IS TO COME, SHE CANNOT BE ALLOWED TO TRIUMPH HERE TODAY.
CAPTAIN AMERICA WILL SORT HER OUT.
CAPTAIN AMERICA IS AWESOME.
YOUR MAJESTY, I'M GOING TO HAVE TO ASK THAT YOU LEAVE EARTH AND NEVER COME BACK.
SEE?

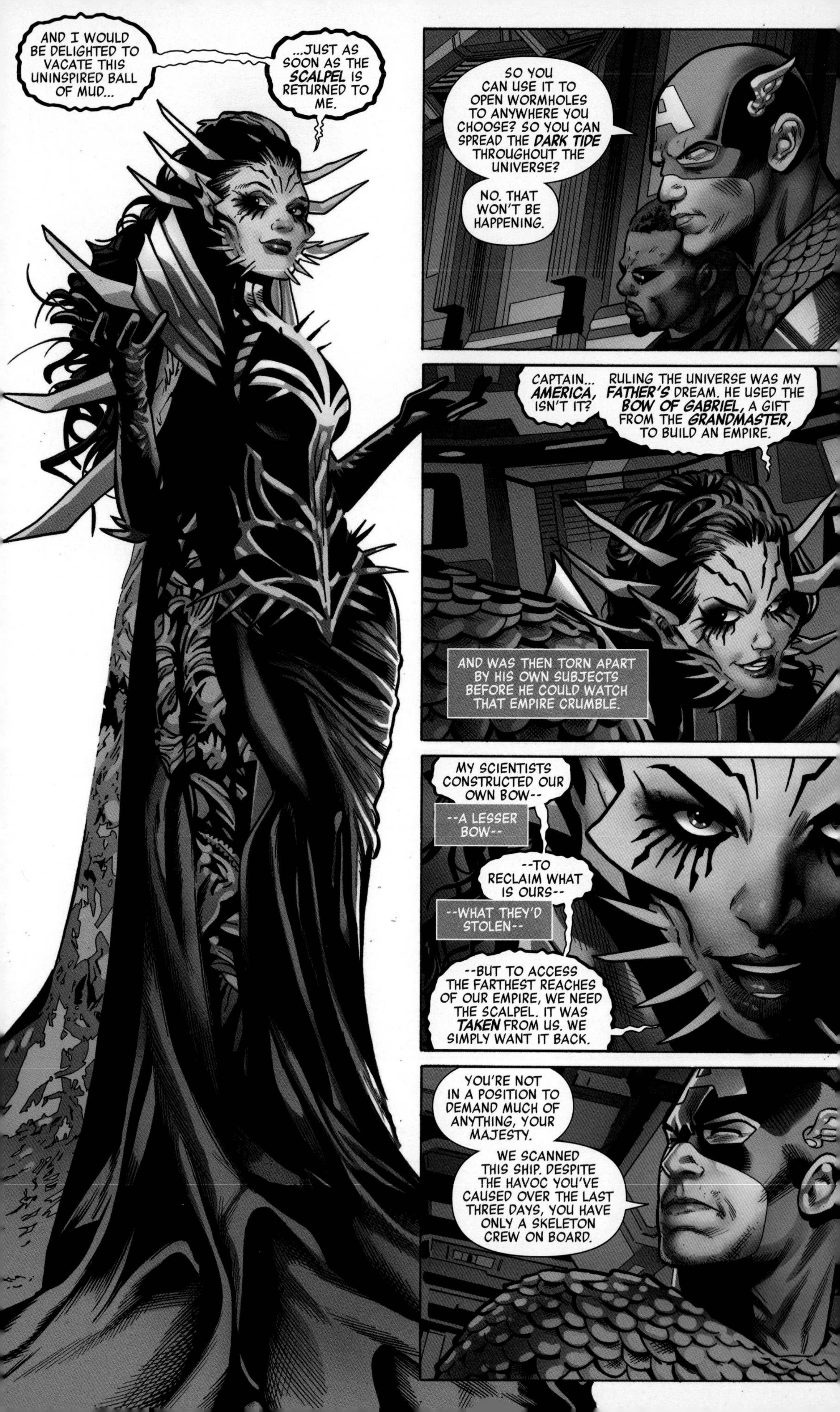
AND I WOULD BE DELIGHTED TO VACATE THIS UNINSPIRED BALL OF MUD...
...JUST AS SOON AS THE *SCALPEL* IS RETURNED TO ME.
SO YOU CAN USE IT TO OPEN WORMHOLES TO ANYWHERE YOU CHOOSE? SO YOU CAN SPREAD THE *DARK TIDE* THROUGHOUT THE UNIVERSE?
NO. THAT WON'T BE HAPPENING.
CAPTAIN... *AMERICA,* ISN'T IT?
RULING THE UNIVERSE WAS MY *FATHER'S* DREAM. HE USED THE *BOW OF GABRIEL,* A GIFT FROM THE *GRANDMASTER,* TO BUILD AN EMPIRE.
AND WAS THEN TORN APART BY HIS OWN SUBJECTS BEFORE HE COULD WATCH THAT EMPIRE CRUMBLE.
MY SCIENTISTS CONSTRUCTED OUR OWN BOW--
--A LESSER BOW--
--TO RECLAIM WHAT IS OURS--
--WHAT THEY'D STOLEN--
--BUT TO ACCESS THE FARTHEST REACHES OF OUR EMPIRE, WE NEED THE SCALPEL. IT WAS *TAKEN* FROM US. WE SIMPLY WANT IT BACK.
YOU'RE NOT IN A POSITION TO DEMAND MUCH OF ANYTHING, YOUR MAJESTY.
WE SCANNED THIS SHIP. DESPITE THE HAVOC YOU'VE CAUSED OVER THE LAST THREE DAYS, YOU HAVE ONLY A SKELETON CREW ON BOARD.

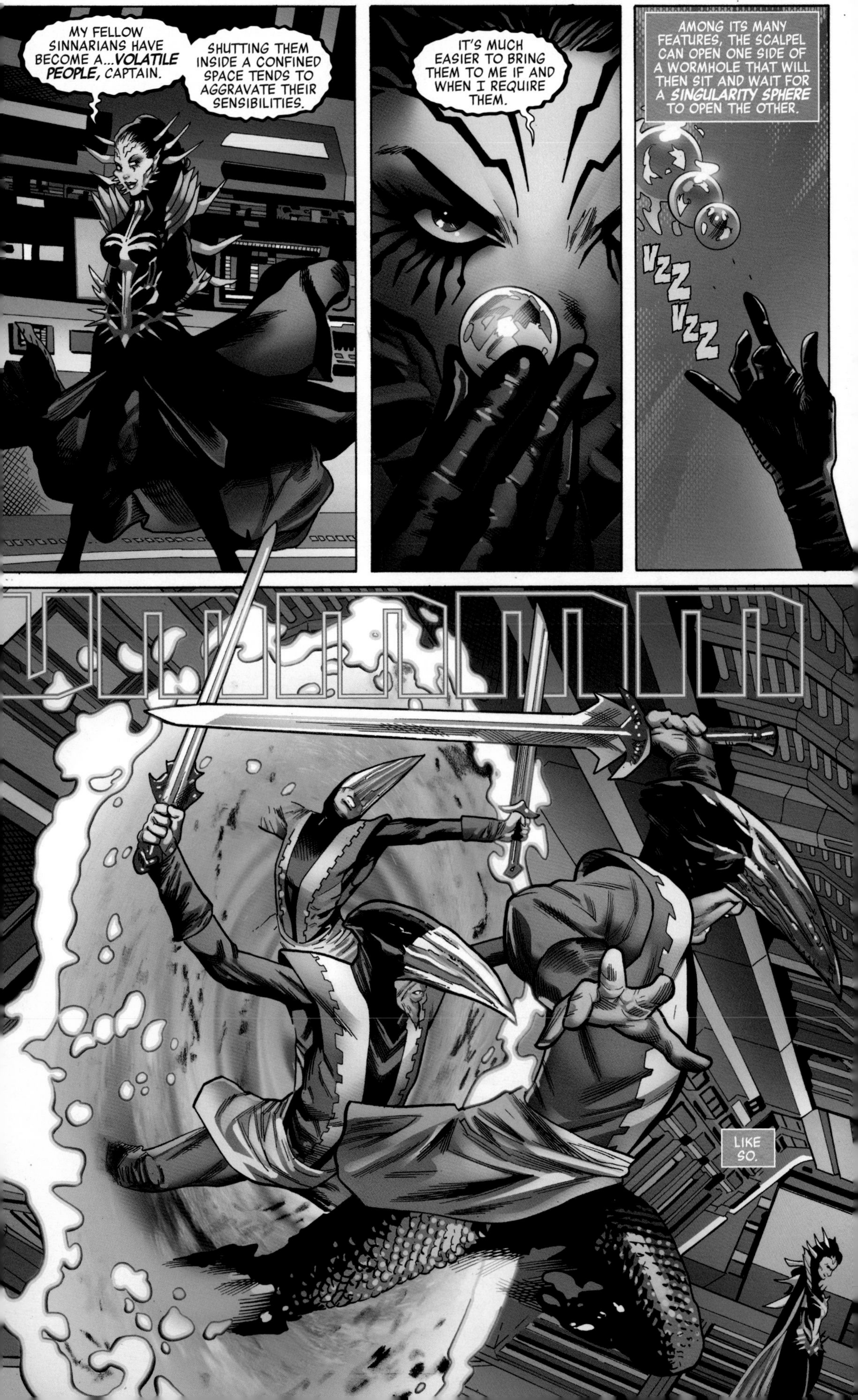
MY FELLOW SINNARIANS HAVE BECOME A...**VOLATILE PEOPLE,** CAPTAIN.
SHUTTING THEM INSIDE A CONFINED SPACE TENDS TO AGGRAVATE THEIR SENSIBILITIES.
IT'S MUCH EASIER TO BRING THEM TO ME IF AND WHEN I REQUIRE THEM.
AMONG ITS MANY FEATURES, THE SCALPEL CAN OPEN ONE SIDE OF A WORMHOLE THAT WILL THEN SIT AND WAIT FOR A ***SINGULARITY SPHERE*** TO OPEN THE OTHER.
VZZ VZZ
LIKE SO.

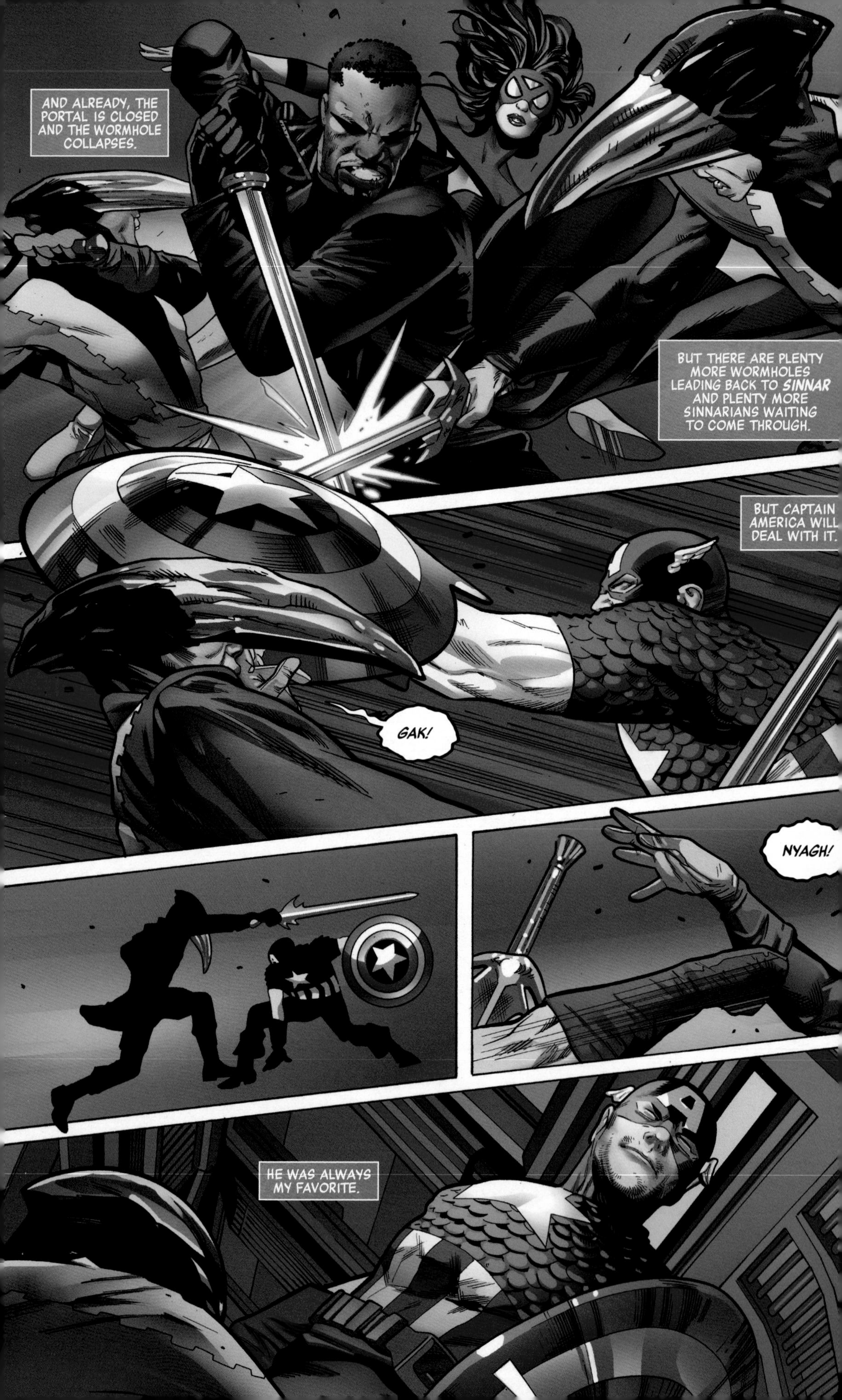
AND ALREADY, THE PORTAL IS CLOSED AND THE WORMHOLE COLLAPSES.
BUT THERE ARE PLENTY MORE WORMHOLES LEADING BACK TO SINNAR AND PLENTY MORE SINNARIANS WAITING TO COME THROUGH.
BUT CAPTAIN AMERICA WILL DEAL WITH IT.
GAK!
NYAGH!
HE WAS ALWAYS MY FAVORITE.

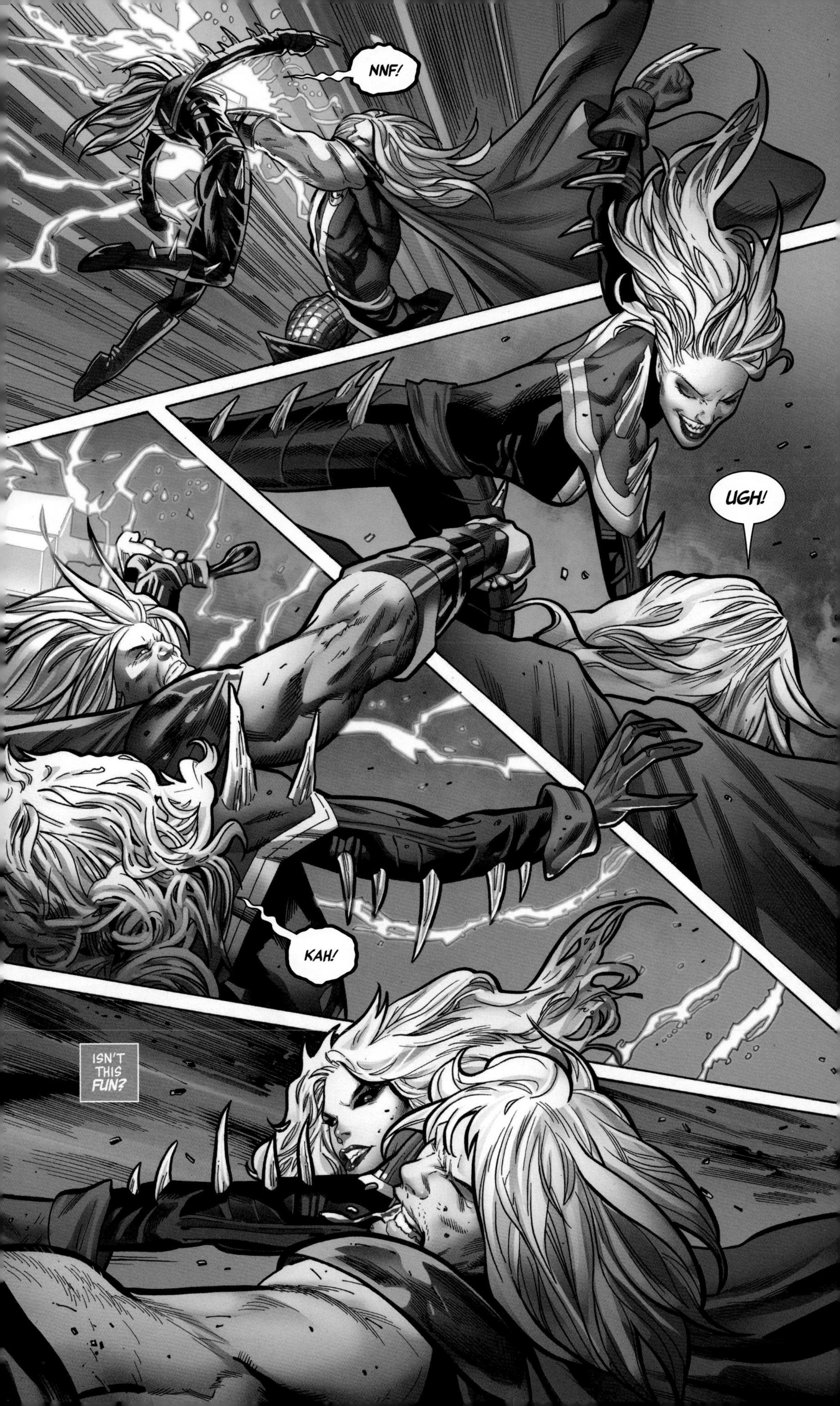
NNF!
UGH!
KAH!
ISN'T THIS FUN?

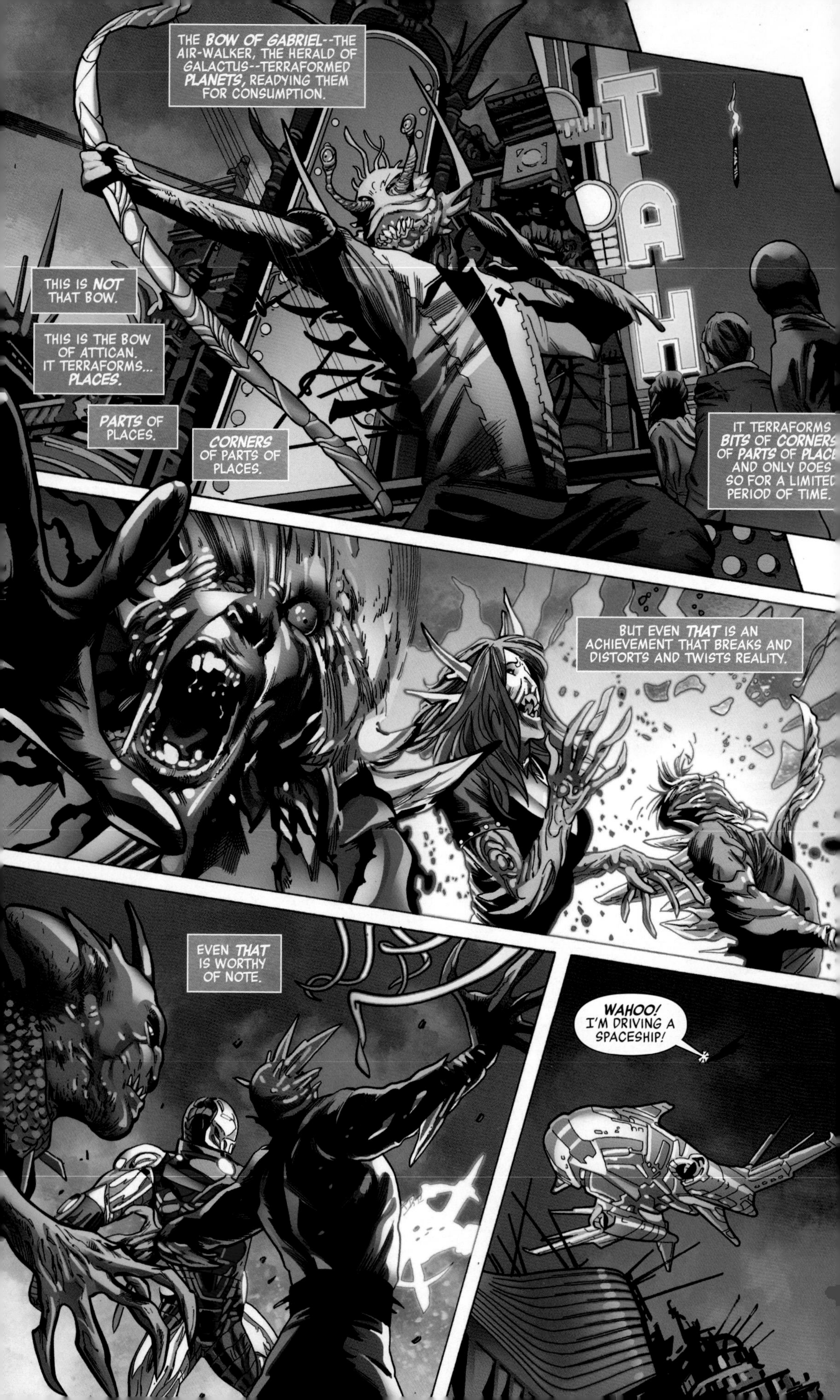
THE BOW OF GABRIEL--THE AIR-WALKER, THE HERALD OF GALACTUS--TERRAFORMED PLANETS, READYING THEM FOR CONSUMPTION.
THIS IS NOT THAT BOW.
THIS IS THE BOW OF ATTICAN. IT TERRAFORMS... PLACES.
PARTS OF PLACES.
CORNERS OF PARTS OF PLACES.
IT TERRAFORMS BITS OF CORNERS OF PARTS OF PLACE AND ONLY DOES SO FOR A LIMITED PERIOD OF TIME.
BUT EVEN THAT IS AN ACHIEVEMENT THAT BREAKS AND DISTORTS AND TWISTS REALITY.
EVEN THAT IS WORTHY OF NOTE.
WAHOO! I'M DRIVING A SPACESHIP!

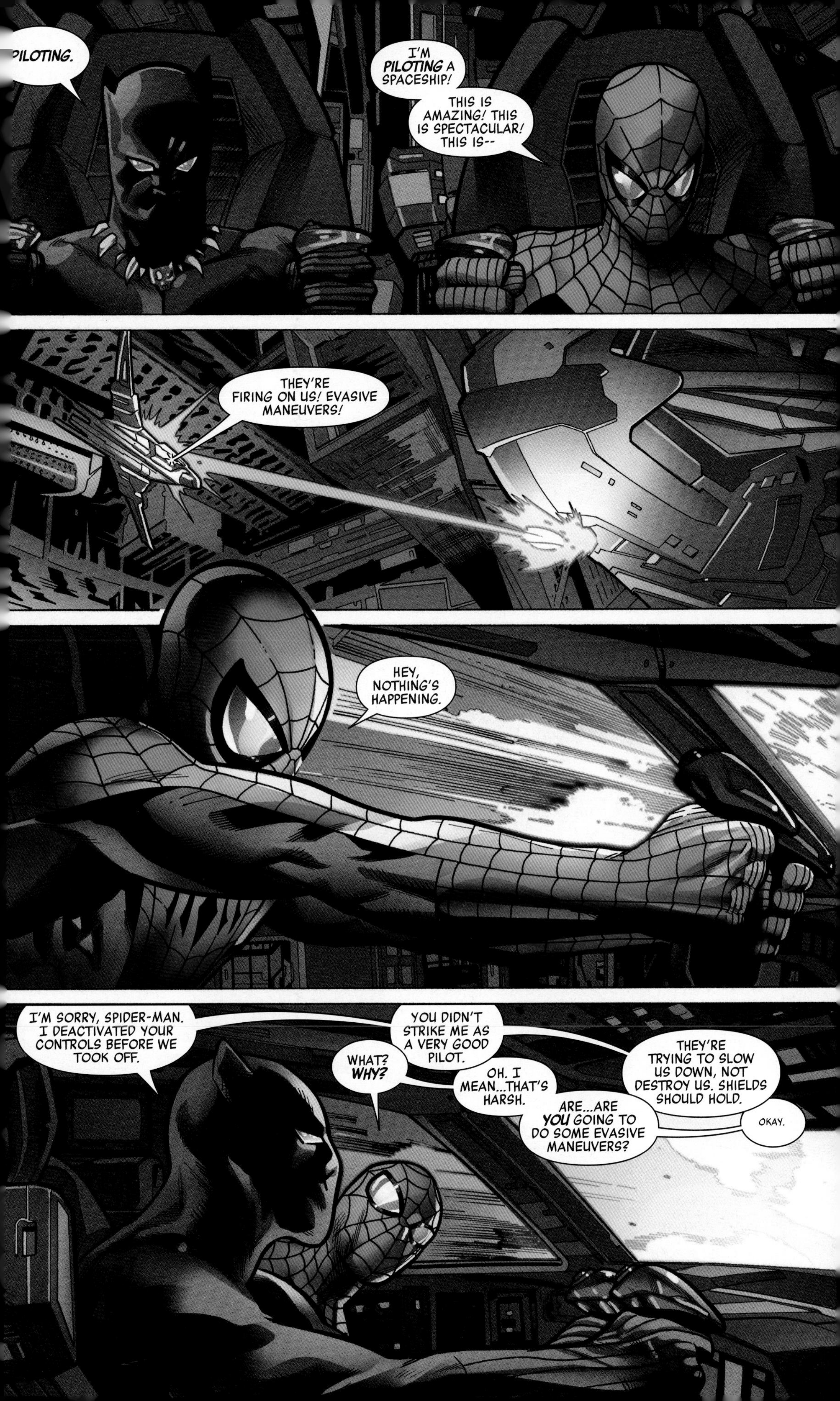

PILOTING.
I'M PILOTING A SPACESHIP!
THIS IS AMAZING! THIS IS SPECTACULAR! THIS IS--
THEY'RE FIRING ON US! EVASIVE MANEUVERS!
HEY, NOTHING'S HAPPENING.
I'M SORRY, SPIDER-MAN. I DEACTIVATED YOUR CONTROLS BEFORE WE TOOK OFF.
WHAT? WHY?
YOU DIDN'T STRIKE ME AS A VERY GOOD PILOT.
OH. I MEAN...THAT'S HARSH.
THEY'RE TRYING TO SLOW US DOWN, NOT DESTROY US. SHIELDS SHOULD HOLD.
ARE...ARE YOU GOING TO DO SOME EVASIVE MANEUVERS?
OKAY.

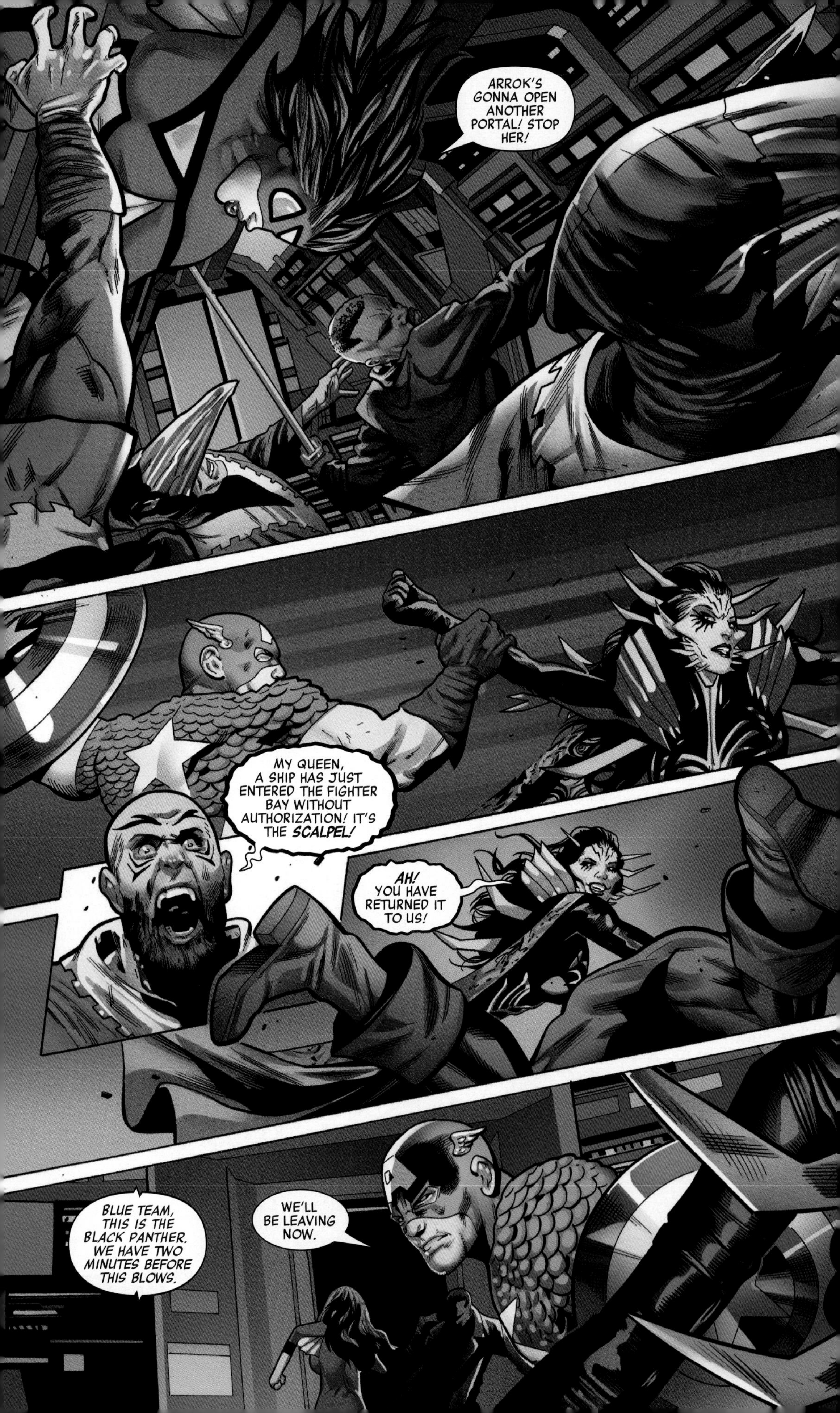
ARROK'S GONNA OPEN ANOTHER PORTAL! STOP HER!
MY QUEEN, A SHIP HAS JUST ENTERED THE FIGHTER BAY WITHOUT AUTHORIZATION! IT'S THE SCALPEL!
AH! YOU HAVE RETURNED IT TO US!
BLUE TEAM, THIS IS THE BLACK PANTHER. WE HAVE TWO MINUTES BEFORE THIS BLOWS.
WE'LL BE LEAVING NOW.

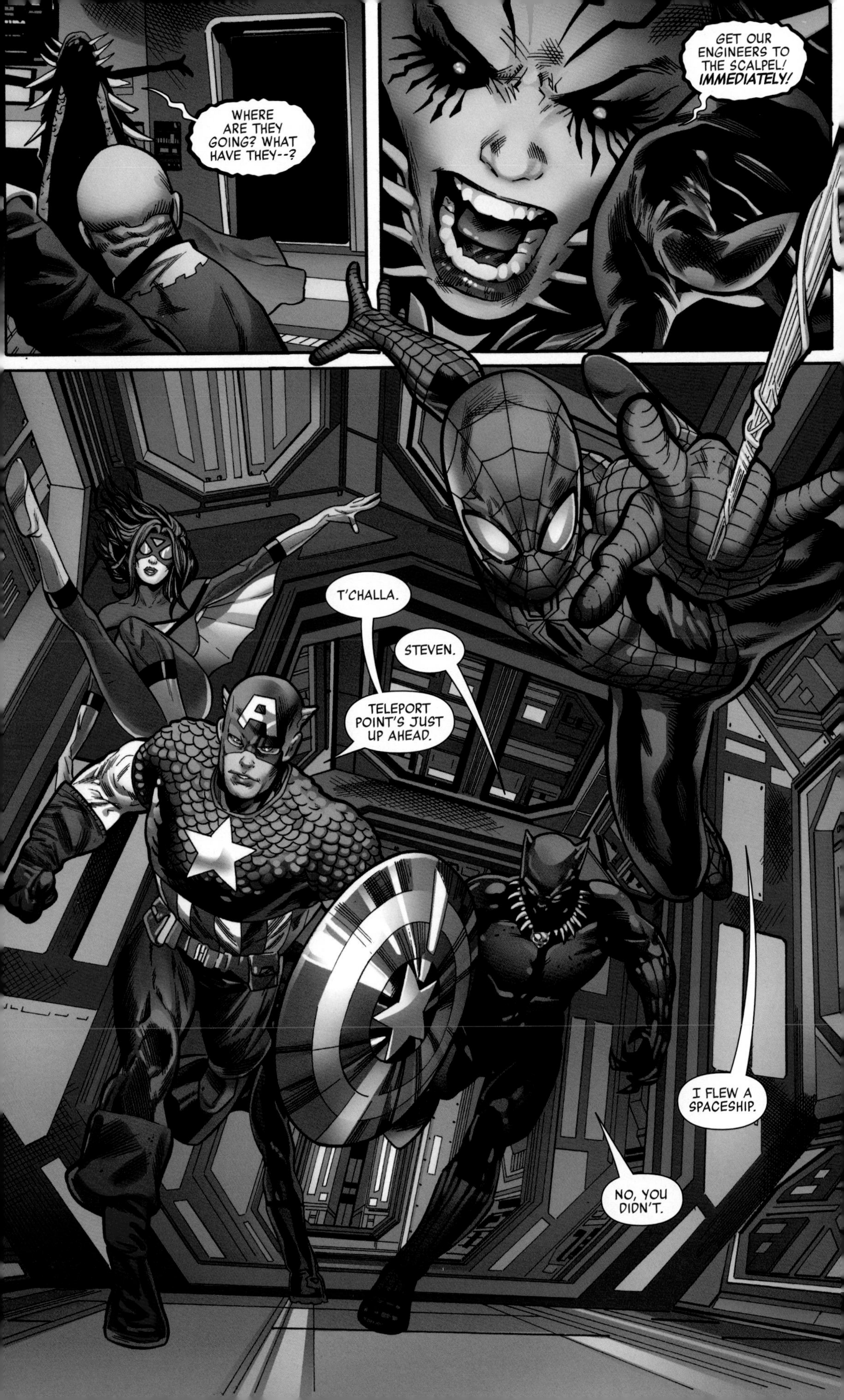
WHERE ARE THEY GOING? WHAT HAVE THEY--?
GET OUR ENGINEERS TO THE SCALPEL! **IMMEDIATELY!**
T'CHALLA.
TELEPORT POINT'S JUST UP AHEAD.
STEVEN.
I FLEW A SPACESHIP.
NO, YOU DIDN'T.

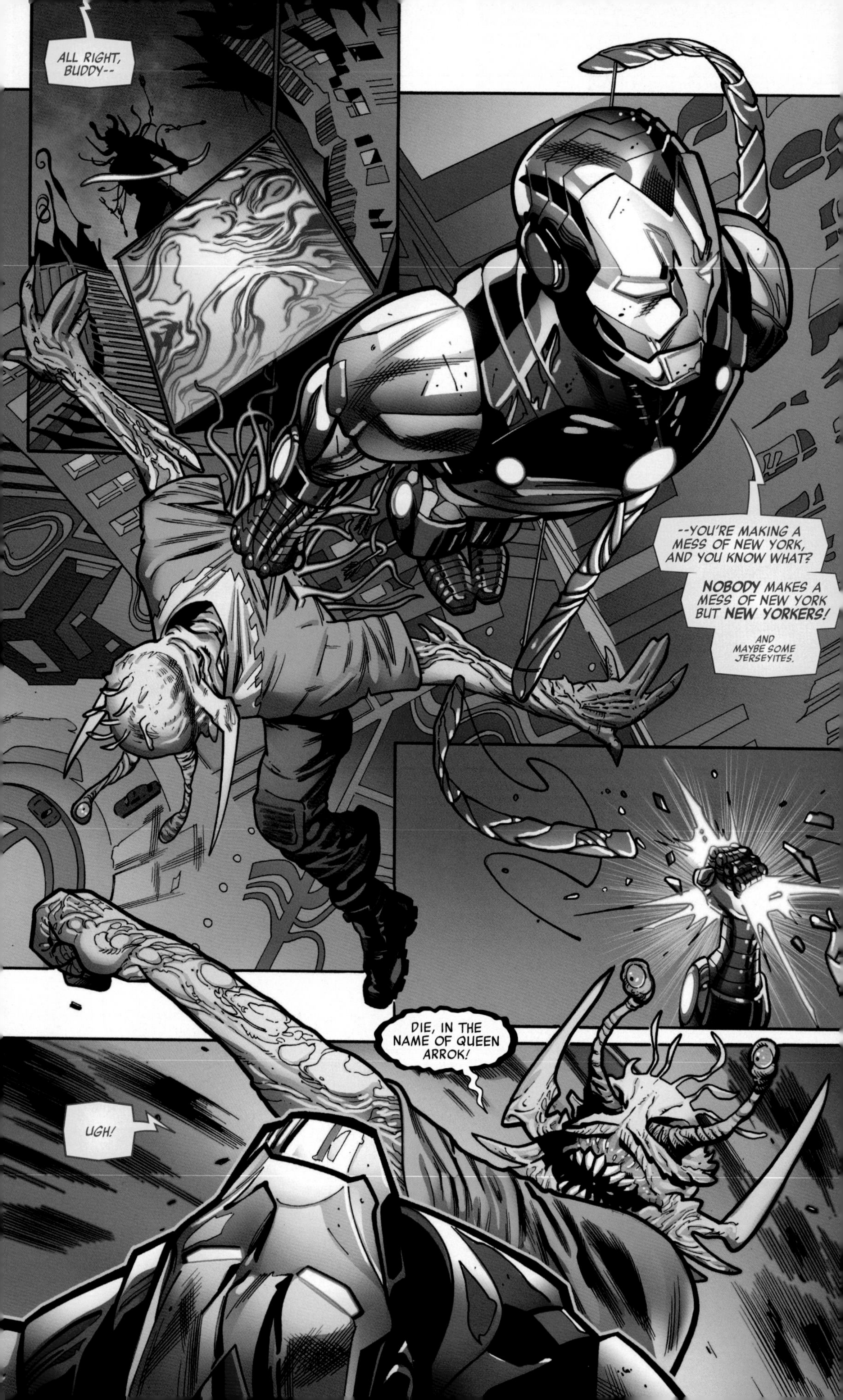
ALL RIGHT, BUDDY--
--YOU'RE MAKING A MESS OF NEW YORK, AND YOU KNOW WHAT?
NOBODY MAKES A MESS OF NEW YORK BUT NEW YORKERS!
AND MAYBE SOME JERSEYITES.
DIE, IN THE NAME OF QUEEN ARROK!
UGH!

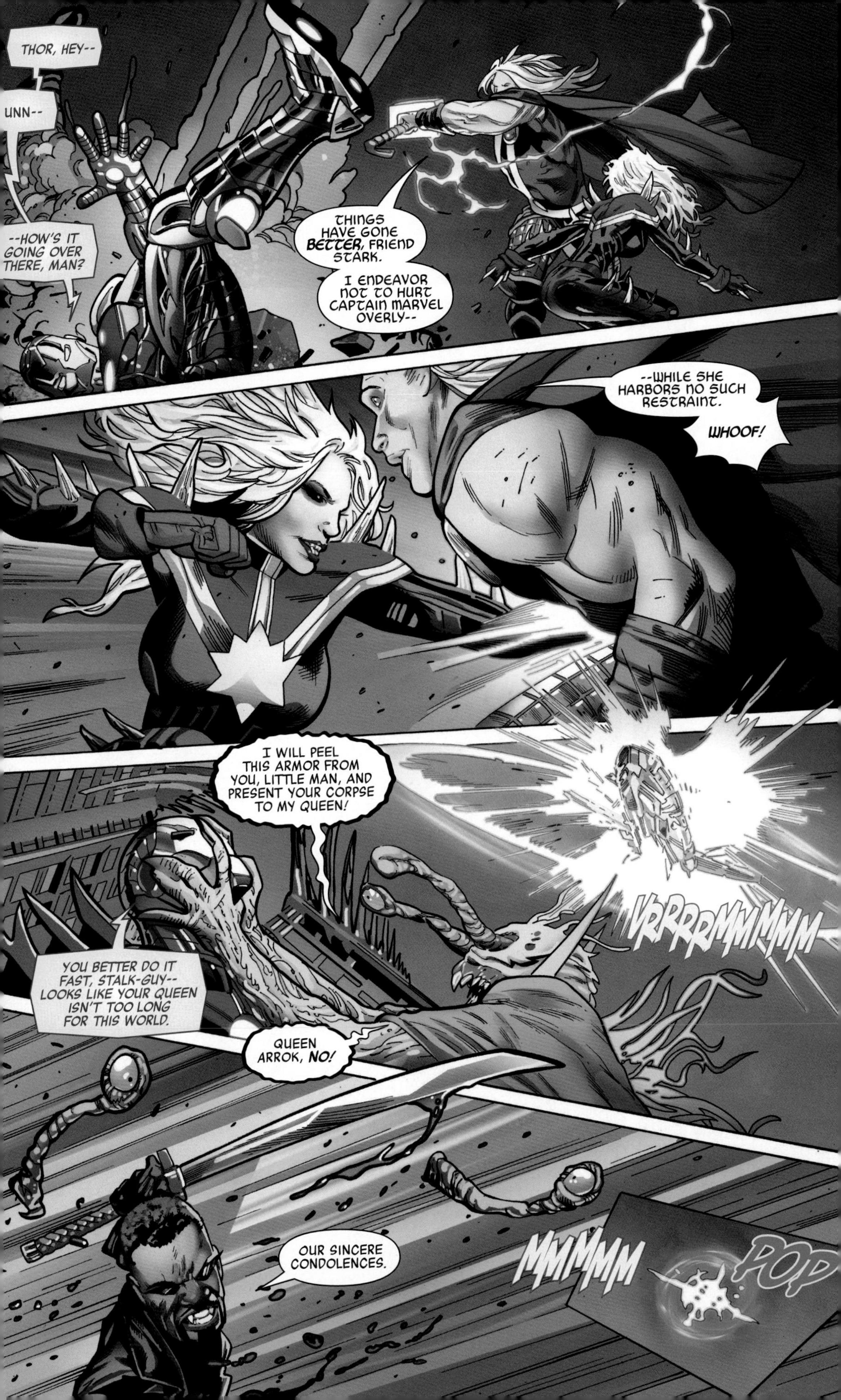

THOR, HEY--
UNN--
--HOW'S IT GOING OVER THERE, MAN?
THINGS HAVE GONE BETTER, FRIEND STARK.
I ENDEAVOR NOT TO HURT CAPTAIN MARVEL OVERLY--
--WHILE SHE HARBORS NO SUCH RESTRAINT.
WHOOF!
I WILL PEEL THIS ARMOR FROM YOU, LITTLE MAN, AND PRESENT YOUR CORPSE TO MY QUEEN!
VRRRRMMMMMM
YOU BETTER DO IT FAST, STALK-GUY-- LOOKS LIKE YOUR QUEEN ISN'T TOO LONG FOR THIS WORLD.
QUEEN ARROK, NO!
OUR SINCERE CONDOLENCES.
MMMMM
POP

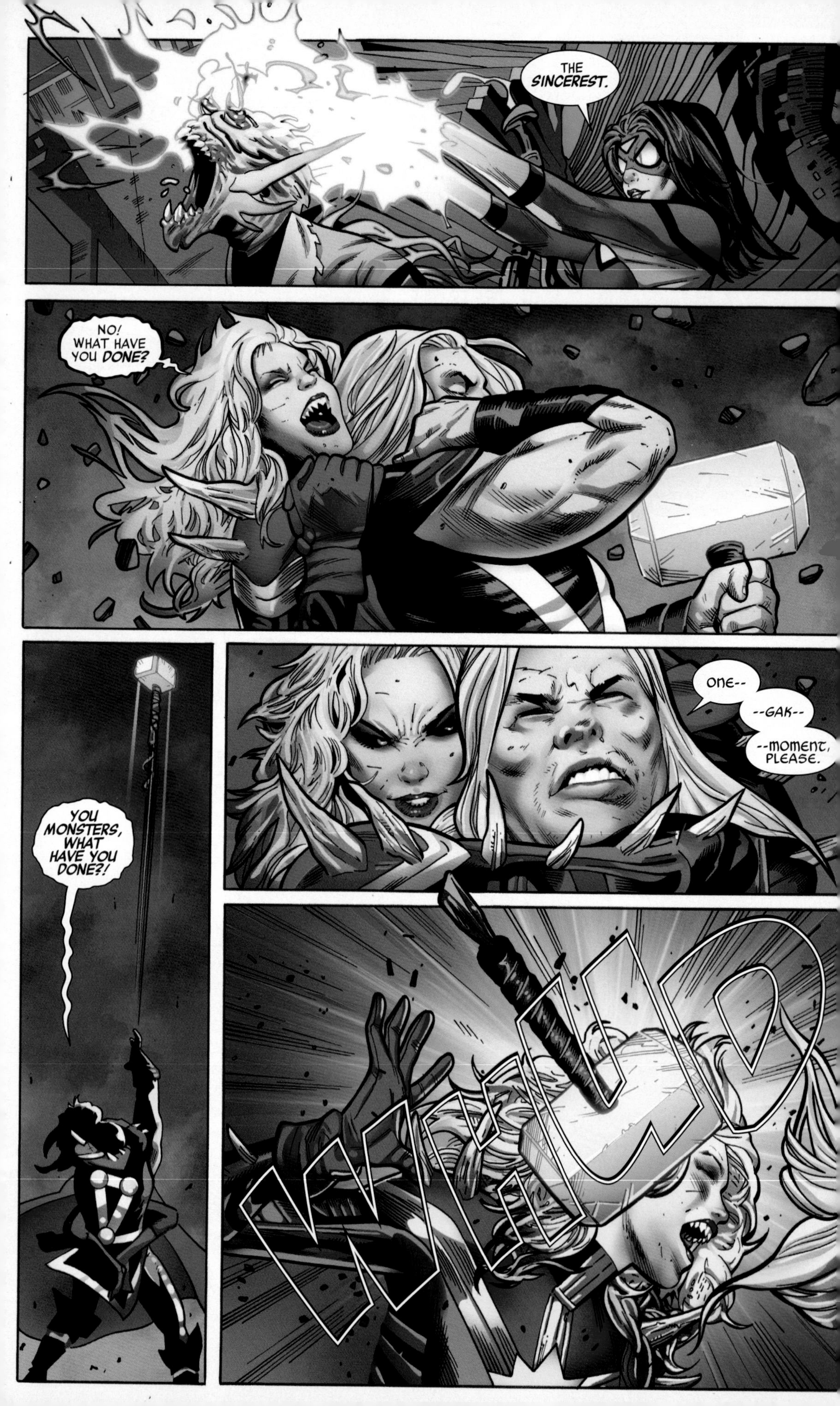
THE SINCEREST.
NO! WHAT HAVE YOU DONE?
ONE--
--GAK--
--MOMENT, PLEASE.
YOU MONSTERS, WHAT HAVE YOU DONE?!

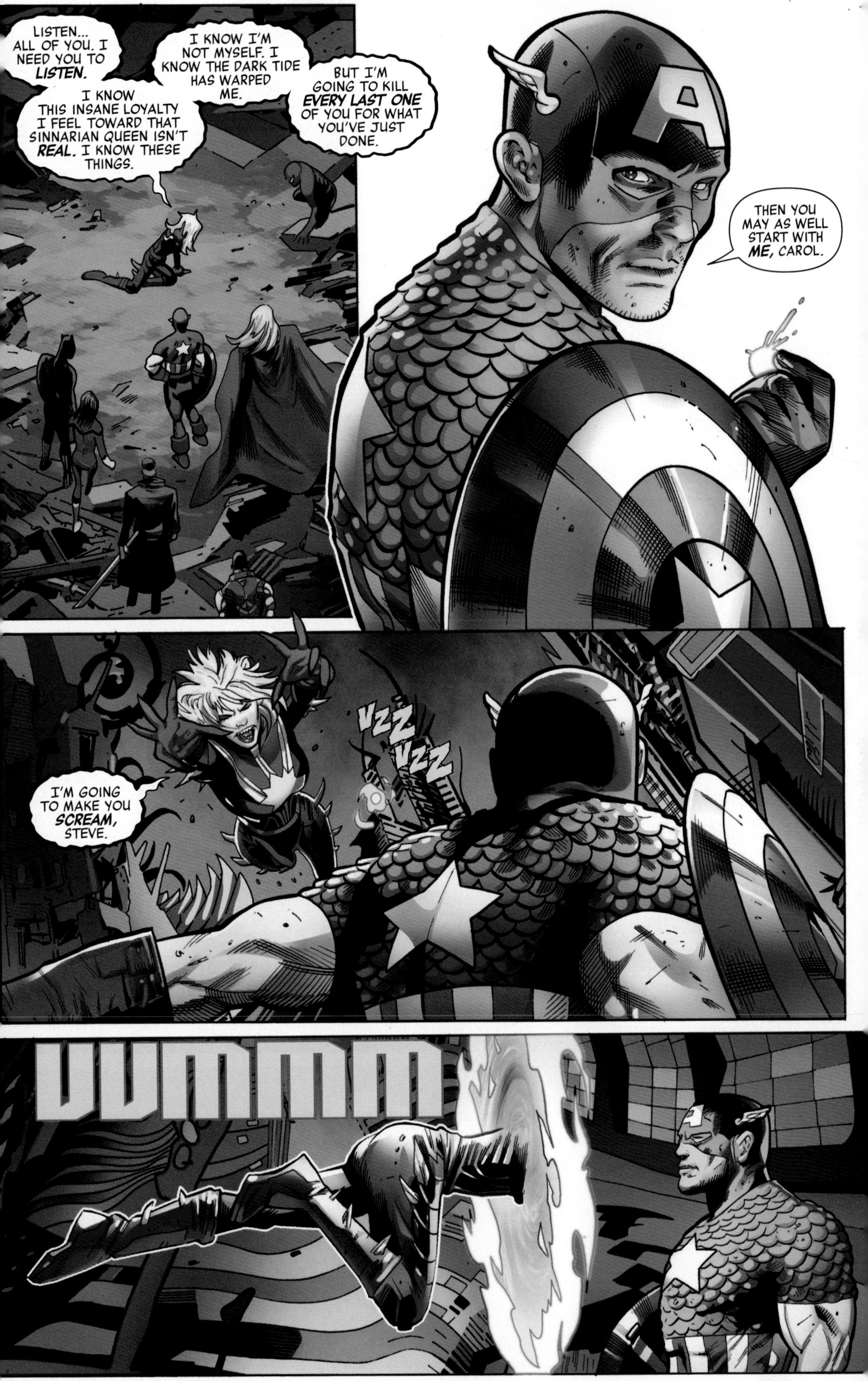
LISTEN... ALL OF YOU. I NEED YOU TO LISTEN.
I KNOW THIS INSANE LOYALTY I FEEL TOWARD THAT SINNARIAN QUEEN ISN'T REAL. I KNOW THESE THINGS.
I KNOW I'M NOT MYSELF. I KNOW THE DARK TIDE HAS WARPED ME.
BUT I'M GOING TO KILL EVERY LAST ONE OF YOU FOR WHAT YOU'VE JUST DONE.
THEN YOU MAY AS WELL START WITH ME, CAROL.
I'M GOING TO MAKE YOU SCREAM, STEVE.
VZZ
VZZ
VVMMM

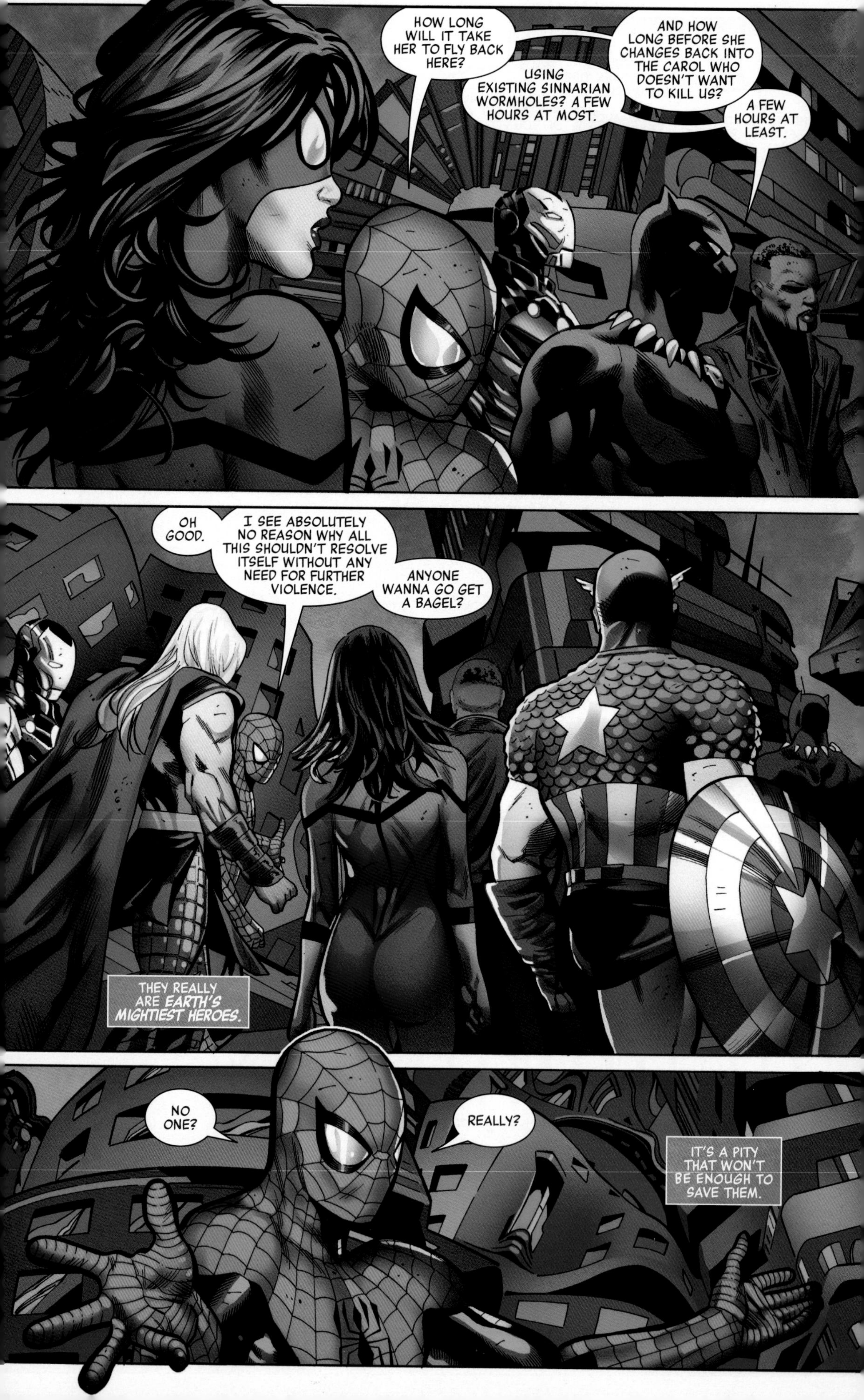
HOW LONG WILL IT TAKE HER TO FLY BACK HERE?
AND HOW LONG BEFORE SHE CHANGES BACK INTO THE CAROL WHO DOESN'T WANT TO KILL US?
USING EXISTING SINNARIAN WORMHOLES? A FEW HOURS AT MOST.
A FEW HOURS AT LEAST.
OH GOOD.
I SEE ABSOLUTELY NO REASON WHY ALL THIS SHOULDN'T RESOLVE ITSELF WITHOUT ANY NEED FOR FURTHER VIOLENCE.
ANYONE WANNA GO GET A BAGEL?
THEY REALLY ARE *EARTH'S MIGHTIEST HEROES.*
NO ONE?
REALLY?
IT'S A PITY THAT WON'T BE ENOUGH TO SAVE THEM.

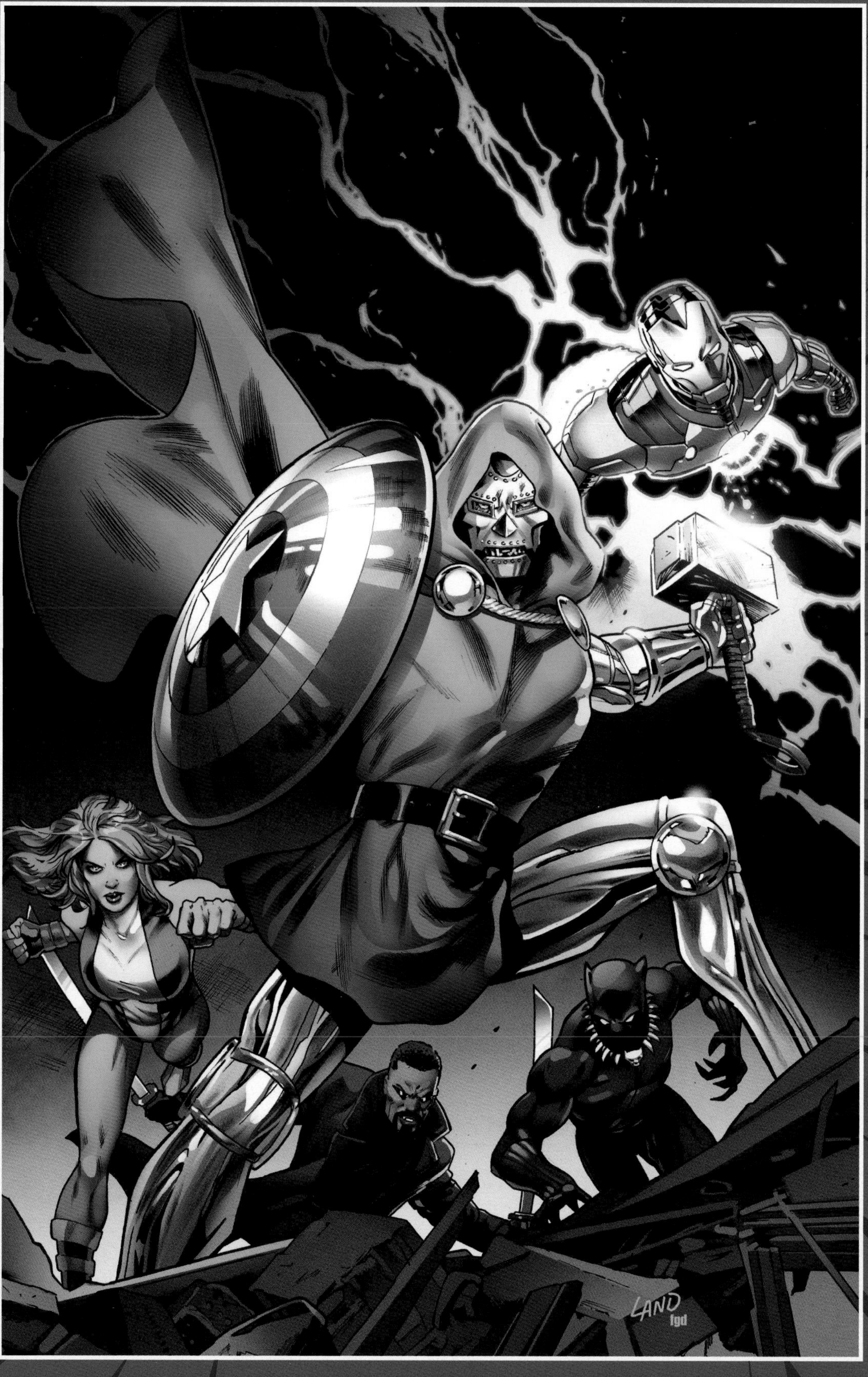
LAND
fgd

Z

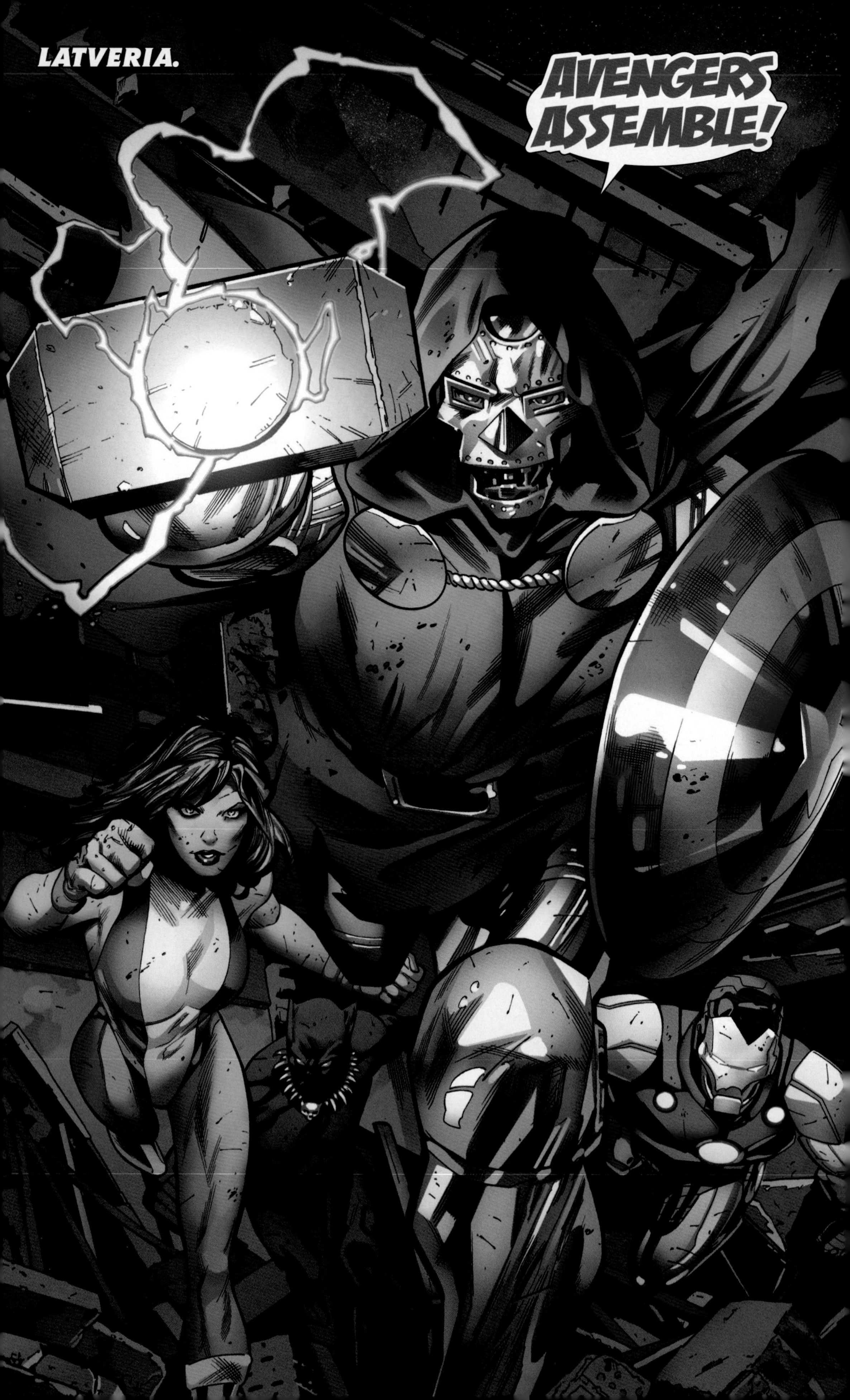
LATVERIA.
AVENGERS ASSEMBLE!

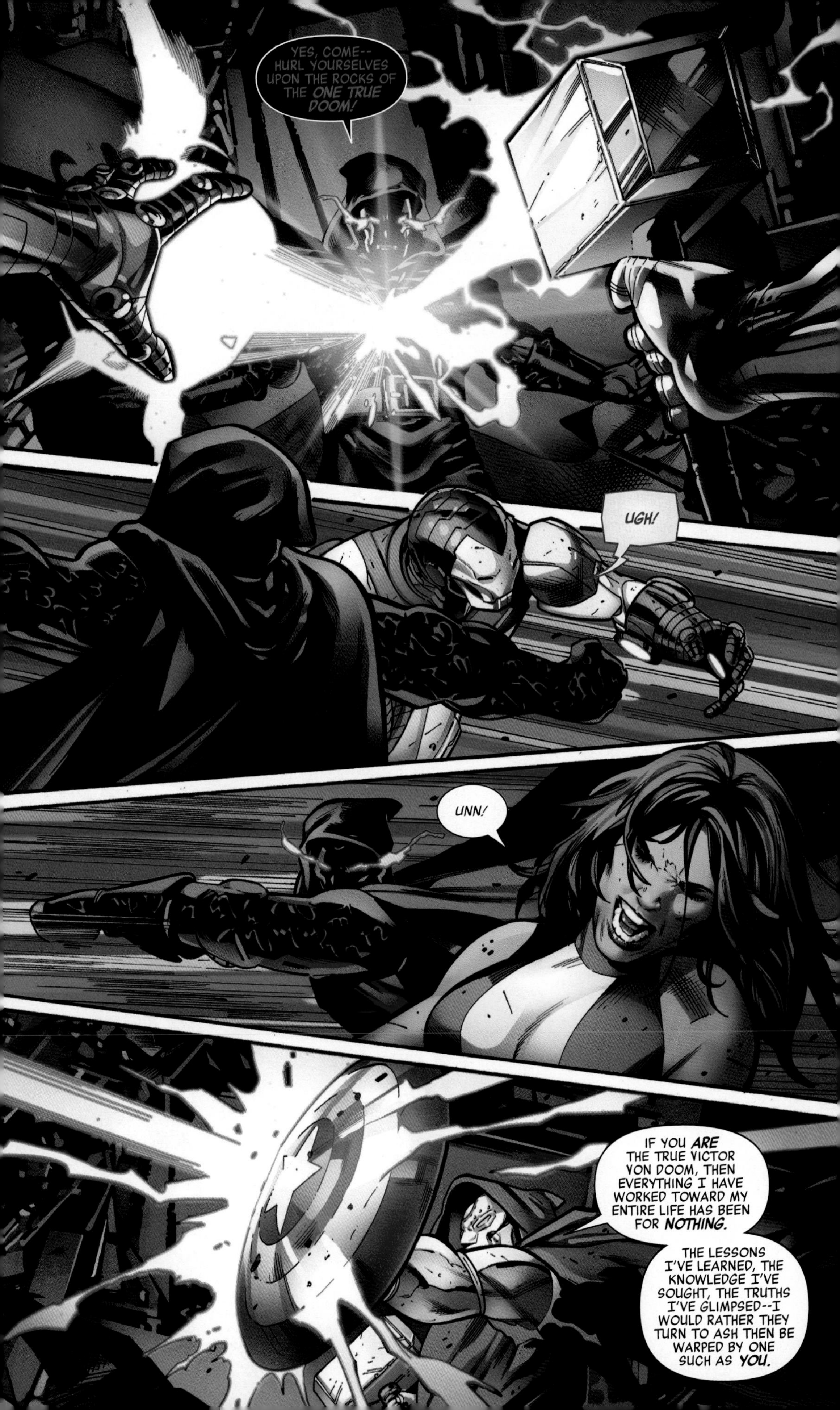

YES, COME-- HURL YOURSELVES UPON THE ROCKS OF THE ONE TRUE DOOM!
UGH!
UNN!
IF YOU ARE THE TRUE VICTOR VON DOOM, THEN EVERYTHING I HAVE WORKED TOWARD MY ENTIRE LIFE HAS BEEN FOR NOTHING.
THE LESSONS I'VE LEARNED, THE KNOWLEDGE I'VE SOUGHT, THE TRUTHS I'VE GLIMPSED--I WOULD RATHER THEY TURN TO ASH THEN BE WARPED BY ONE SUCH AS YOU.

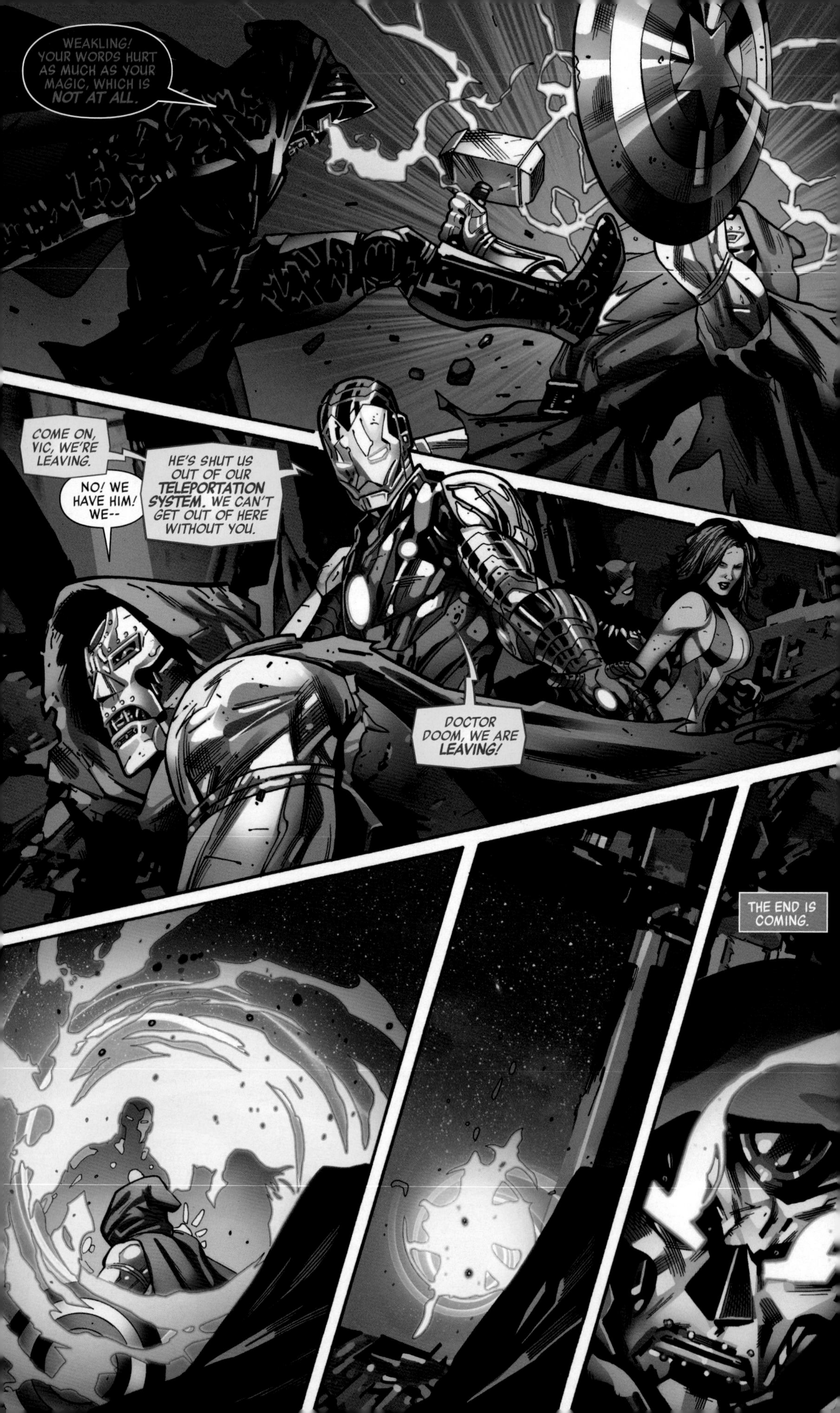
WEAKLING! YOUR WORDS HURT AS MUCH AS YOUR MAGIC, WHICH IS **NOT AT ALL**.
COME ON, VIC, WE'RE LEAVING.
NO! WE HAVE HIM! WE--
HE'S SHUT US OUT OF OUR **TELEPORTATION SYSTEM**. WE CAN'T GET OUT OF HERE WITHOUT YOU.
DOCTOR DOOM, WE ARE **LEAVING!**
THE END IS COMING.

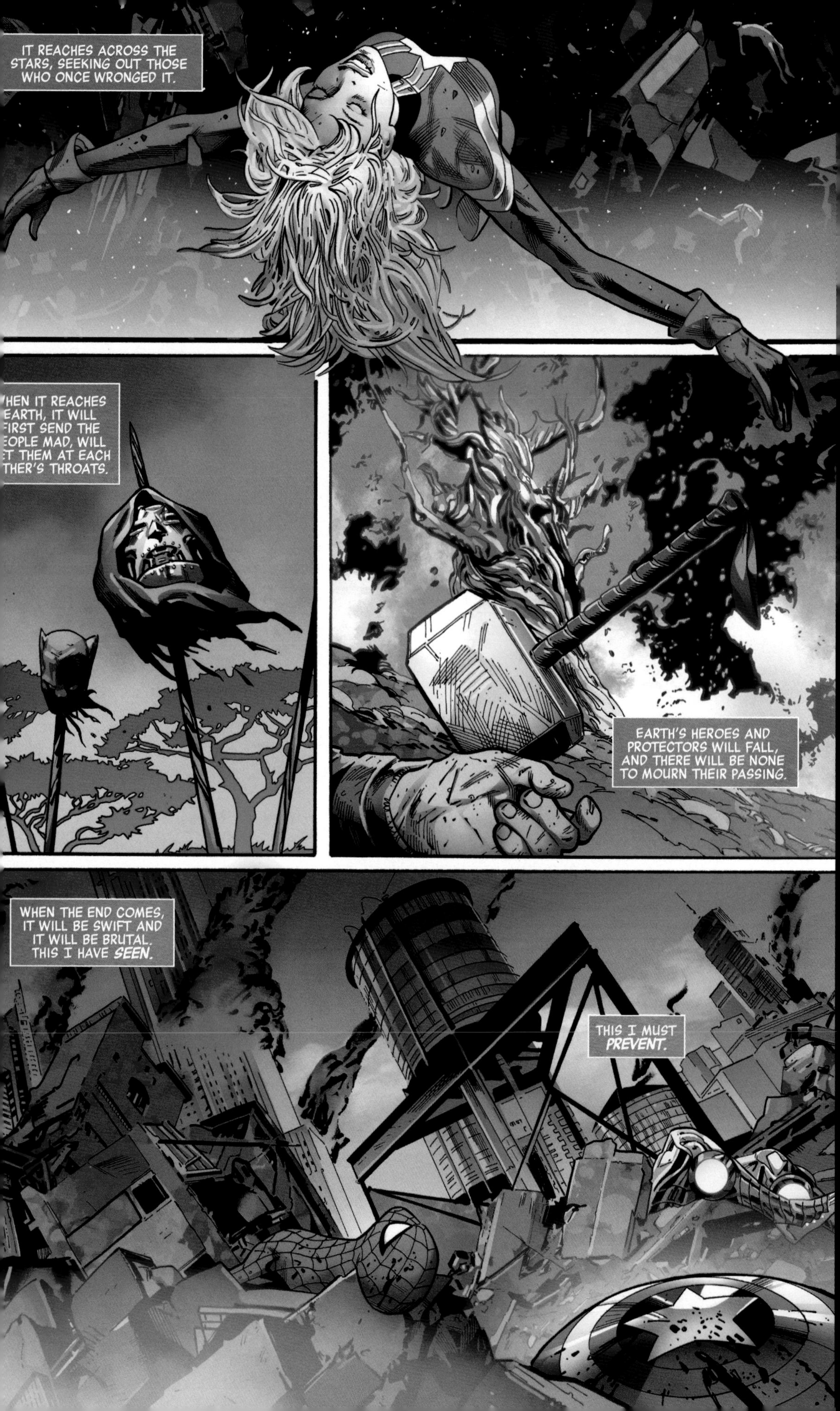
IT REACHES ACROSS THE STARS, SEEKING OUT THOSE WHO ONCE WRONGED IT.
HEN IT REACHES EARTH, IT WILL FIRST SEND THE EOPLE MAD, WILL T THEM AT EACH THER'S THROATS.
EARTH'S HEROES AND PROTECTORS WILL FALL, AND THERE WILL BE NONE TO MOURN THEIR PASSING.
WHEN THE END COMES, IT WILL BE SWIFT AND IT WILL BE BRUTAL. THIS I HAVE *SEEN*.
THIS I MUST *PREVENT*.

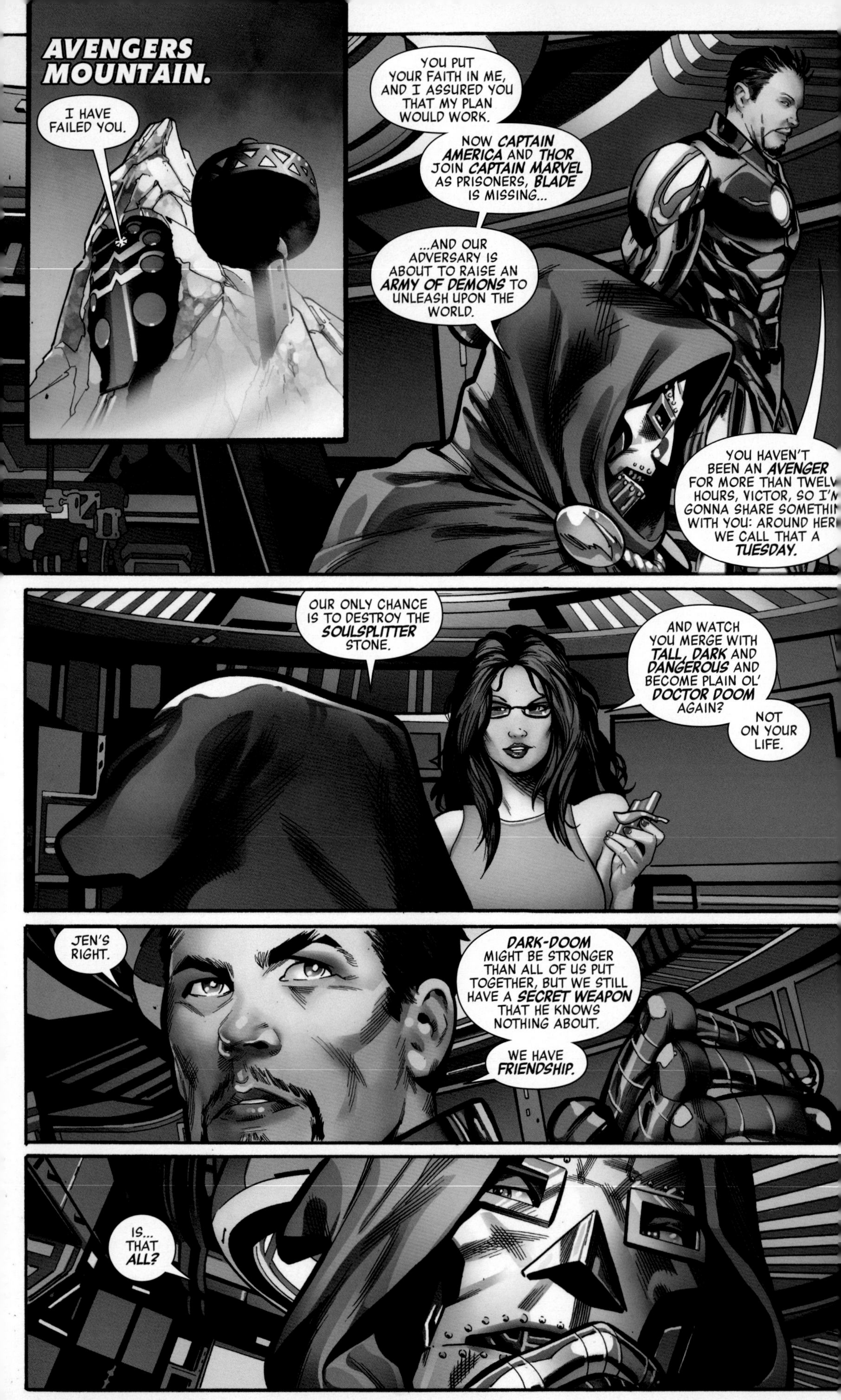
AVENGERS MOUNTAIN.
I HAVE FAILED YOU.
YOU PUT YOUR FAITH IN ME, AND I ASSURED YOU THAT MY PLAN WOULD WORK.
NOW CAPTAIN AMERICA AND THOR JOIN CAPTAIN MARVEL AS PRISONERS, BLADE IS MISSING...
...AND OUR ADVERSARY IS ABOUT TO RAISE AN ARMY OF DEMONS TO UNLEASH UPON THE WORLD.
YOU HAVEN'T BEEN AN AVENGER FOR MORE THAN TWELV HOURS, VICTOR, SO I'M GONNA SHARE SOMETHI WITH YOU: AROUND HER WE CALL THAT A TUESDAY.
OUR ONLY CHANCE IS TO DESTROY THE SOULSPLITTER STONE.
AND WATCH YOU MERGE WITH TALL, DARK AND DANGEROUS AND BECOME PLAIN OL' DOCTOR DOOM AGAIN?
NOT ON YOUR LIFE.
JEN'S RIGHT.
DARK-DOOM MIGHT BE STRONGER THAN ALL OF US PUT TOGETHER, BUT WE STILL HAVE A SECRET WEAPON THAT HE KNOWS NOTHING ABOUT.
WE HAVE FRIENDSHIP.
IS... THAT ALL?

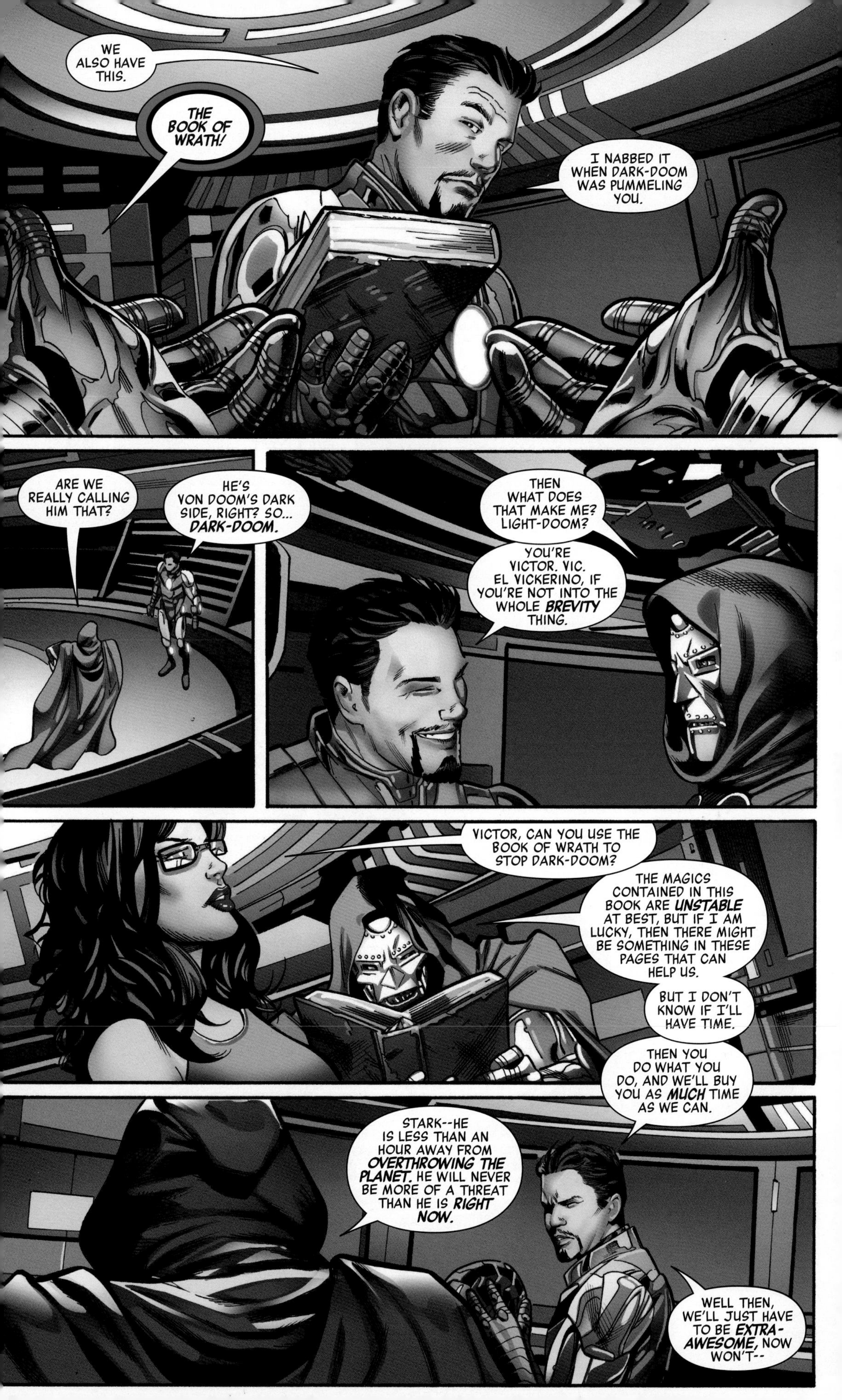
WE ALSO HAVE THIS.
THE BOOK OF WRATH!
I NABBED IT WHEN DARK-DOOM WAS PUMMELING YOU.
ARE WE REALLY CALLING HIM THAT?
HE'S VON DOOM'S DARK SIDE, RIGHT? SO... DARK-DOOM.
THEN WHAT DOES THAT MAKE ME? LIGHT-DOOM?
YOU'RE VICTOR. VIC. EL VICKERINO, IF YOU'RE NOT INTO THE WHOLE BREVITY THING.
VICTOR, CAN YOU USE THE BOOK OF WRATH TO STOP DARK-DOOM?
THE MAGICS CONTAINED IN THIS BOOK ARE UNSTABLE AT BEST, BUT IF I AM LUCKY, THEN THERE MIGHT BE SOMETHING IN THESE PAGES THAT CAN HELP US.
BUT I DON'T KNOW IF I'LL HAVE TIME.
THEN YOU DO WHAT YOU DO, AND WE'LL BUY YOU AS MUCH TIME AS WE CAN.
STARK--HE IS LESS THAN AN HOUR AWAY FROM OVERTHROWING THE PLANET. HE WILL NEVER BE MORE OF A THREAT THAN HE IS RIGHT NOW.
WELL THEN, WE'LL JUST HAVE TO BE EXTRA-AWESOME, NOW WON'T--

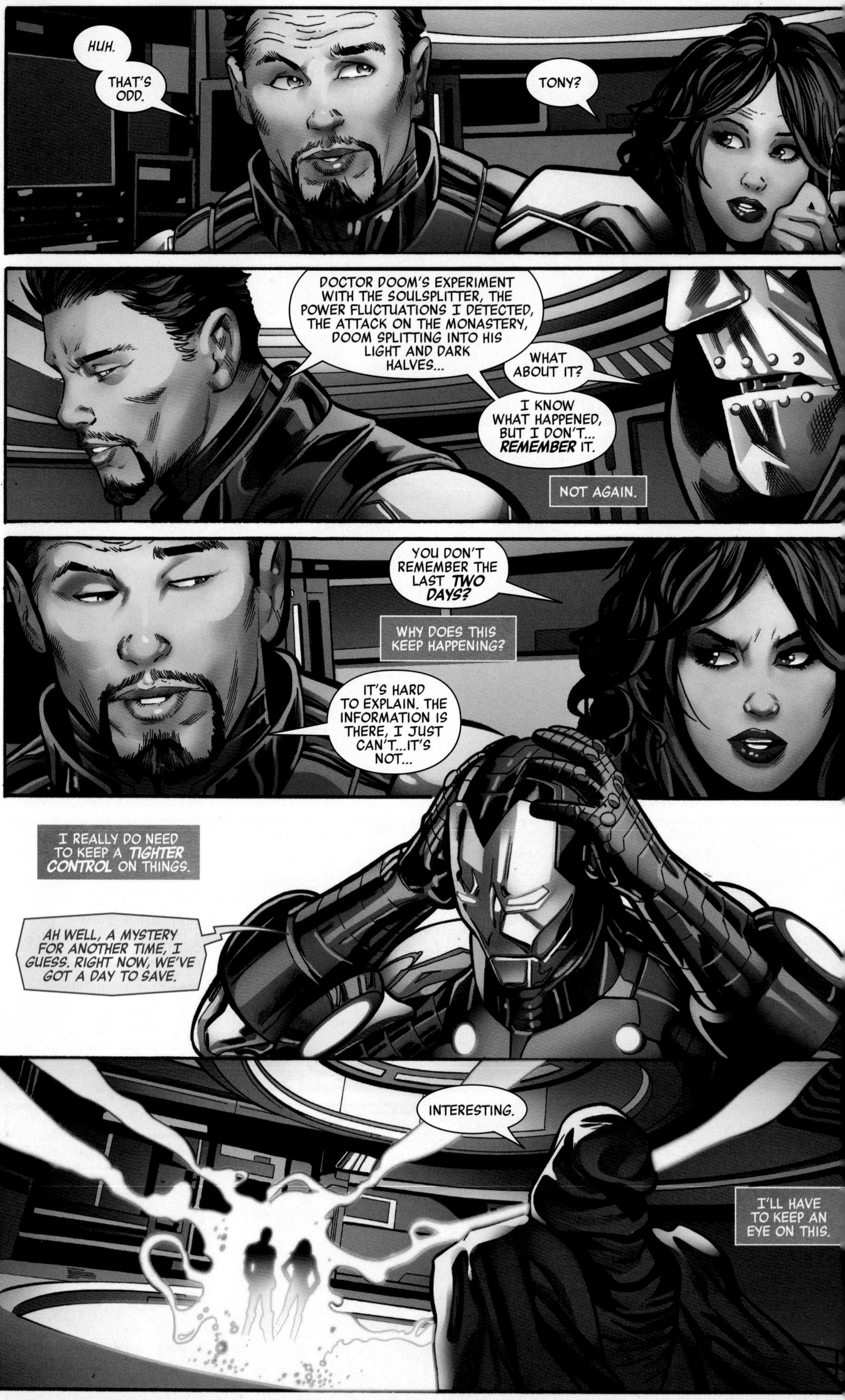
HUH.
THAT'S ODD.
TONY?
DOCTOR DOOM'S EXPERIMENT WITH THE SOULSPLITTER, THE POWER FLUCTUATIONS I DETECTED, THE ATTACK ON THE MONASTERY, DOOM SPLITTING INTO HIS LIGHT AND DARK HALVES...
WHAT ABOUT IT?
I KNOW WHAT HAPPENED, BUT I DON'T... REMEMBER IT.
NOT AGAIN.
YOU DON'T REMEMBER THE LAST TWO DAYS?
WHY DOES THIS KEEP HAPPENING?
IT'S HARD TO EXPLAIN. THE INFORMATION IS THERE, I JUST CAN'T...IT'S NOT...
I REALLY DO NEED TO KEEP A TIGHTER CONTROL ON THINGS.
AH WELL, A MYSTERY FOR ANOTHER TIME, I GUESS. RIGHT NOW, WE'VE GOT A DAY TO SAVE.
INTERESTING.
I'LL HAVE TO KEEP AN EYE ON THIS.

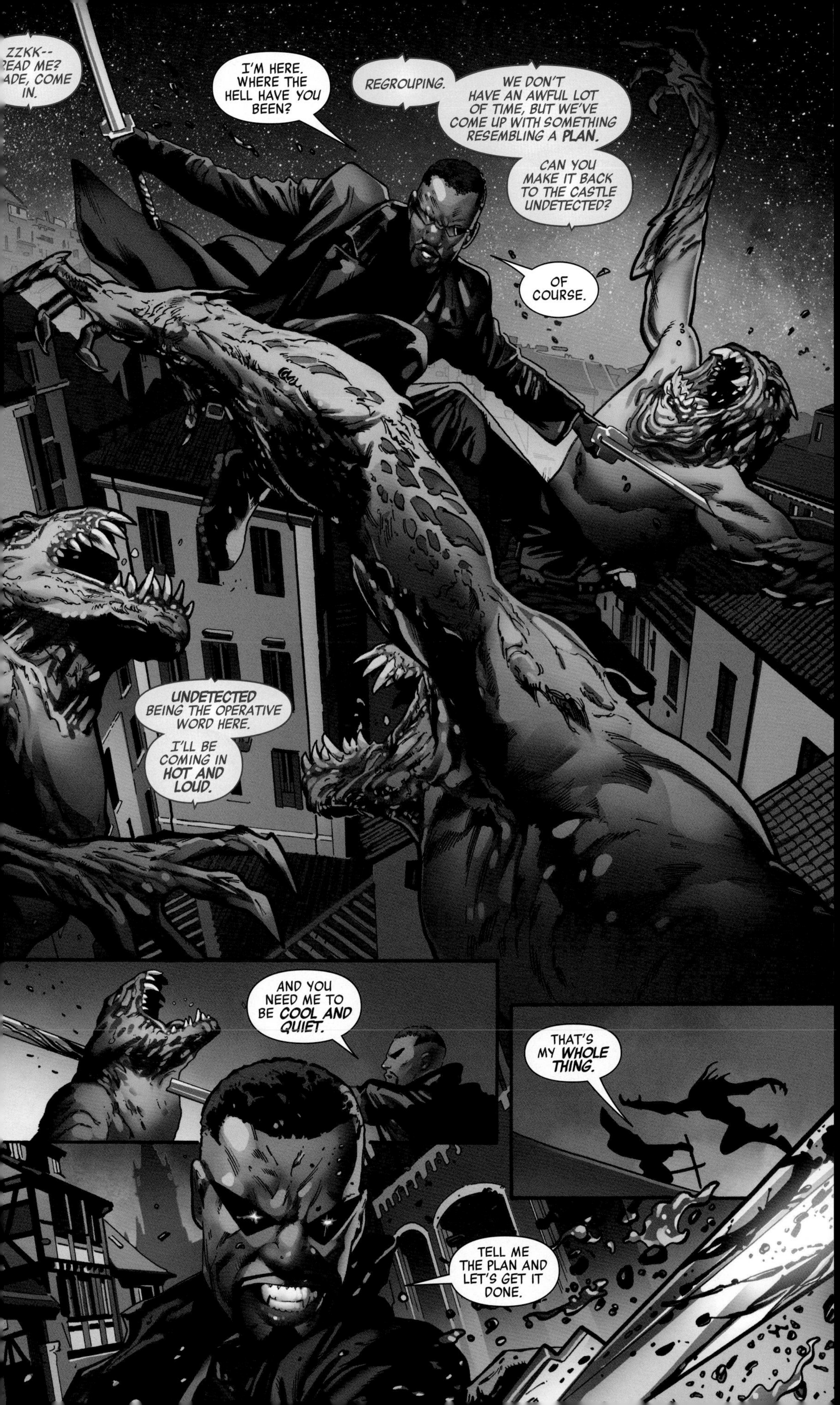
ZZKK-- READ ME? ADE, COME IN.
I'M HERE. WHERE THE HELL HAVE YOU BEEN?
REGROUPING.
WE DON'T HAVE AN AWFUL LOT OF TIME, BUT WE'VE COME UP WITH SOMETHING RESEMBLING A PLAN.
CAN YOU MAKE IT BACK TO THE CASTLE UNDETECTED?
OF COURSE.
UNDETECTED BEING THE OPERATIVE WORD HERE.
I'LL BE COMING IN HOT AND LOUD.
AND YOU NEED ME TO BE COOL AND QUIET.
THAT'S MY WHOLE THING.
TELL ME THE PLAN AND LET'S GET IT DONE.

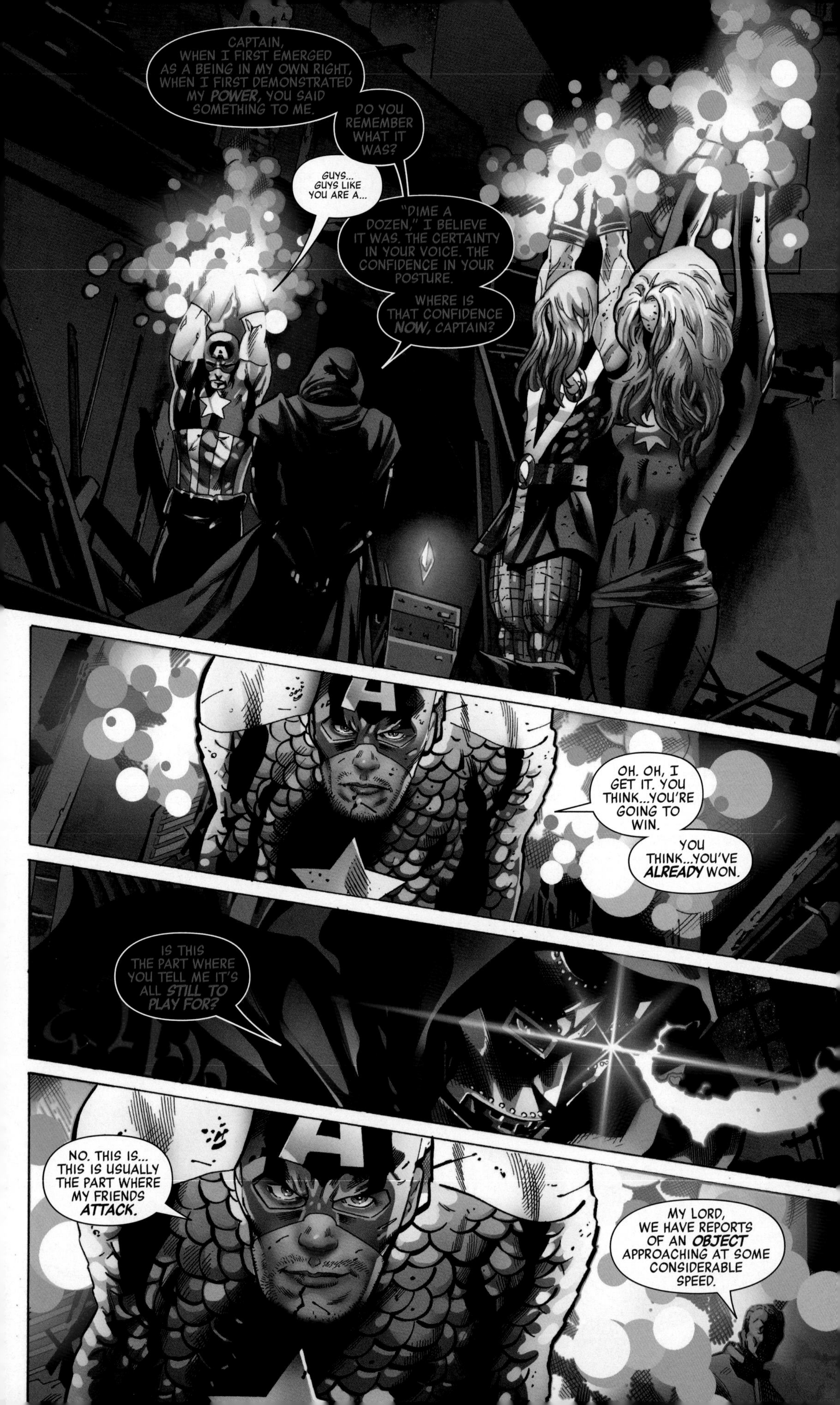
CAPTAIN, WHEN I FIRST EMERGED AS A BEING IN MY OWN RIGHT, WHEN I FIRST DEMONSTRATED MY POWER, YOU SAID SOMETHING TO ME.
DO YOU REMEMBER WHAT IT WAS?
GUYS... GUYS LIKE YOU ARE A...
"DIME A DOZEN," I BELIEVE IT WAS. THE CERTAINTY IN YOUR VOICE. THE CONFIDENCE IN YOUR POSTURE.
WHERE IS THAT CONFIDENCE NOW, CAPTAIN?
OH. OH, I GET IT. YOU THINK...YOU'RE GOING TO WIN.
YOU THINK...YOU'VE ALREADY WON.
IS THIS THE PART WHERE YOU TELL ME IT'S ALL STILL TO PLAY FOR?
NO. THIS IS... THIS IS USUALLY THE PART WHERE MY FRIENDS ATTACK.
MY LORD, WE HAVE REPORTS OF AN OBJECT APPROACHING AT SOME CONSIDERABLE SPEED.

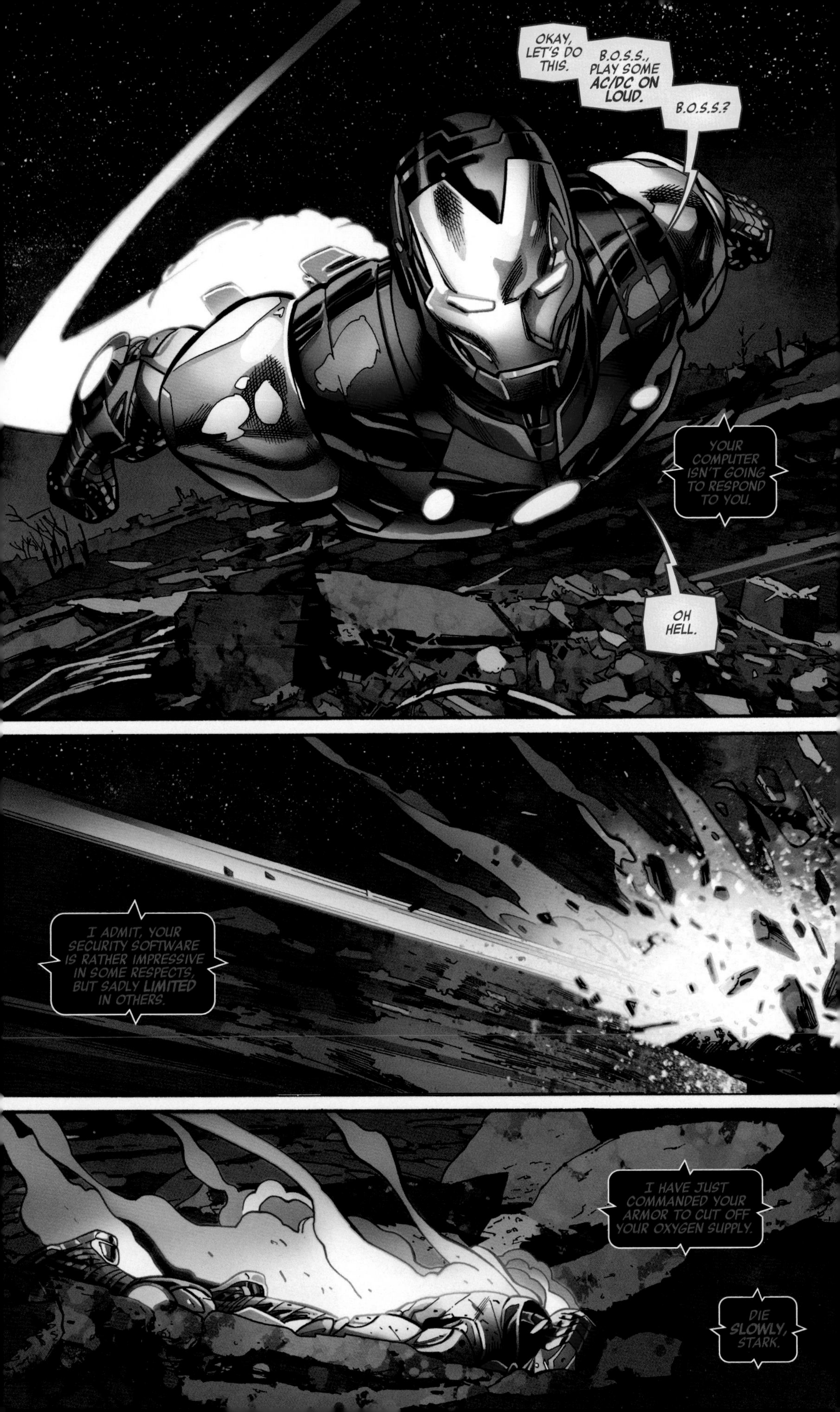
OKAY, LET'S DO THIS.
B.O.S.S., PLAY SOME AC/DC ON LOUD.
B.O.S.S.?
YOUR COMPUTER ISN'T GOING TO RESPOND TO YOU.
OH HELL.
I ADMIT, YOUR SECURITY SOFTWARE IS RATHER IMPRESSIVE IN SOME RESPECTS, BUT SADLY LIMITED IN OTHERS.
I HAVE JUST COMMANDED YOUR ARMOR TO CUT OFF YOUR OXYGEN SUPPLY.
DIE SLOWLY, STARK.

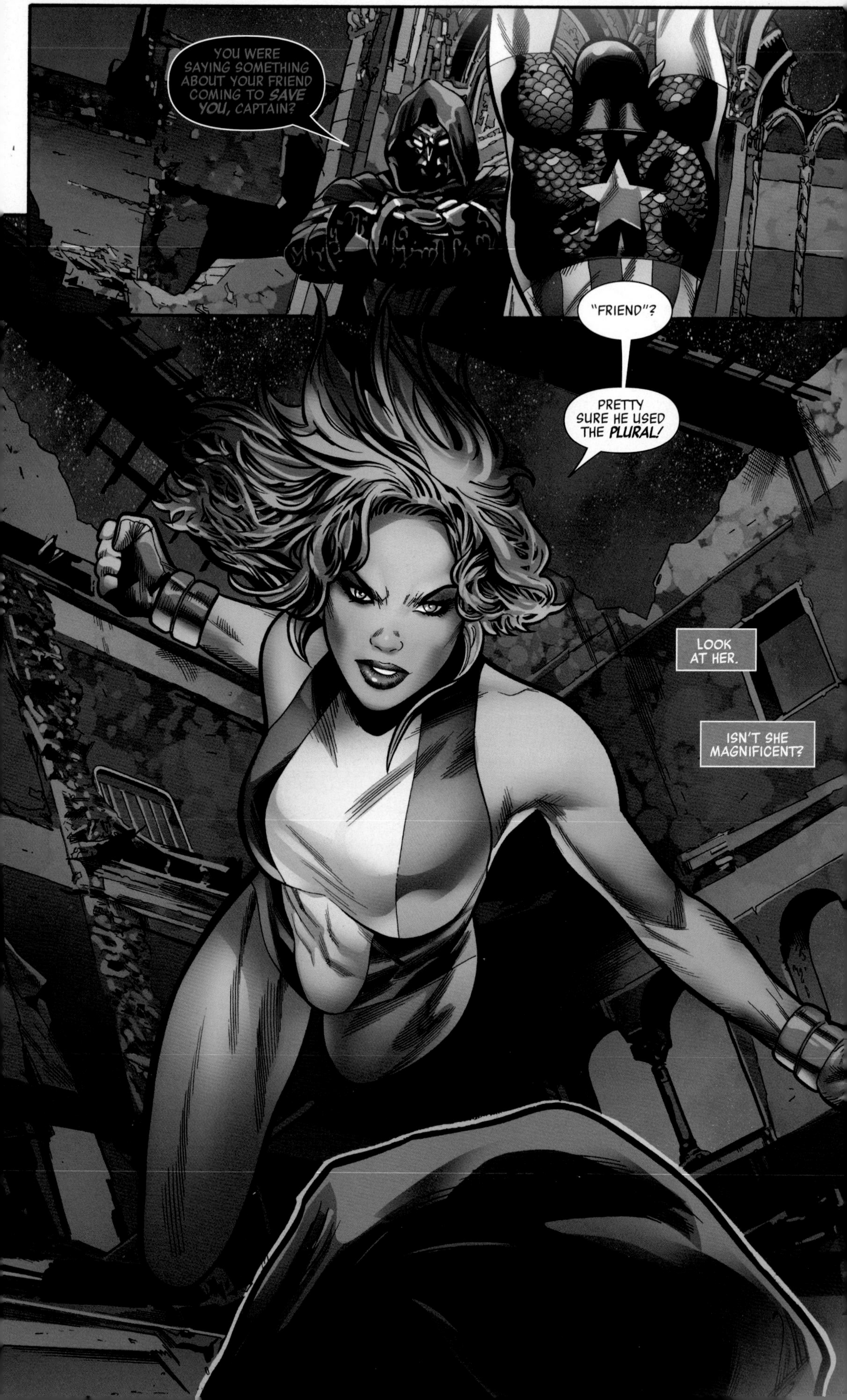
YOU WERE SAYING SOMETHING ABOUT YOUR FRIEND COMING TO SAVE YOU, CAPTAIN?
"FRIEND"?
PRETTY SURE HE USED THE PLURAL!
LOOK AT HER.
ISN'T SHE MAGNIFICENT?

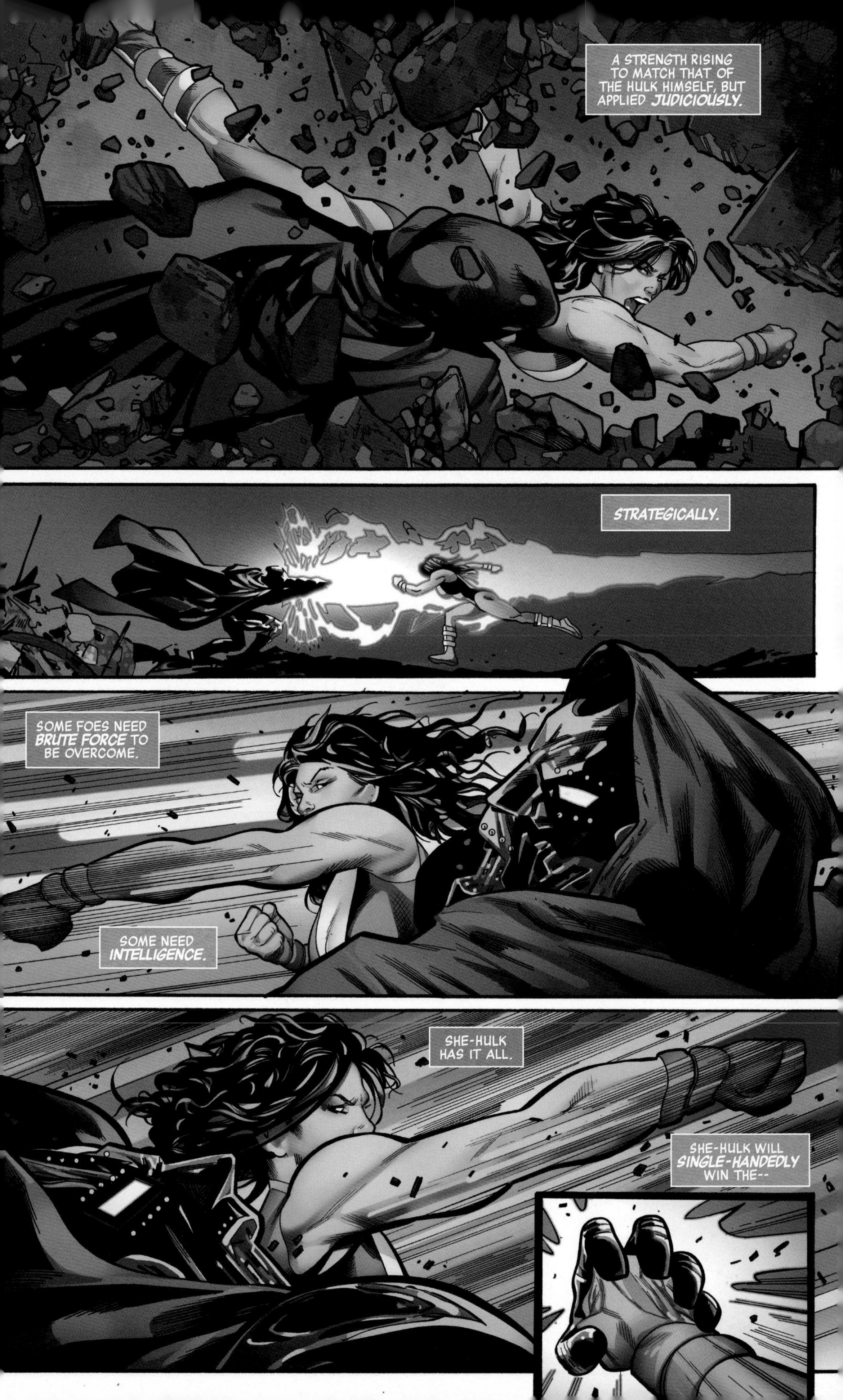
A STRENGTH RISING TO MATCH THAT OF THE HULK HIMSELF, BUT APPLIED JUDICIOUSLY.
STRATEGICALLY.
SOME FOES NEED BRUTE FORCE TO BE OVERCOME.
SOME NEED INTELLIGENCE.
SHE-HULK HAS IT ALL.
SHE-HULK WILL SINGLE-HANDEDLY WIN THE--

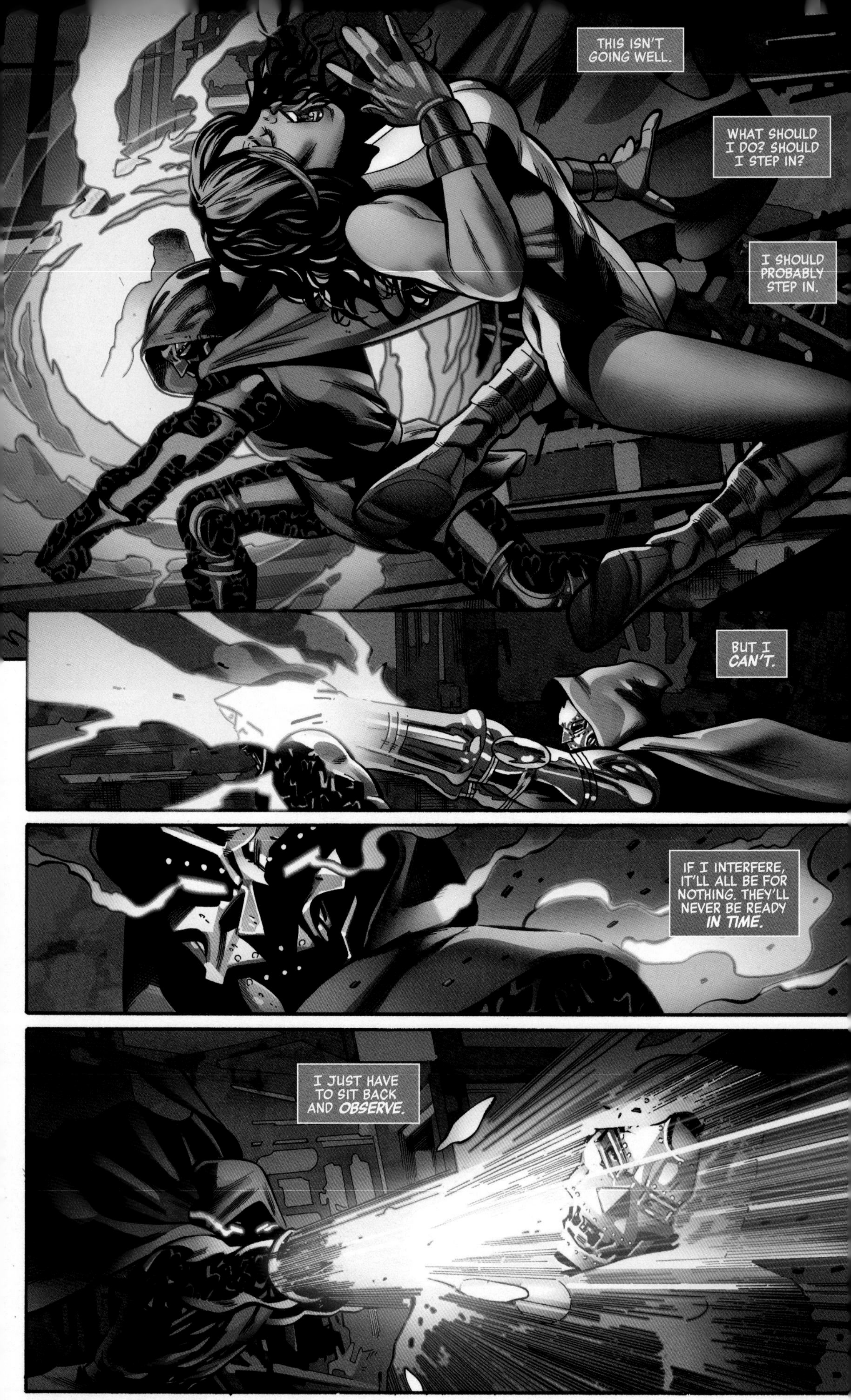
THIS ISN'T GOING WELL.
WHAT SHOULD I DO? SHOULD I STEP IN?
I SHOULD PROBABLY STEP IN.
BUT I *CAN'T*.
IF I INTERFERE, IT'LL ALL BE FOR NOTHING. THEY'LL NEVER BE READY *IN TIME*.
I JUST HAVE TO SIT BACK AND *OBSERVE*.

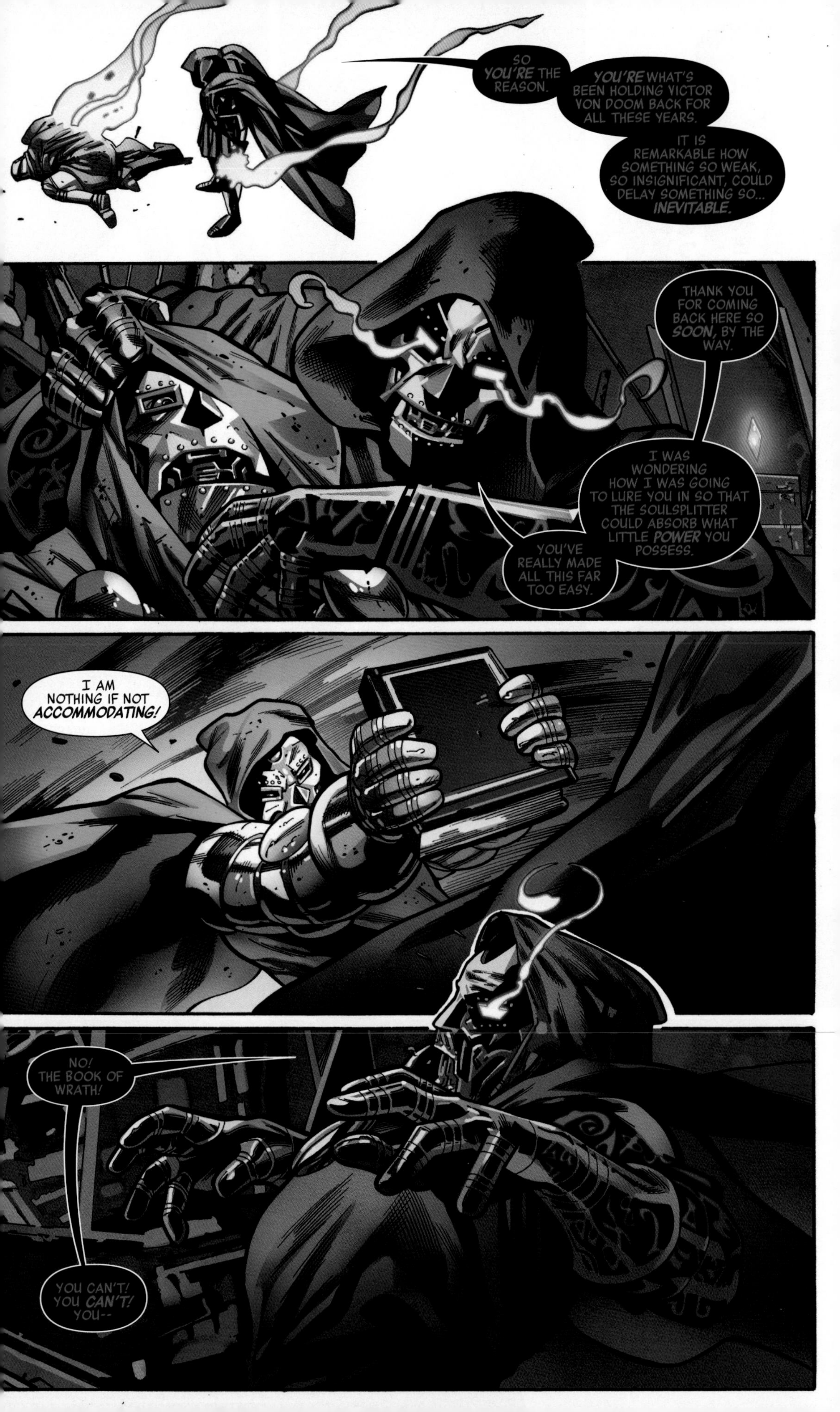
SO YOU'RE THE REASON.
YOU'RE WHAT'S BEEN HOLDING VICTOR VON DOOM BACK FOR ALL THESE YEARS.
IT IS REMARKABLE HOW SOMETHING SO WEAK, SO INSIGNIFICANT, COULD DELAY SOMETHING SO... INEVITABLE.
THANK YOU FOR COMING BACK HERE SO SOON, BY THE WAY.
I WAS WONDERING HOW I WAS GOING TO LURE YOU IN SO THAT THE SOULSPLITTER COULD ABSORB WHAT LITTLE POWER YOU POSSESS.
YOU'VE REALLY MADE ALL THIS FAR TOO EASY.
I AM NOTHING IF NOT ACCOMMODATING!
NO! THE BOOK OF WRATH!
YOU CAN'T! YOU CAN'T! YOU--

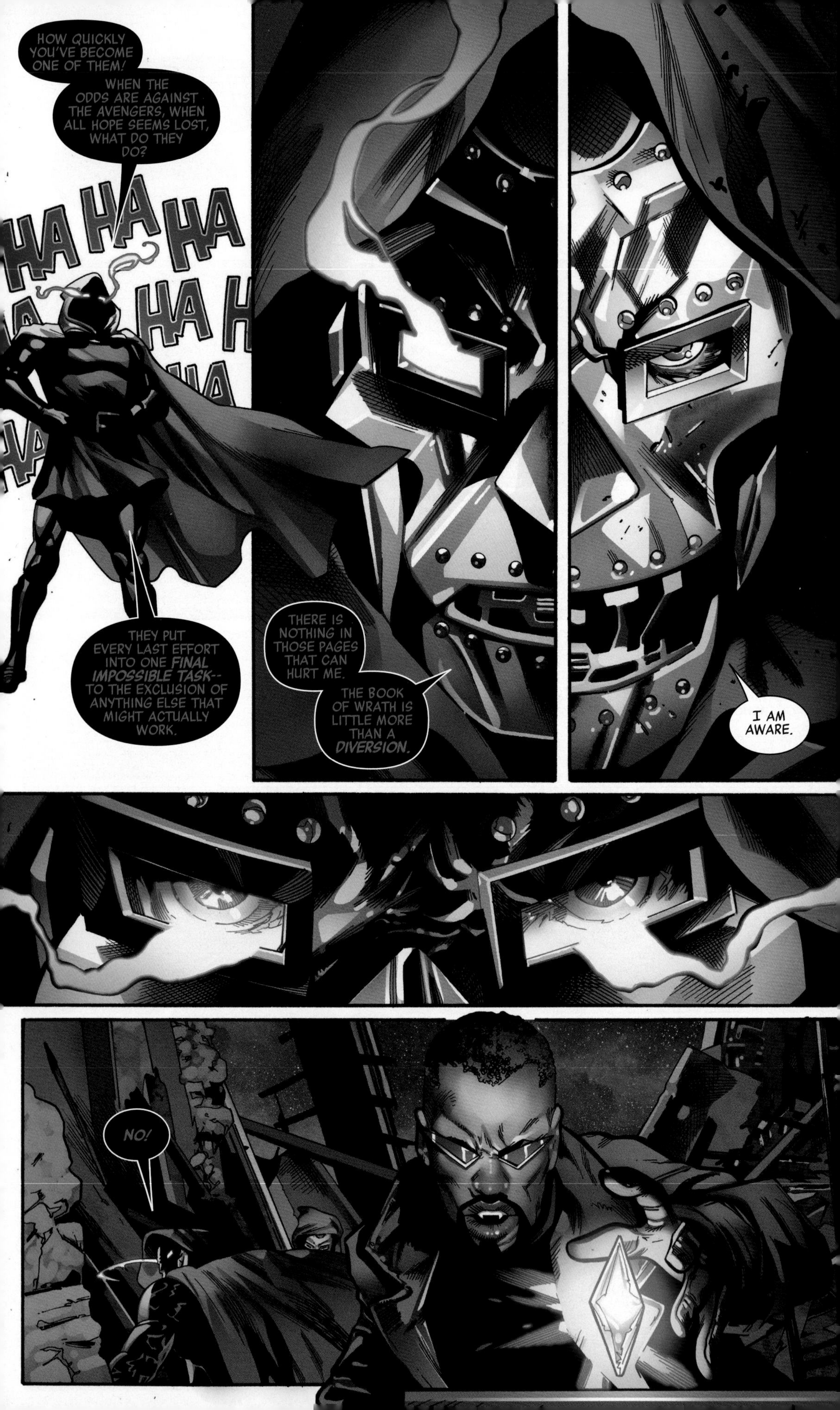

HOW QUICKLY YOU'VE BECOME ONE OF THEM!
WHEN THE ODDS ARE AGAINST THE AVENGERS, WHEN ALL HOPE SEEMS LOST, WHAT DO THEY DO?
HA HA HA HA
HA HA H
HA
THEY PUT EVERY LAST EFFORT INTO ONE FINAL IMPOSSIBLE TASK-- TO THE EXCLUSION OF ANYTHING ELSE THAT MIGHT ACTUALLY WORK.
THERE IS NOTHING IN THOSE PAGES THAT CAN HURT ME.
THE BOOK OF WRATH IS LITTLE MORE THAN A DIVERSION.
I AM AWARE.
NO!

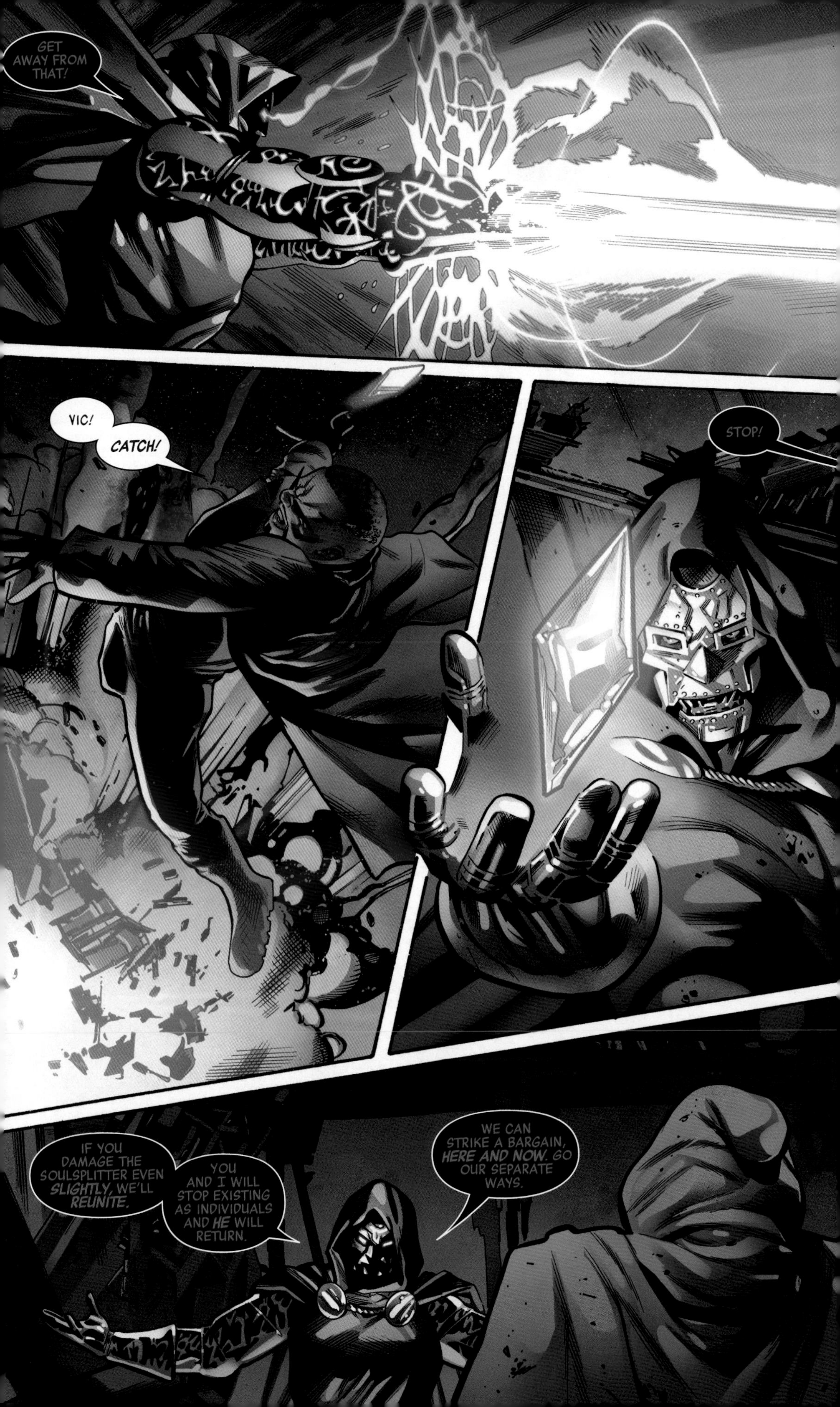

GET AWAY FROM THAT!
VIC!
CATCH!
STOP!
IF YOU DAMAGE THE SOULSPLITTER EVEN SLIGHTLY, WE'LL REUNITE.
YOU AND I WILL STOP EXISTING AS INDIVIDUALS AND HE WILL RETURN.
WE CAN STRIKE A BARGAIN, HERE AND NOW. GO OUR SEPARATE WAYS.

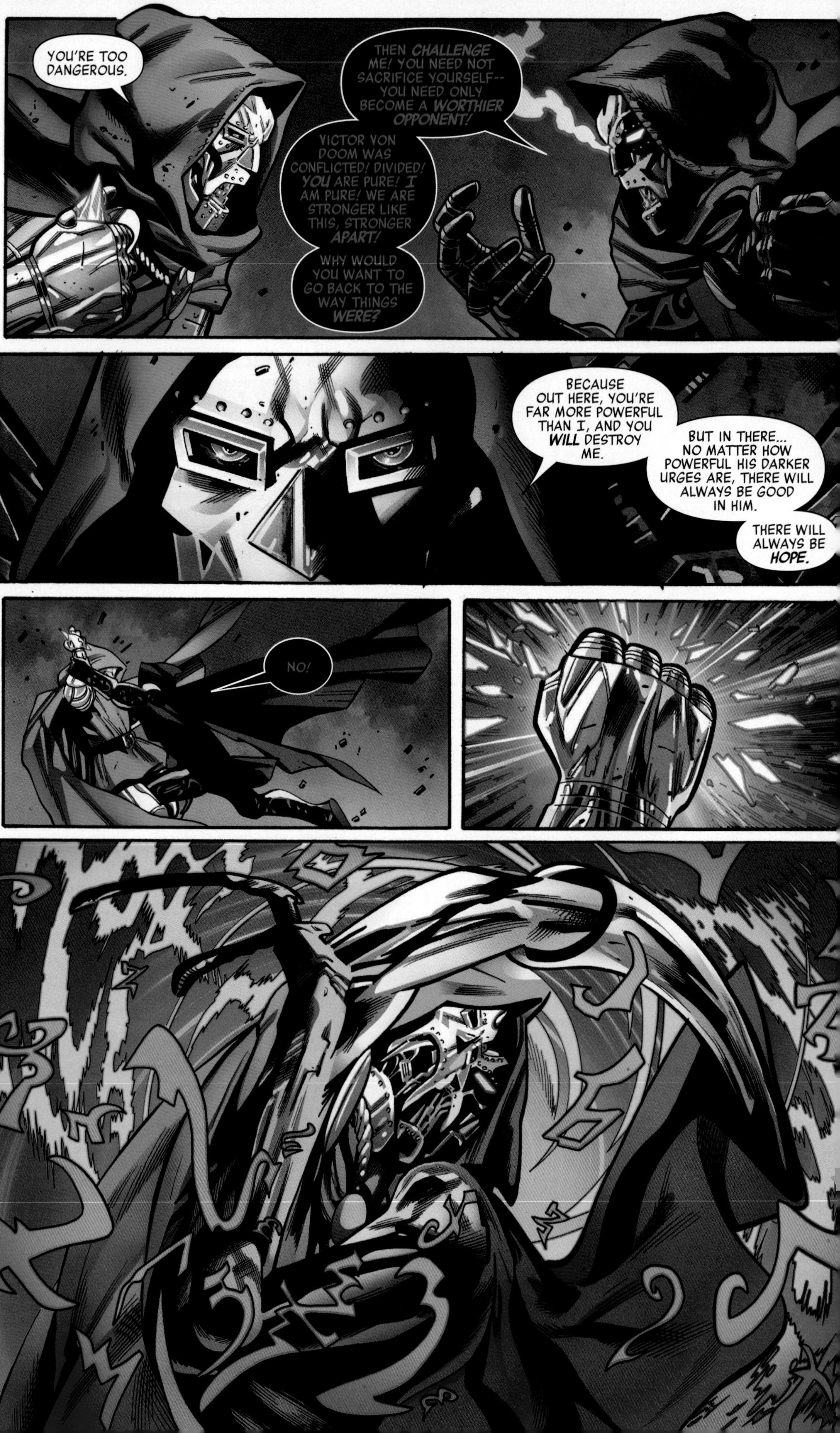

YOU'RE TOO DANGEROUS.
THEN CHALLENGE ME! YOU NEED NOT SACRIFICE YOURSELF-- YOU NEED ONLY BECOME A WORTHIER OPPONENT!
VICTOR VON DOOM WAS CONFLICTED! DIVIDED! YOU ARE PURE! I AM PURE! WE ARE STRONGER LIKE THIS, STRONGER APART!
WHY WOULD YOU WANT TO GO BACK TO THE WAY THINGS WERE?
BECAUSE OUT HERE, YOU'RE FAR MORE POWERFUL THAN I, AND YOU WILL DESTROY ME.
BUT IN THERE... NO MATTER HOW POWERFUL HIS DARKER URGES ARE, THERE WILL ALWAYS BE GOOD IN HIM.
THERE WILL ALWAYS BE HOPE.
NO!

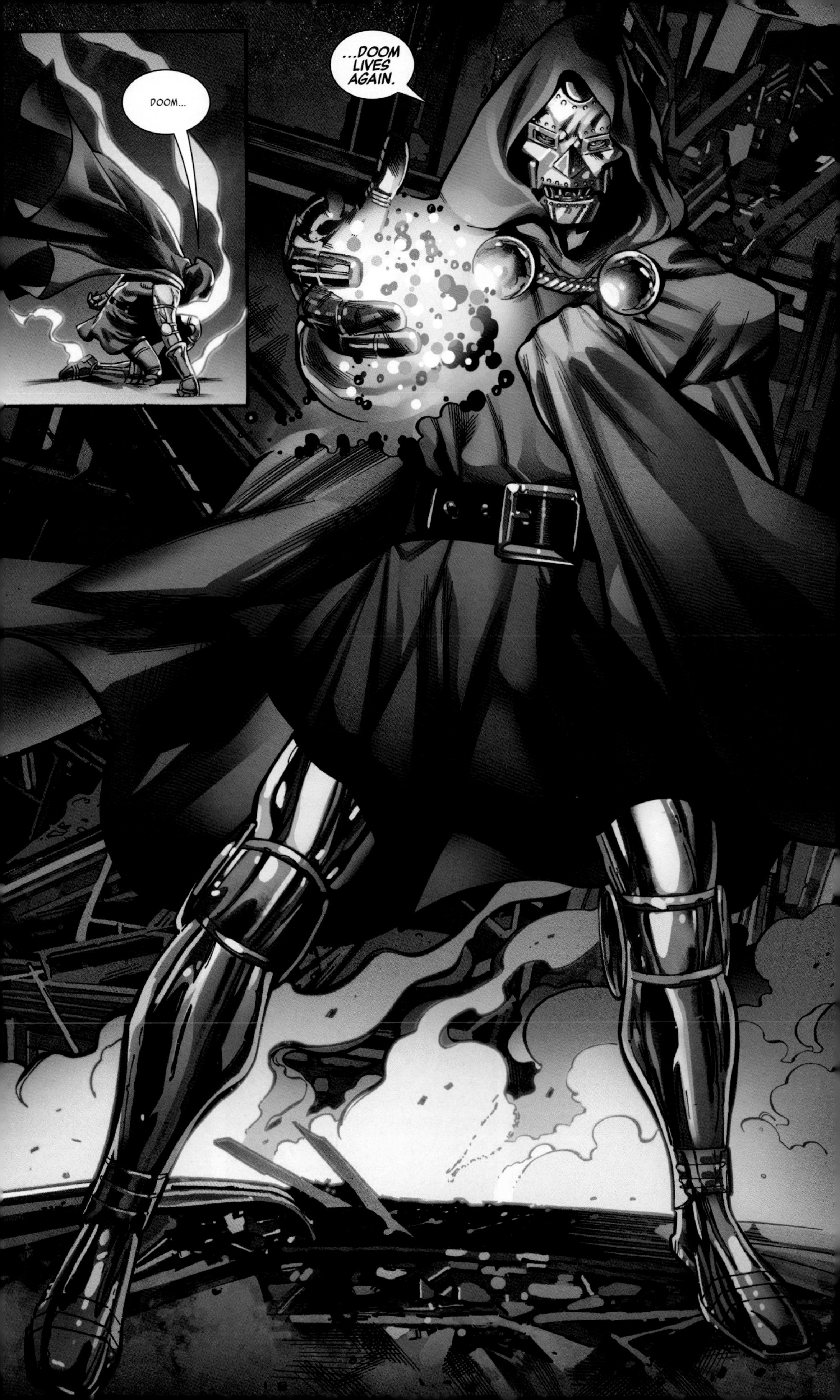
DOOM...
...DOOM LIVES AGAIN.

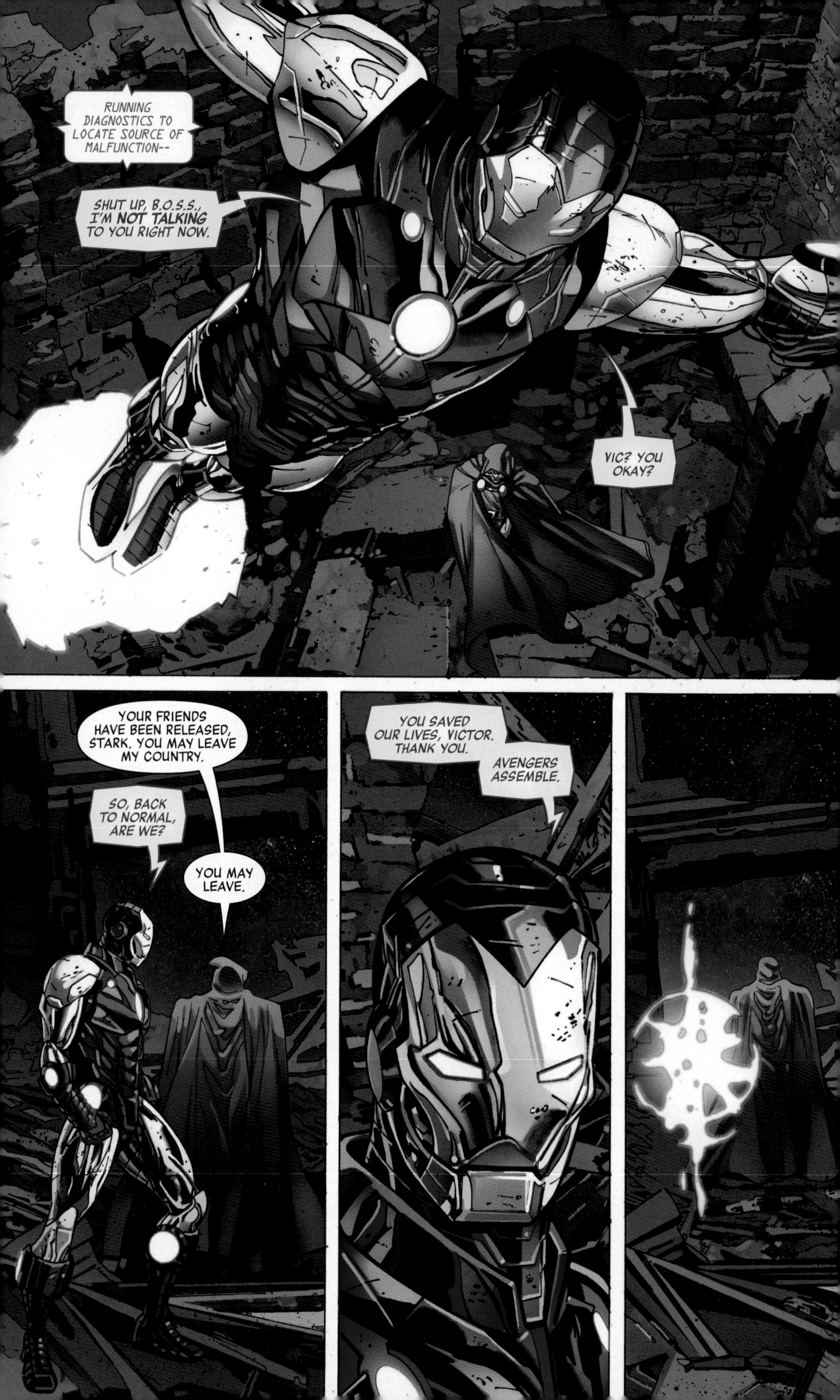
RUNNING DIAGNOSTICS TO LOCATE SOURCE OF MALFUNCTION--
SHUT UP, B.O.S.S., I'M **NOT TALKING** TO YOU RIGHT NOW.
VIC? YOU OKAY?
YOUR FRIENDS HAVE BEEN RELEASED, STARK. YOU MAY LEAVE MY COUNTRY.
SO, BACK TO NORMAL, ARE WE?
YOU MAY LEAVE.
YOU SAVED OUR LIVES, VICTOR. THANK YOU.
AVENGERS ASSEMBLE.

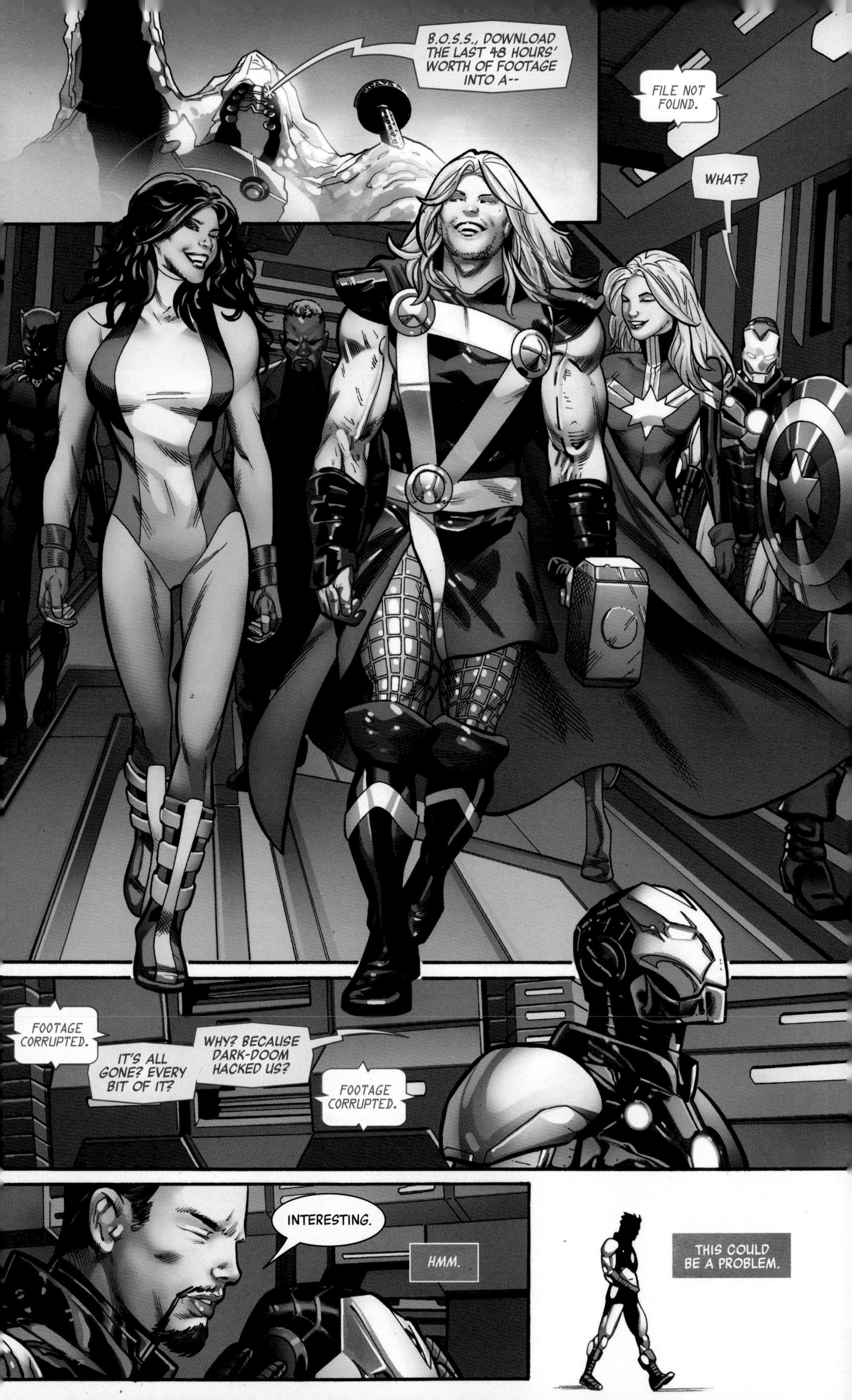
B.O.S.S., DOWNLOAD THE LAST 48 HOURS' WORTH OF FOOTAGE INTO A--
FILE NOT FOUND.
WHAT?
FOOTAGE CORRUPTED.
IT'S ALL GONE? EVERY BIT OF IT?
WHY? BECAUSE DARK-DOOM HACKED US?
FOOTAGE CORRUPTED.
INTERESTING.
HMM.
THIS COULD BE A PROBLEM.

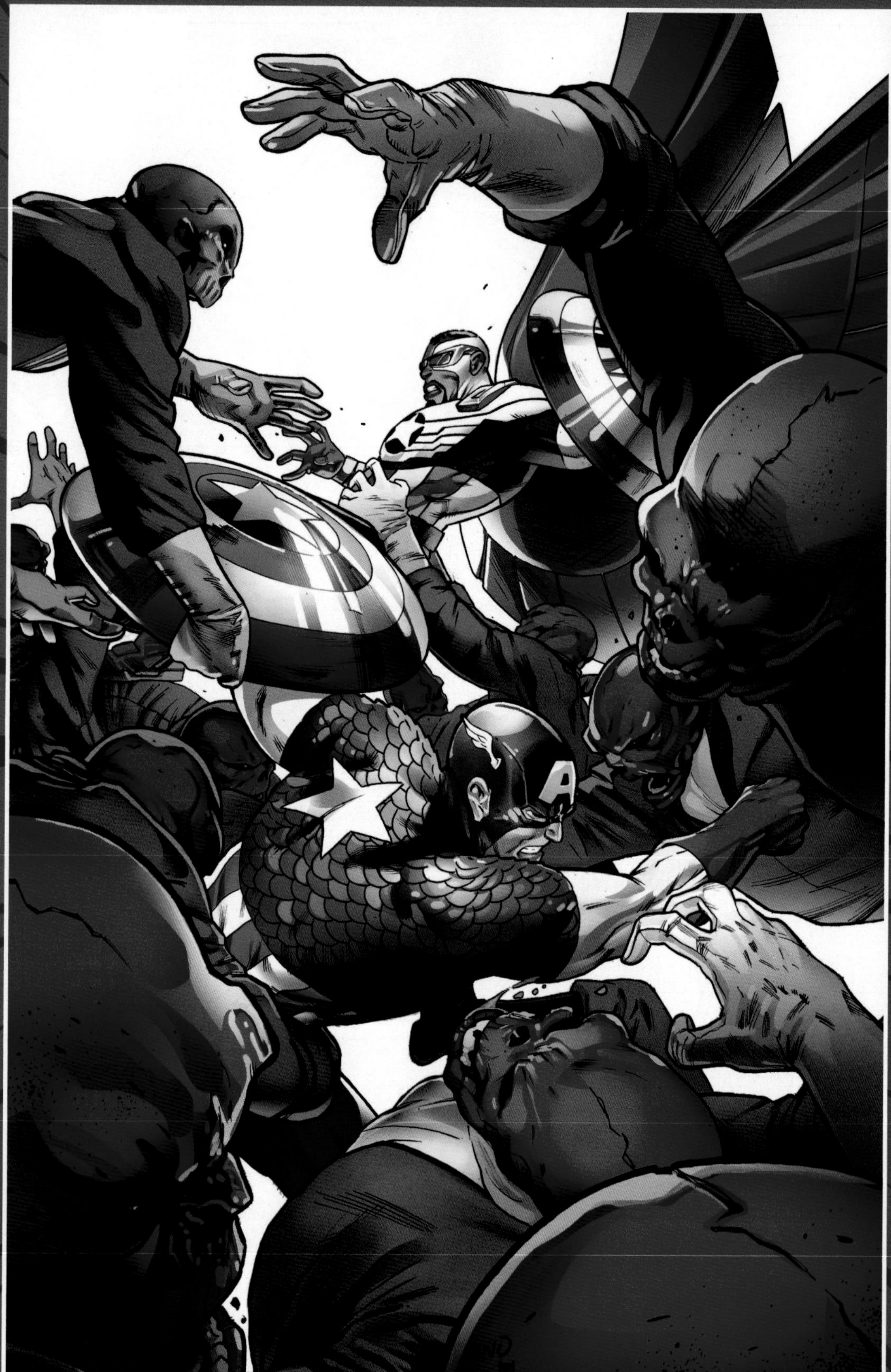

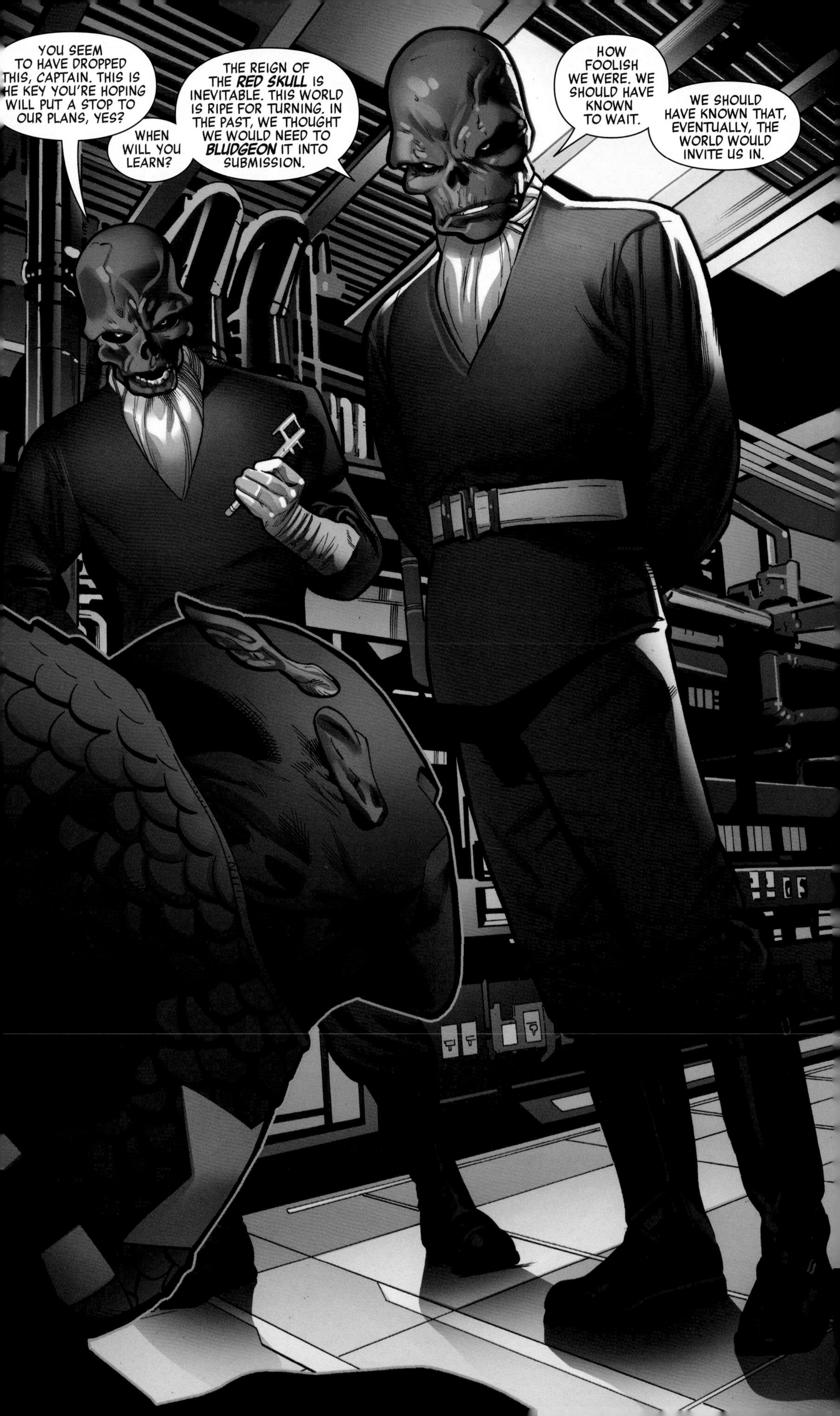
YOU SEEM TO HAVE DROPPED THIS, CAPTAIN. THIS IS HE KEY YOU'RE HOPING WILL PUT A STOP TO OUR PLANS, YES?
WHEN WILL YOU LEARN?
THE REIGN OF THE RED SKULL IS INEVITABLE. THIS WORLD IS RIPE FOR TURNING. IN THE PAST, WE THOUGHT WE WOULD NEED TO BLUDGEON IT INTO SUBMISSION.
HOW FOOLISH WE WERE. WE SHOULD HAVE KNOWN TO WAIT.
WE SHOULD HAVE KNOWN THAT, EVENTUALLY, THE WORLD WOULD INVITE US IN.

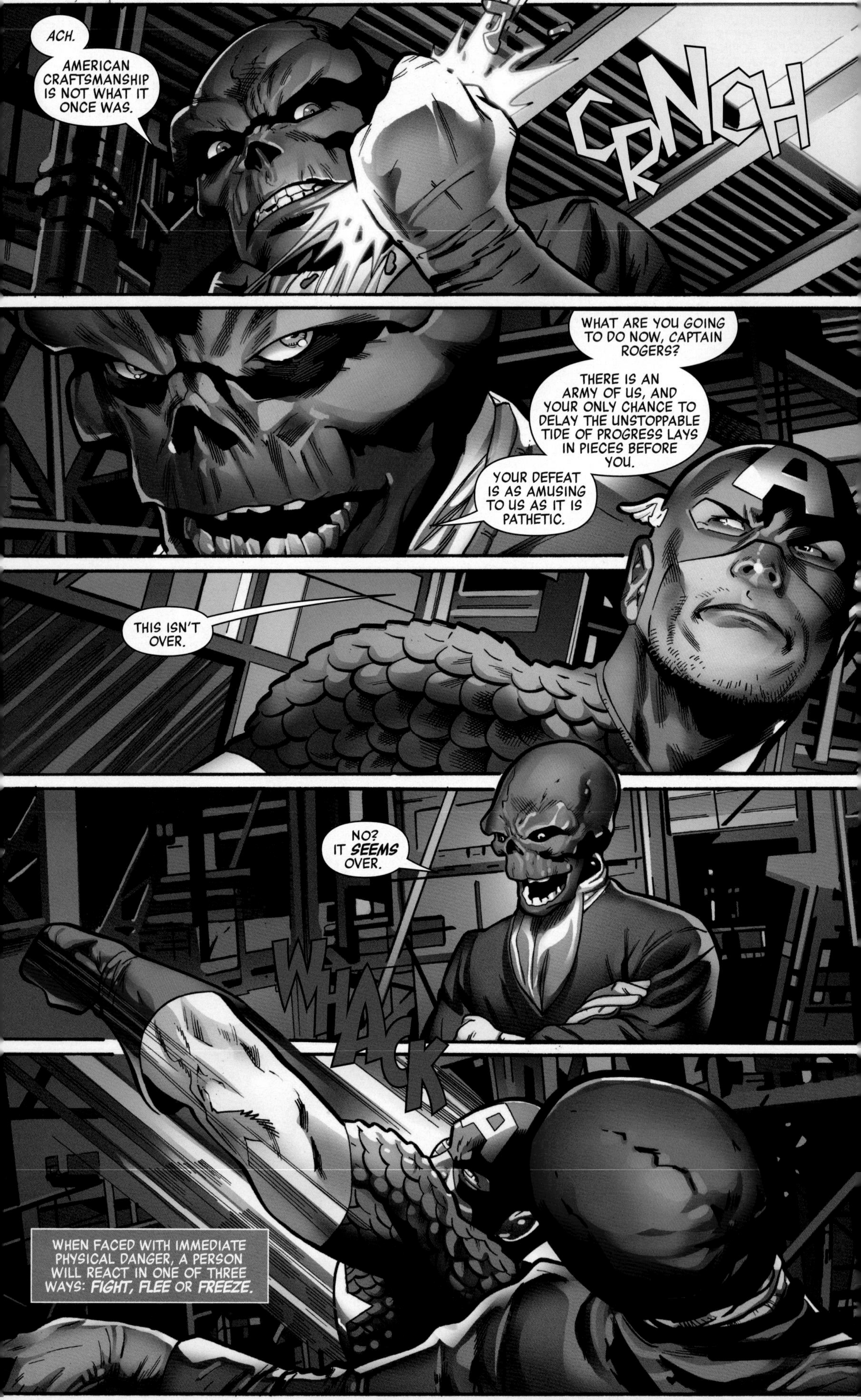
ACH.
AMERICAN CRAFTSMANSHIP IS NOT WHAT IT ONCE WAS.
CRNCH
WHAT ARE YOU GOING TO DO NOW, CAPTAIN ROGERS?
THERE IS AN ARMY OF US, AND YOUR ONLY CHANCE TO DELAY THE UNSTOPPABLE TIDE OF PROGRESS LAYS IN PIECES BEFORE YOU.
YOUR DEFEAT IS AS AMUSING TO US AS IT IS PATHETIC.
THIS ISN'T OVER.
NO? IT *SEEMS* OVER.
WHACK
WHEN FACED WITH IMMEDIATE PHYSICAL DANGER, A PERSON WILL REACT IN ONE OF THREE WAYS: ***FIGHT, FLEE*** OR ***FREEZE.***

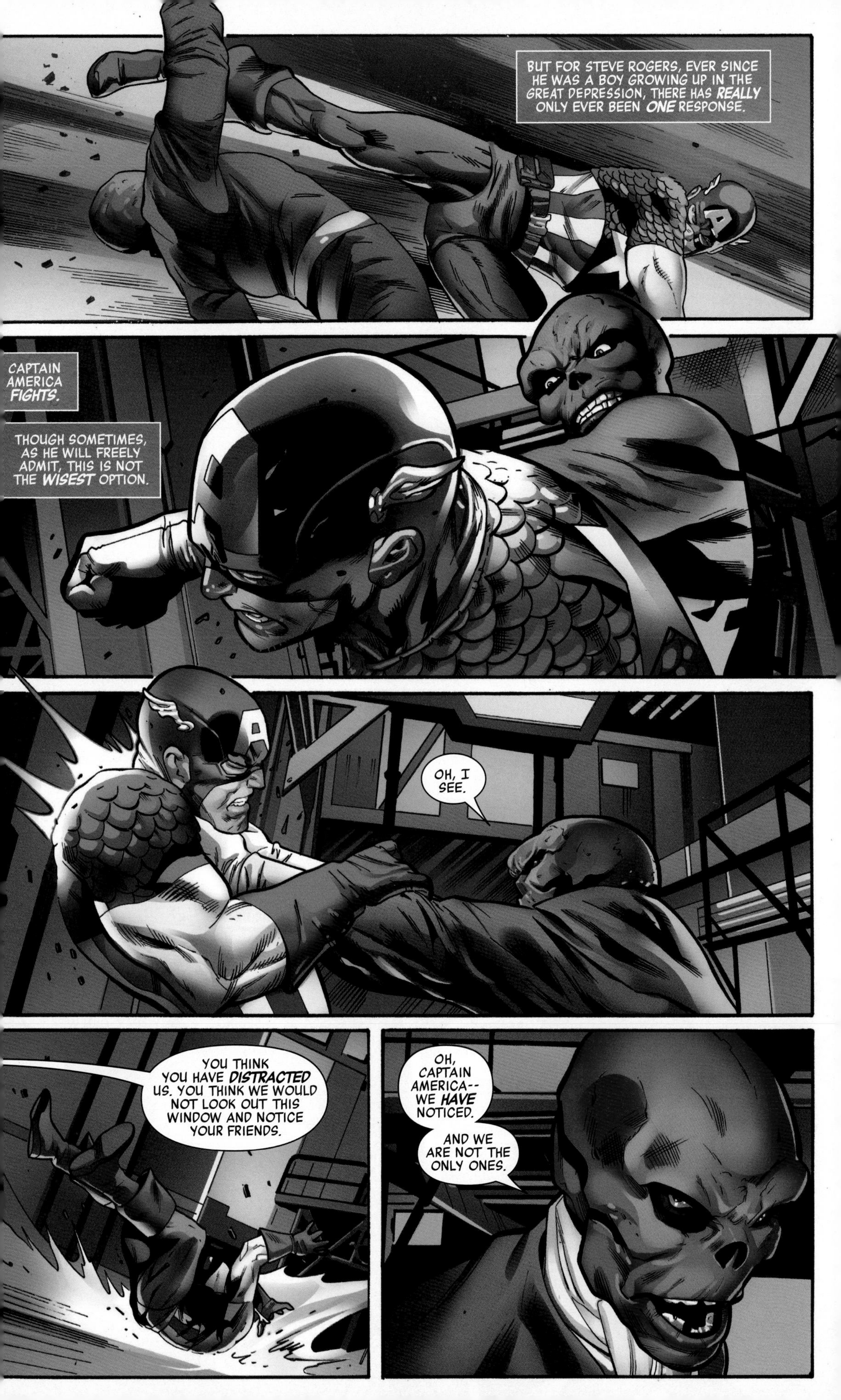
BUT FOR STEVE ROGERS, EVER SINCE HE WAS A BOY GROWING UP IN THE GREAT DEPRESSION, THERE HAS REALLY ONLY EVER BEEN ONE RESPONSE.
CAPTAIN AMERICA FIGHTS.
THOUGH SOMETIMES, AS HE WILL FREELY ADMIT, THIS IS NOT THE WISEST OPTION.
OH, I SEE.
YOU THINK YOU HAVE DISTRACTED US. YOU THINK WE WOULD NOT LOOK OUT THIS WINDOW AND NOTICE YOUR FRIENDS.
OH, CAPTAIN AMERICA-- WE HAVE NOTICED.
AND WE ARE NOT THE ONLY ONES.

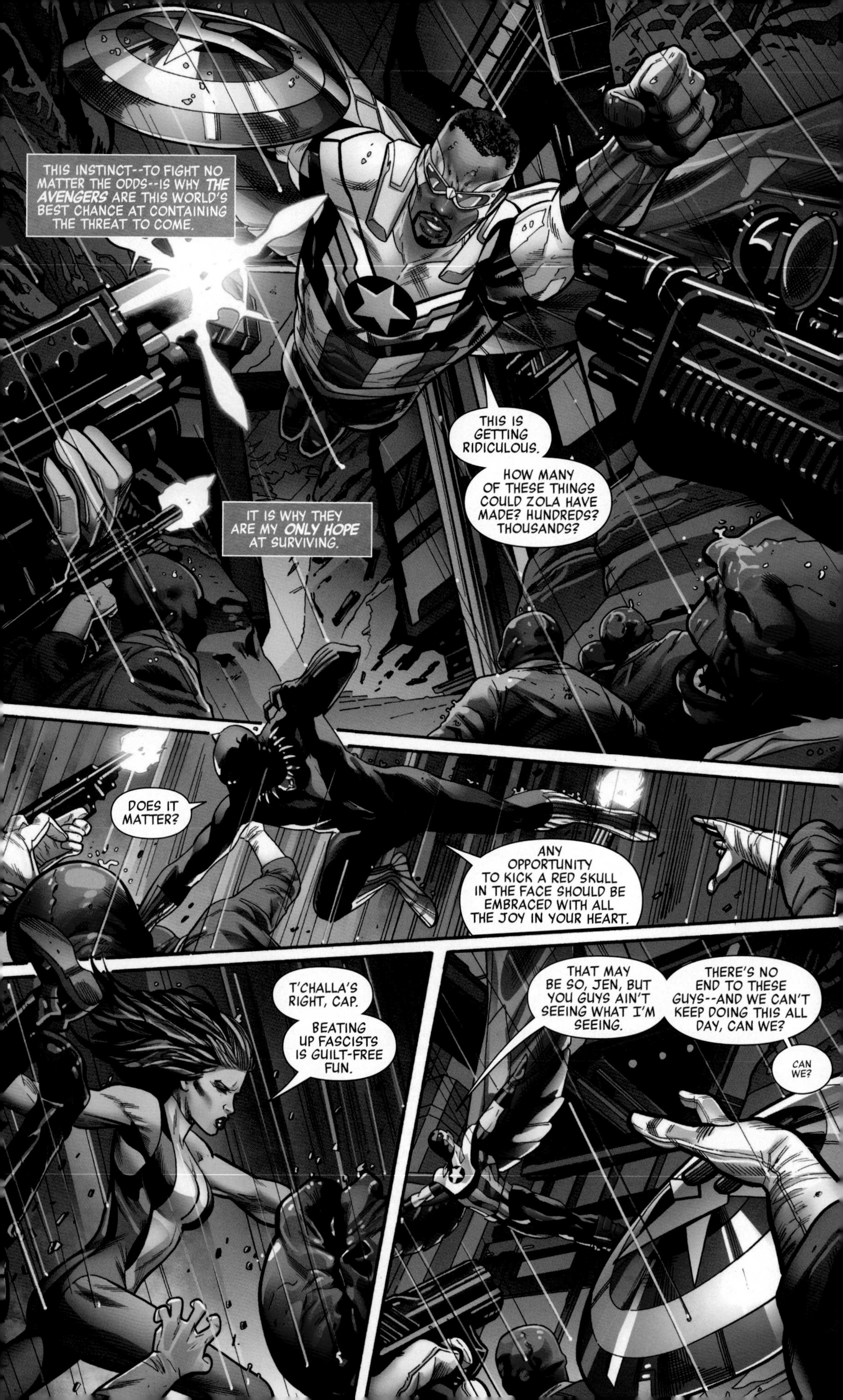
THIS INSTINCT--TO FIGHT NO MATTER THE ODDS--IS WHY THE AVENGERS ARE THIS WORLD'S BEST CHANCE AT CONTAINING THE THREAT TO COME.
IT IS WHY THEY ARE MY ONLY HOPE AT SURVIVING.
THIS IS GETTING RIDICULOUS.
HOW MANY OF THESE THINGS COULD ZOLA HAVE MADE? HUNDREDS? THOUSANDS?
DOES IT MATTER?
ANY OPPORTUNITY TO KICK A RED SKULL IN THE FACE SHOULD BE EMBRACED WITH ALL THE JOY IN YOUR HEART.
T'CHALLA'S RIGHT, CAP.
BEATING UP FASCISTS IS GUILT-FREE FUN.
THAT MAY BE SO, JEN, BUT YOU GUYS AIN'T SEEING WHAT I'M SEEING.
THERE'S NO END TO THESE GUYS--AND WE CAN'T KEEP DOING THIS ALL DAY, CAN WE?
CAN WE?

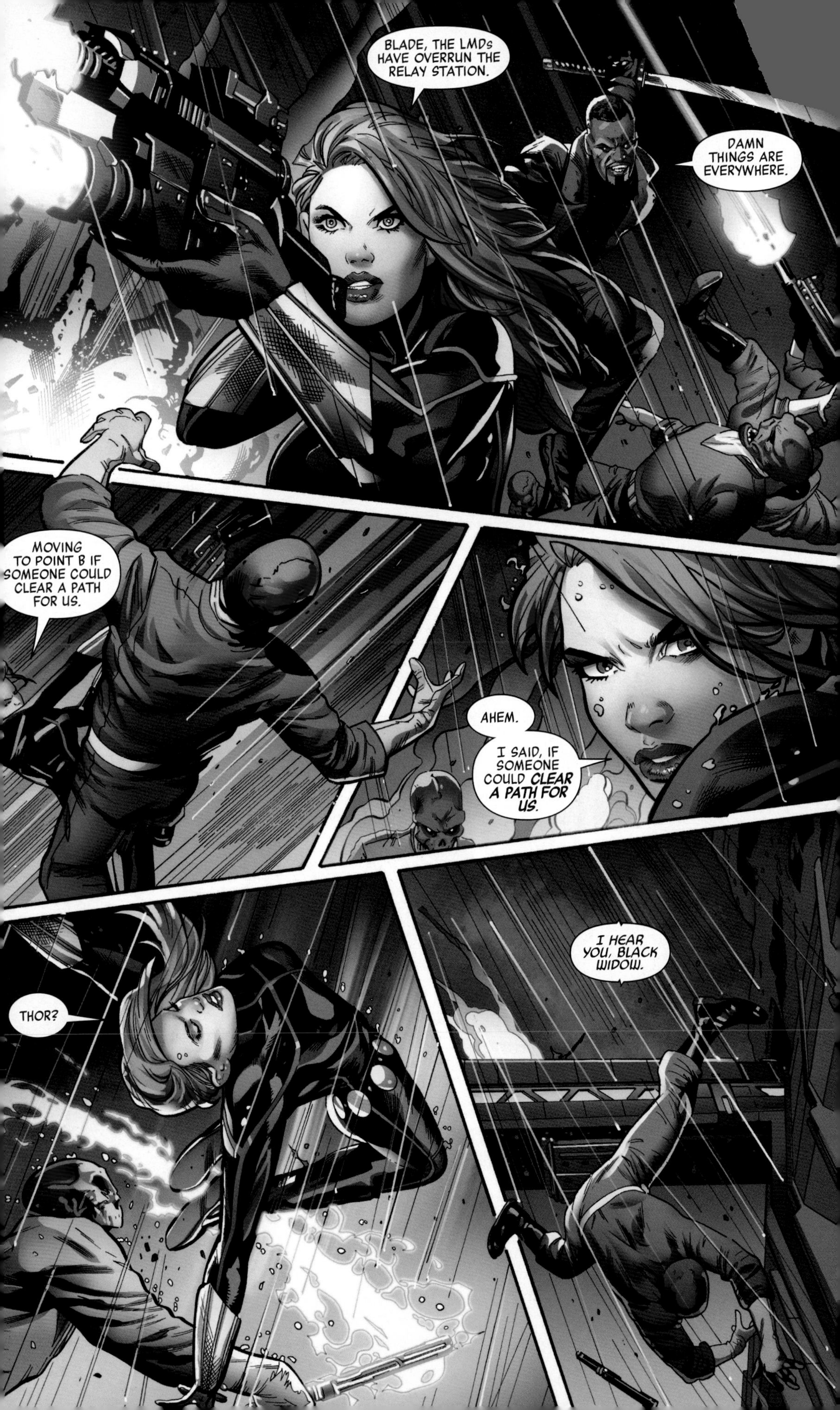
BLADE, THE LMDs HAVE OVERRUN THE RELAY STATION.
DAMN THINGS ARE EVERYWHERE.
MOVING TO POINT B IF SOMEONE COULD CLEAR A PATH FOR US.
AHEM.
I SAID, IF SOMEONE COULD CLEAR A PATH FOR US.
THOR?
I HEAR YOU, BLACK WIDOW.

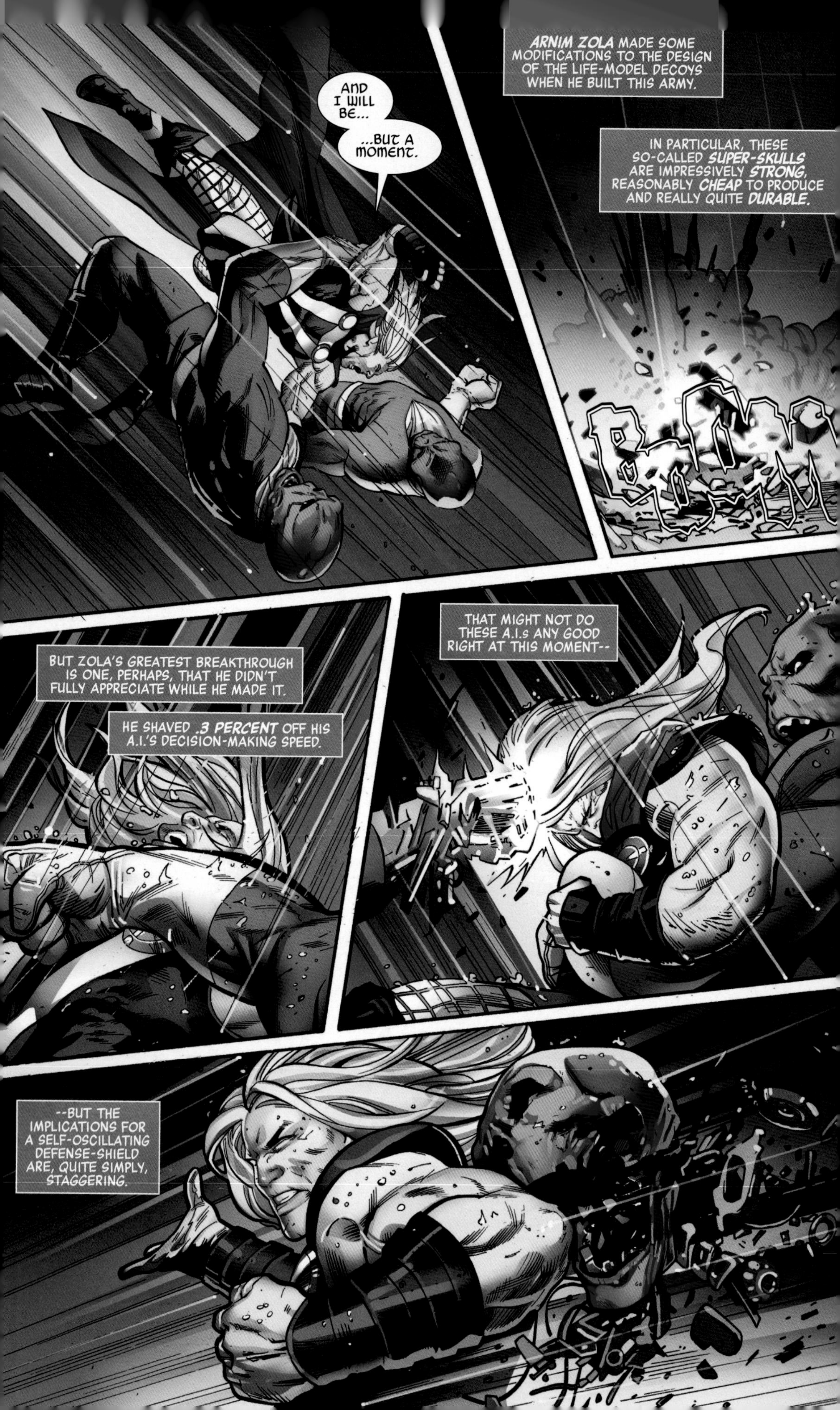
AND I WILL BE...
...BUT A MOMENT.
ARNIM ZOLA MADE SOME MODIFICATIONS TO THE DESIGN OF THE LIFE-MODEL DECOYS WHEN HE BUILT THIS ARMY.
IN PARTICULAR, THESE SO-CALLED SUPER-SKULLS ARE IMPRESSIVELY STRONG, REASONABLY CHEAP TO PRODUCE AND REALLY QUITE DURABLE.
BUT ZOLA'S GREATEST BREAKTHROUGH IS ONE, PERHAPS, THAT HE DIDN'T FULLY APPRECIATE WHILE HE MADE IT.
HE SHAVED .3 PERCENT OFF HIS A.I.'S DECISION-MAKING SPEED.
THAT MIGHT NOT DO THESE A.I.s ANY GOOD RIGHT AT THIS MOMENT--
--BUT THE IMPLICATIONS FOR A SELF-OSCILLATING DEFENSE-SHIELD ARE, QUITE SIMPLY, STAGGERING.

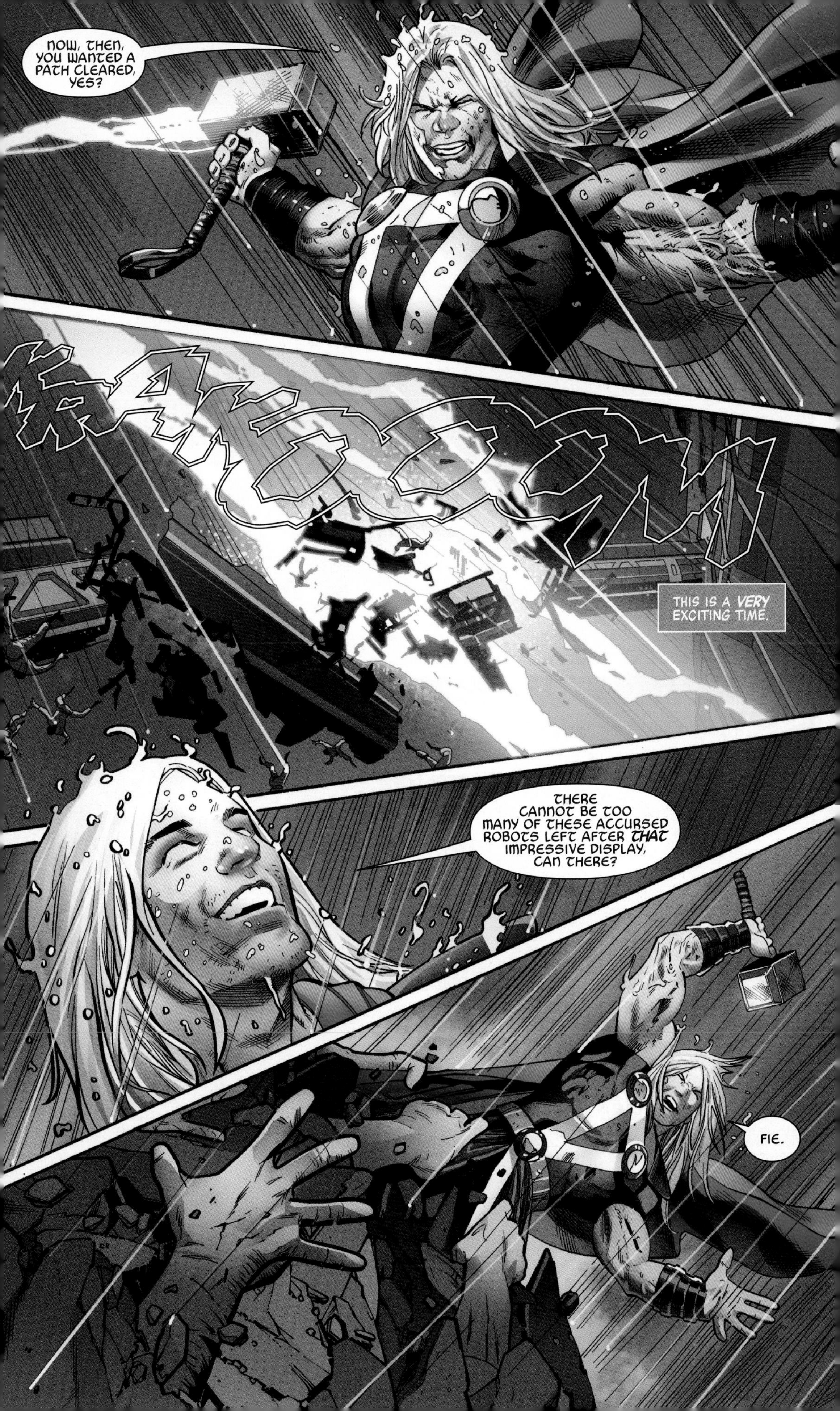
NOW, THEN, YOU WANTED A PATH CLEARED, YES?
KRAKOOM
THIS IS A VERY EXCITING TIME.
THERE CANNOT BE TOO MANY OF THESE ACCURSED ROBOTS LEFT AFTER THAT IMPRESSIVE DISPLAY, CAN THERE?
FIE.

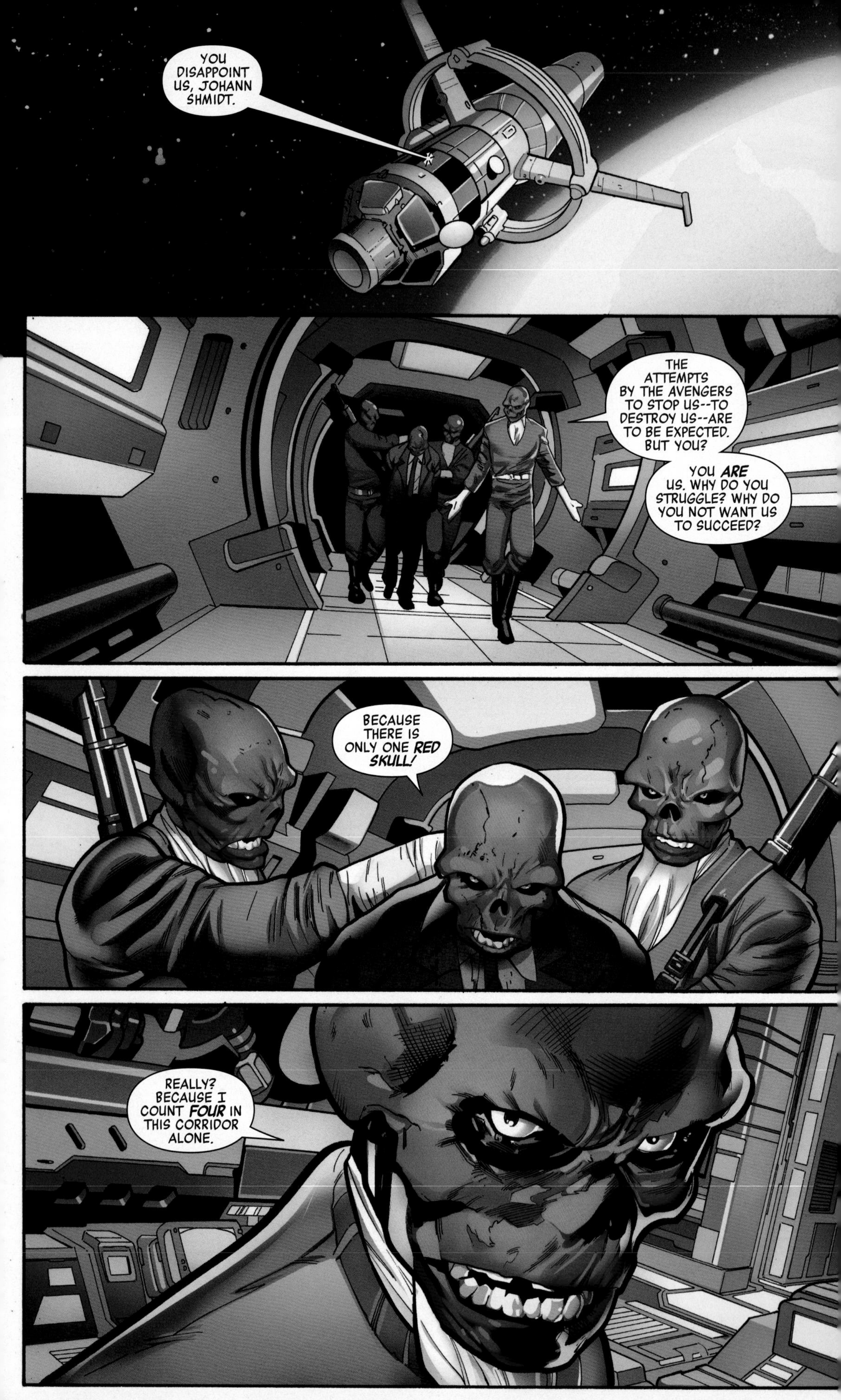
YOU DISAPPOINT US, JOHANN SHMIDT.
THE ATTEMPTS BY THE AVENGERS TO STOP US--TO DESTROY US--ARE TO BE EXPECTED. BUT YOU?
YOU ARE US. WHY DO YOU STRUGGLE? WHY DO YOU NOT WANT US TO SUCCEED?
BECAUSE THERE IS ONLY ONE RED SKULL!
REALLY? BECAUSE I COUNT FOUR IN THIS CORRIDOR ALONE.

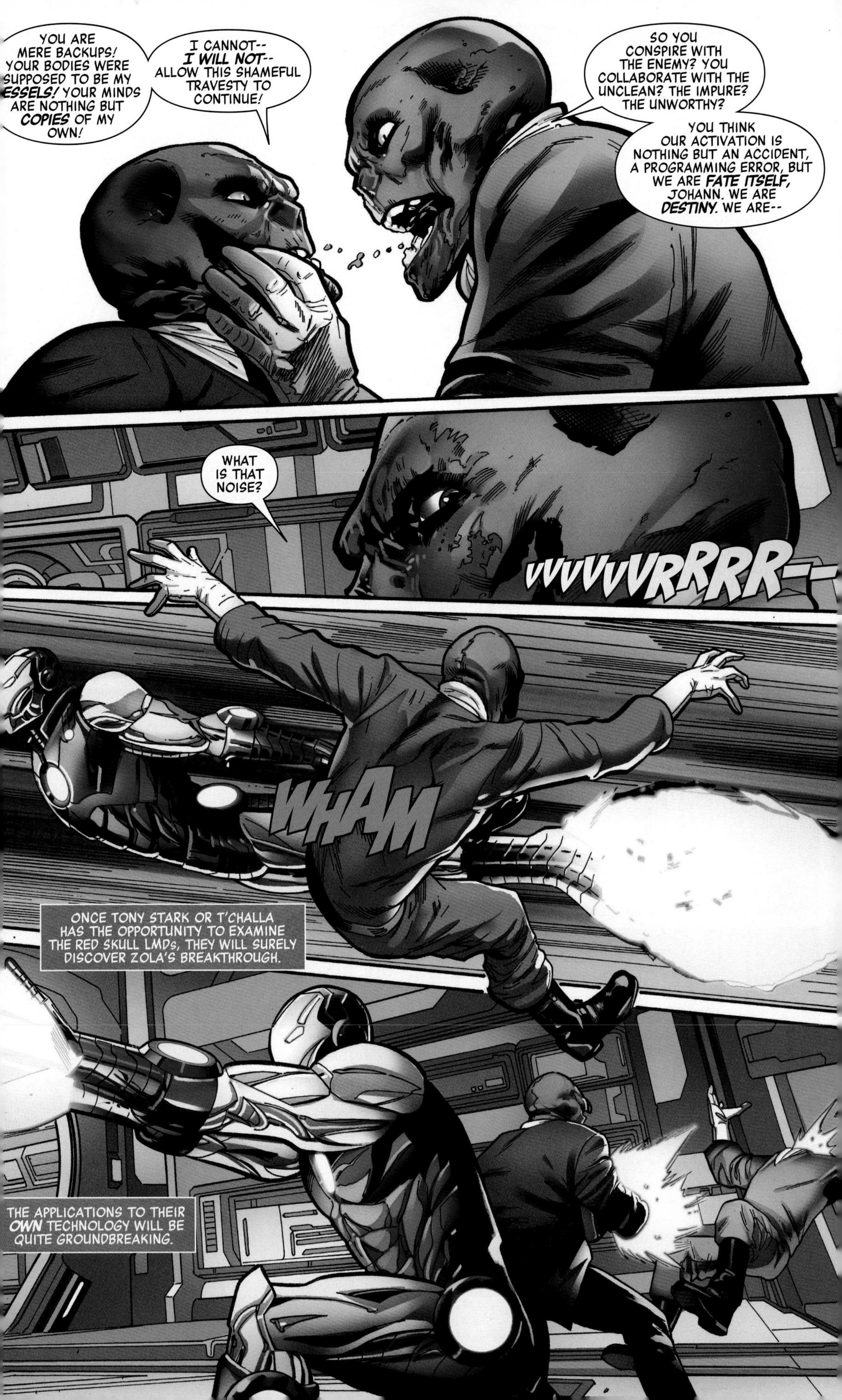

YOU ARE MERE BACKUPS! YOUR BODIES WERE SUPPOSED TO BE MY ESSELS! YOUR MINDS ARE NOTHING BUT COPIES OF MY OWN!
I CANNOT-- I WILL NOT-- ALLOW THIS SHAMEFUL TRAVESTY TO CONTINUE!
SO YOU CONSPIRE WITH THE ENEMY? YOU COLLABORATE WITH THE UNCLEAN? THE IMPURE? THE UNWORTHY?
YOU THINK OUR ACTIVATION IS NOTHING BUT AN ACCIDENT, A PROGRAMMING ERROR, BUT WE ARE FATE ITSELF, JOHANN. WE ARE DESTINY. WE ARE--
WHAT IS THAT NOISE?
VVVVVVRRRR--
WHAM
ONCE TONY STARK OR T'CHALLA HAS THE OPPORTUNITY TO EXAMINE THE RED SKULL LMDs, THEY WILL SURELY DISCOVER ZOLA'S BREAKTHROUGH.
THE APPLICATIONS TO THEIR OWN TECHNOLOGY WILL BE QUITE GROUNDBREAKING.

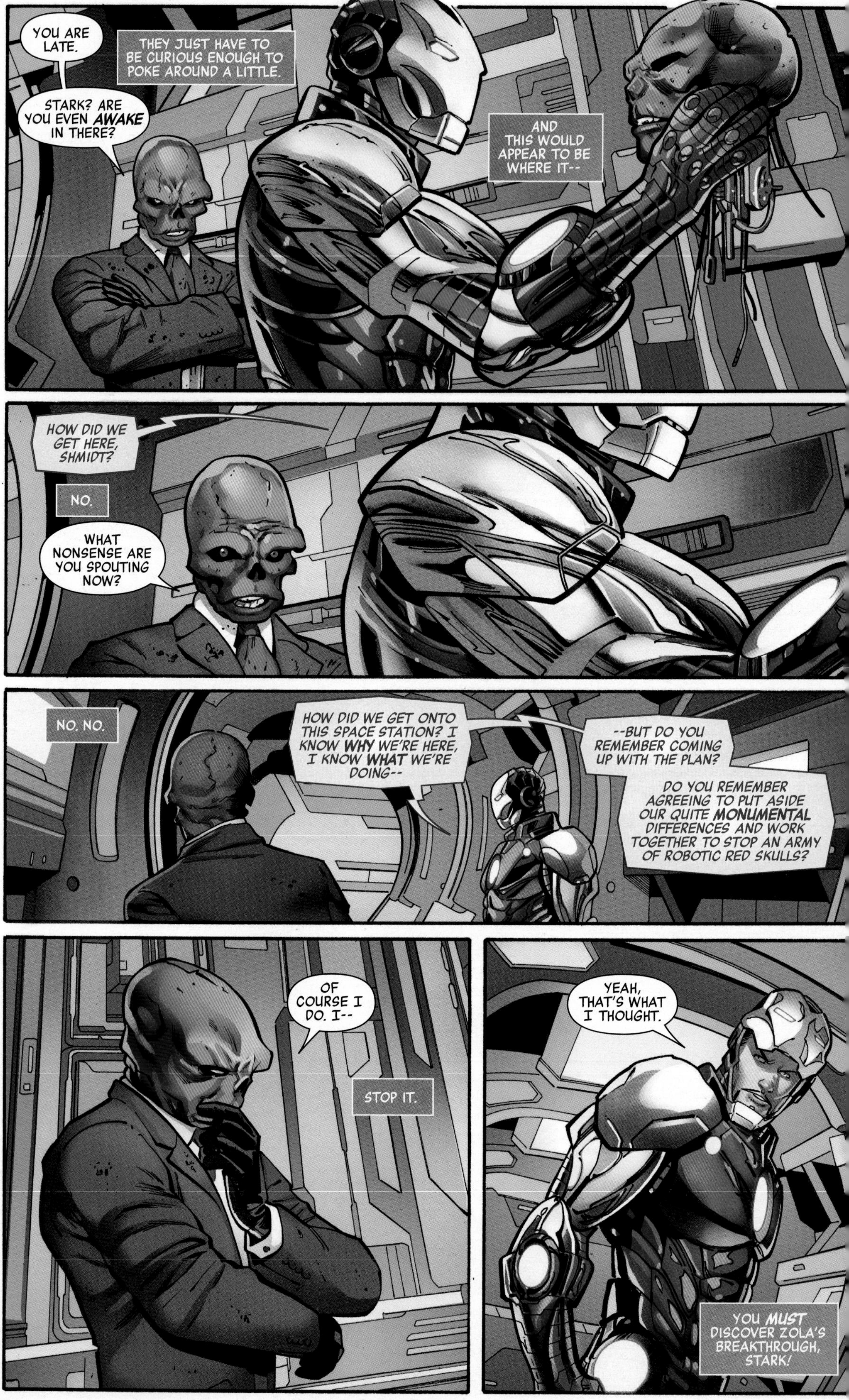

YOU ARE LATE.
THEY JUST HAVE TO BE CURIOUS ENOUGH TO POKE AROUND A LITTLE.
STARK? ARE YOU EVEN AWAKE IN THERE?
AND THIS WOULD APPEAR TO BE WHERE IT--
HOW DID WE GET HERE, SHMIDT?
NO.
WHAT NONSENSE ARE YOU SPOUTING NOW?
NO. NO.
HOW DID WE GET ONTO THIS SPACE STATION? I KNOW WHY WE'RE HERE, I KNOW WHAT WE'RE DOING--
--BUT DO YOU REMEMBER COMING UP WITH THE PLAN?
DO YOU REMEMBER AGREEING TO PUT ASIDE OUR QUITE MONUMENTAL DIFFERENCES AND WORK TOGETHER TO STOP AN ARMY OF ROBOTIC RED SKULLS?
OF COURSE I DO. I--
STOP IT.
YEAH, THAT'S WHAT I THOUGHT.
YOU MUST DISCOVER ZOLA'S BREAKTHROUGH, STARK!

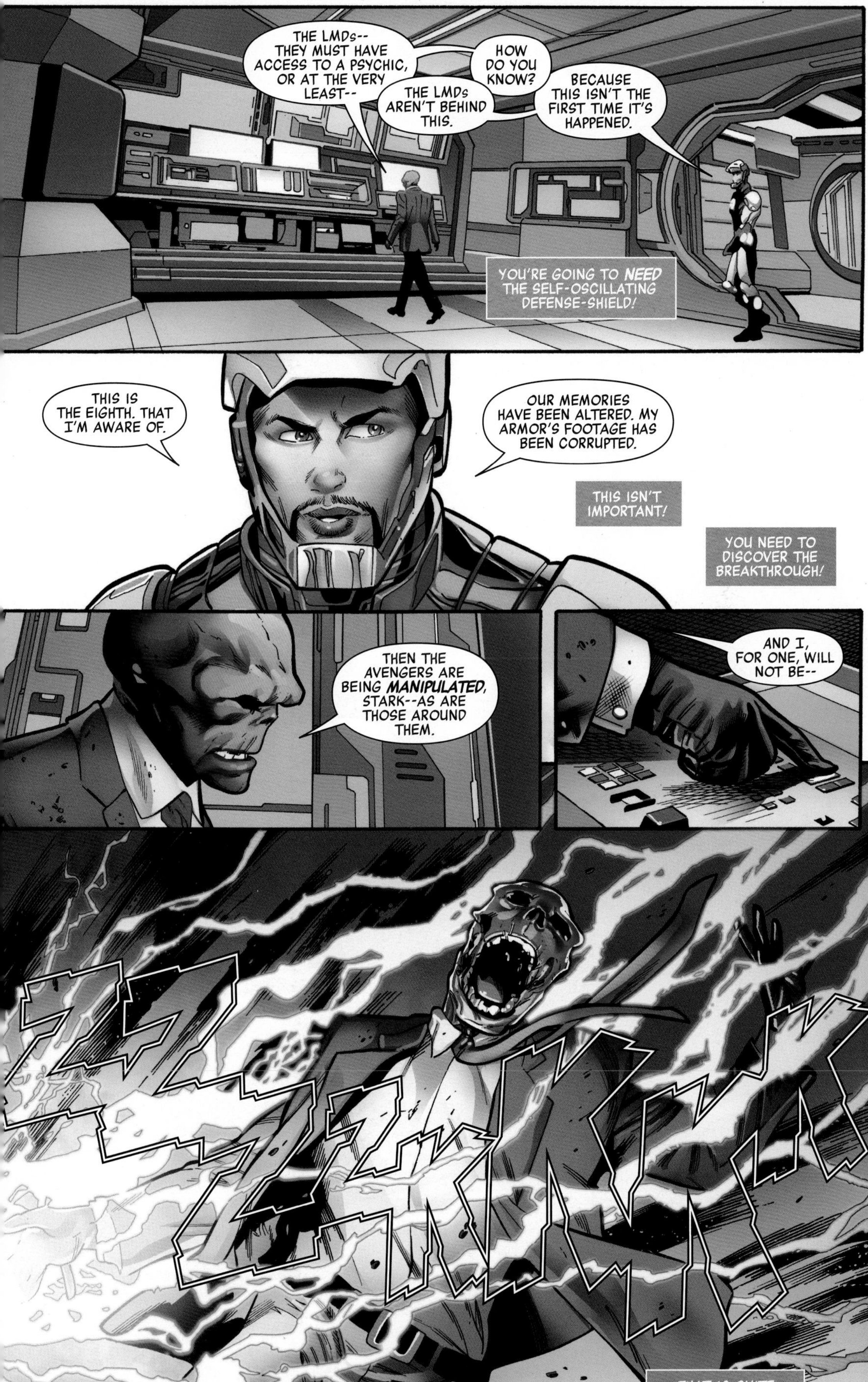
THE LMDs--
THEY MUST HAVE ACCESS TO A PSYCHIC, OR AT THE VERY LEAST--
HOW DO YOU KNOW?
THE LMDs AREN'T BEHIND THIS.
BECAUSE THIS ISN'T THE FIRST TIME IT'S HAPPENED.
YOU'RE GOING TO NEED THE SELF-OSCILLATING DEFENSE-SHIELD!
THIS IS THE EIGHTH. THAT I'M AWARE OF.
OUR MEMORIES HAVE BEEN ALTERED. MY ARMOR'S FOOTAGE HAS BEEN CORRUPTED.
THIS ISN'T IMPORTANT!
YOU NEED TO DISCOVER THE BREAKTHROUGH!
THEN THE AVENGERS ARE BEING MANIPULATED, STARK--AS ARE THOSE AROUND THEM.
AND I, FOR ONE, WILL NOT BE--
ZZZKKKK
THAT IS QUITE ENOUGH OUT OF YOU, HERR SHMIDT.

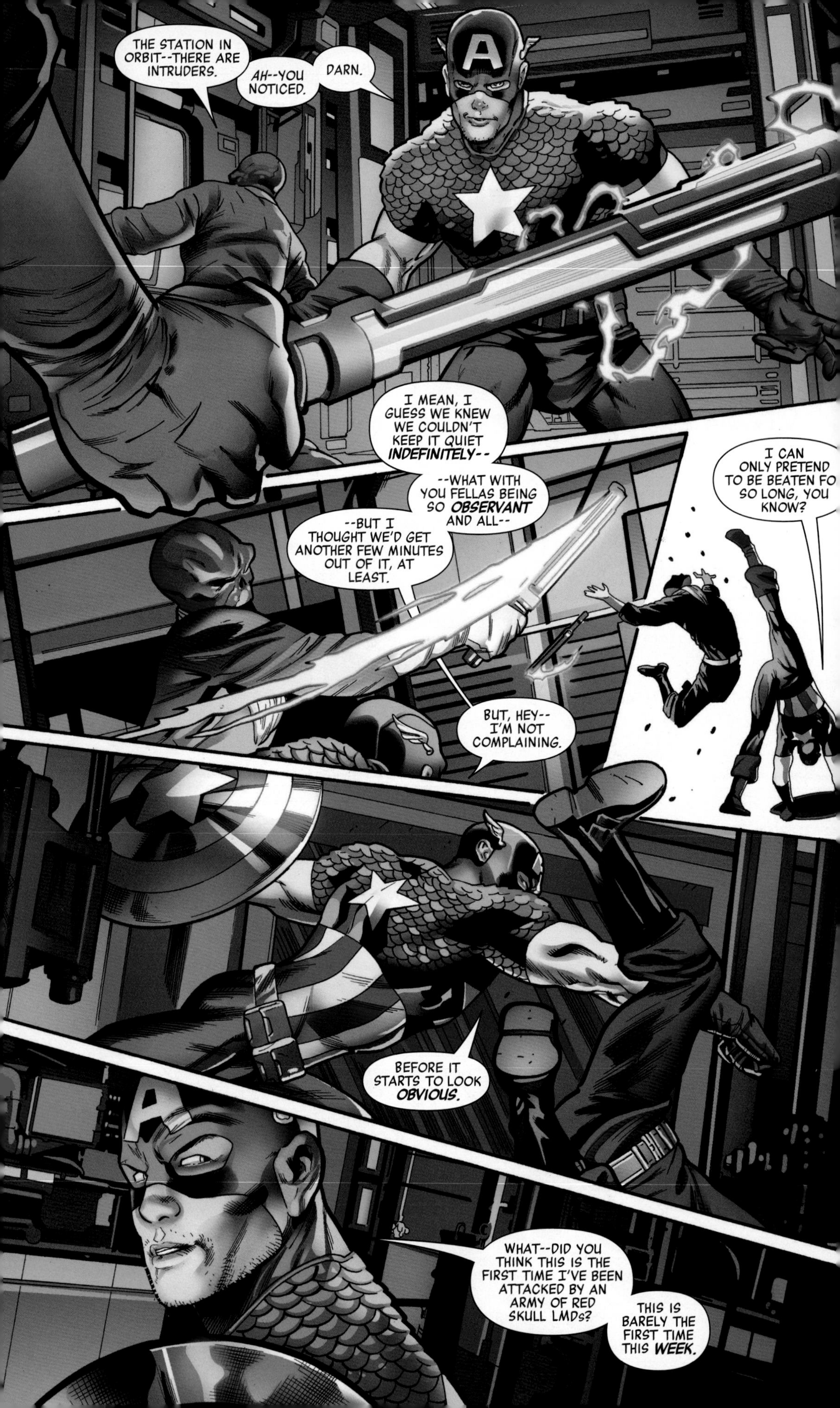
THE STATION IN ORBIT--THERE ARE INTRUDERS.
AH--YOU NOTICED.
DARN.
I MEAN, I GUESS WE KNEW WE COULDN'T KEEP IT QUIET INDEFINITELY--
--WHAT WITH YOU FELLAS BEING SO OBSERVANT AND ALL--
--BUT I THOUGHT WE'D GET ANOTHER FEW MINUTES OUT OF IT, AT LEAST.
BUT, HEY-- I'M NOT COMPLAINING.
I CAN ONLY PRETEND TO BE BEATEN FO SO LONG, YOU KNOW?
BEFORE IT STARTS TO LOOK OBVIOUS.
WHAT--DID YOU THINK THIS IS THE FIRST TIME I'VE BEEN ATTACKED BY AN ARMY OF RED SKULL LMDs?
THIS IS BARELY THE FIRST TIME THIS WEEK.

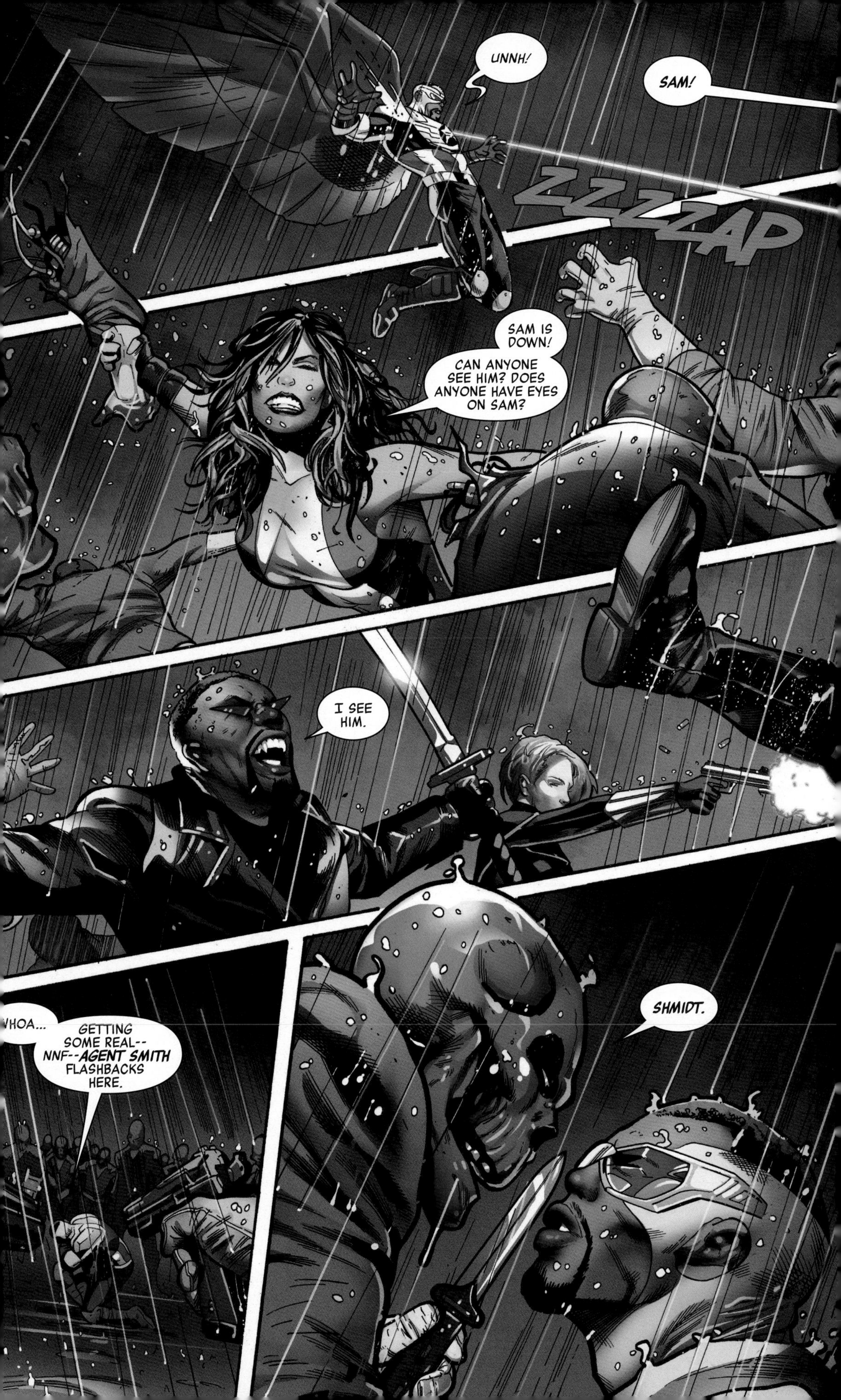
UNNH!
SAM!
ZZZZAP
SAM IS DOWN!
CAN ANYONE SEE HIM? DOES ANYONE HAVE EYES ON SAM?
I SEE HIM.
WHOA...
GETTING SOME REAL-- NNF--AGENT SMITH FLASHBACKS HERE.
SHMIDT.

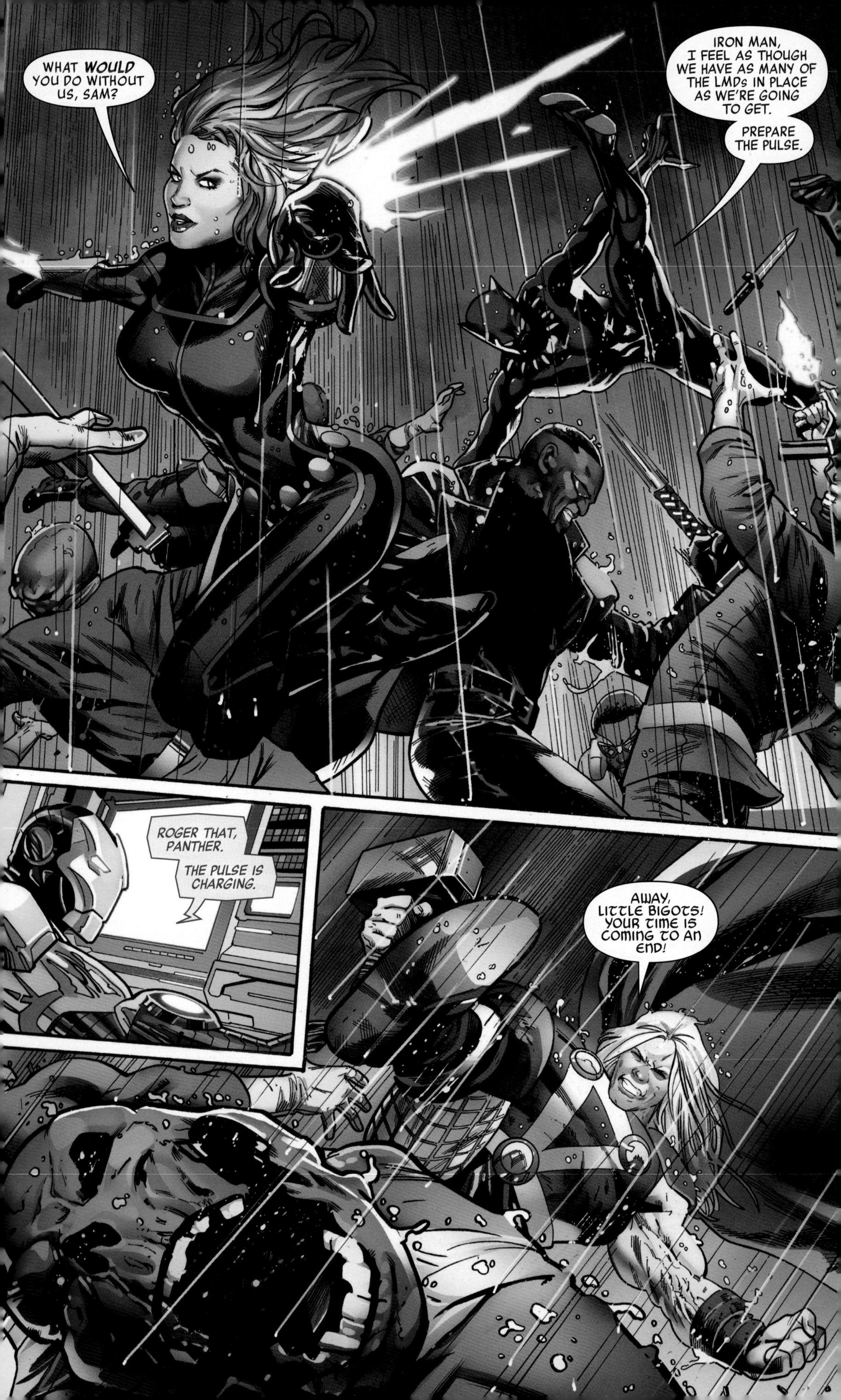

WHAT WOULD YOU DO WITHOUT US, SAM?
IRON MAN, I FEEL AS THOUGH WE HAVE AS MANY OF THE LMDs IN PLACE AS WE'RE GOING TO GET.
PREPARE THE PULSE.
ROGER THAT, PANTHER.
THE PULSE IS CHARGING.
AWAY, LITTLE BIGOTS! YOUR TIME IS COMING TO AN END!

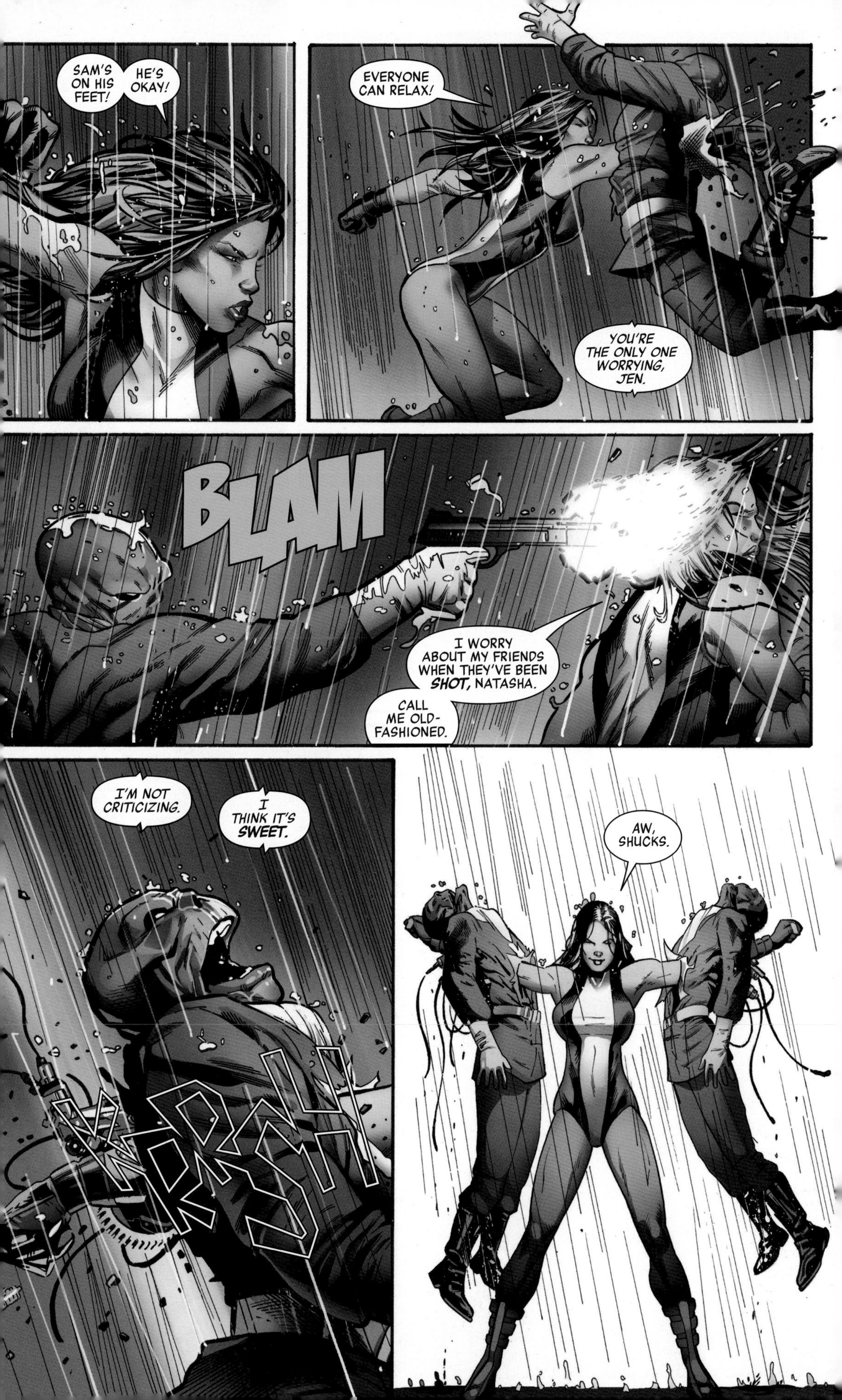
SAM'S ON HIS FEET!
HE'S OKAY!
EVERYONE CAN RELAX!
YOU'RE THE ONLY ONE WORRYING, JEN.
BLAM
I WORRY ABOUT MY FRIENDS WHEN THEY'VE BEEN SHOT, NATASHA.
CALL ME OLD-FASHIONED.
I'M NOT CRITICIZING.
I THINK IT'S SWEET.
KRASH
AW, SHUCKS.

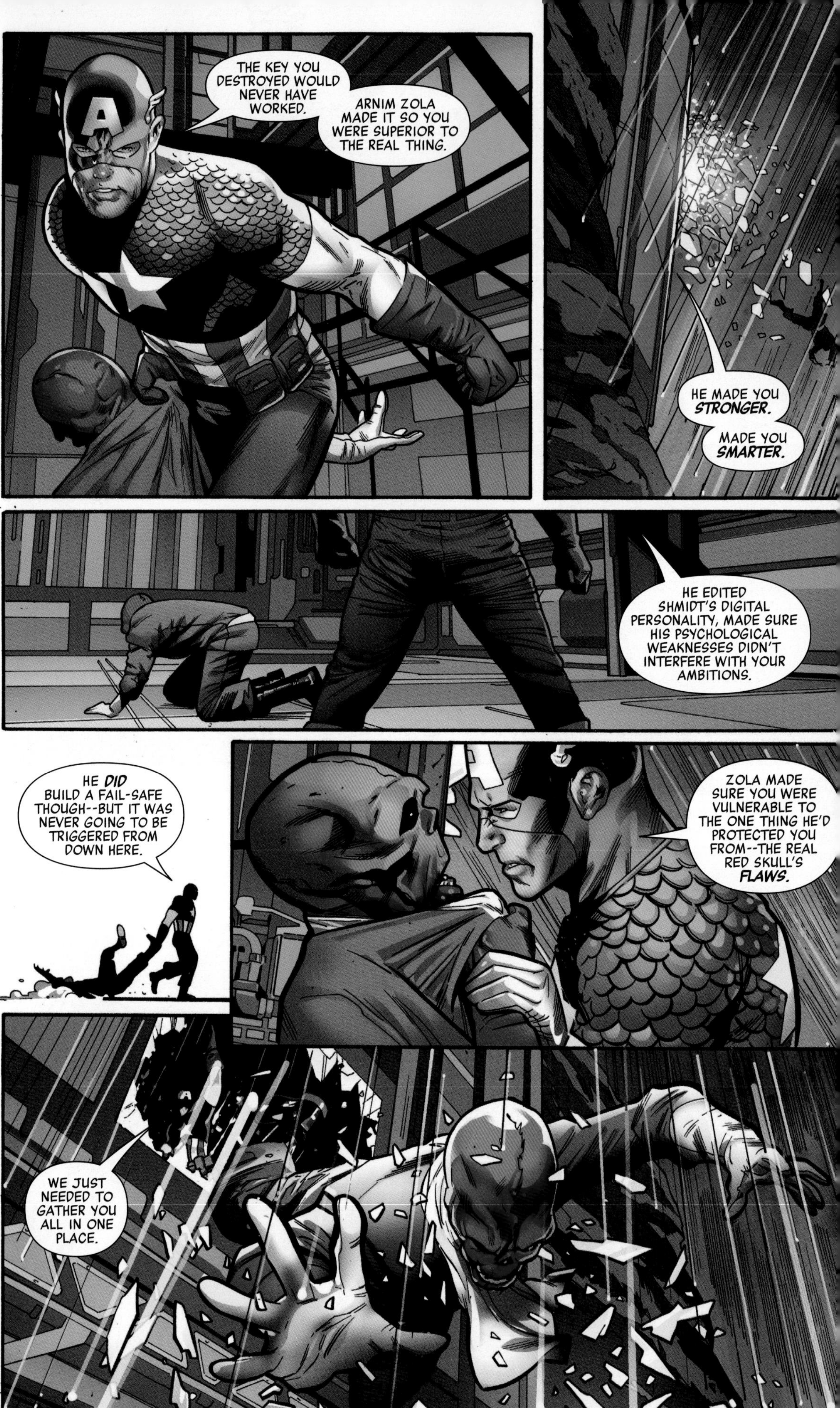
THE KEY YOU DESTROYED WOULD NEVER HAVE WORKED.
ARNIM ZOLA MADE IT SO YOU WERE SUPERIOR TO THE REAL THING.
HE MADE YOU **STRONGER.**
MADE YOU **SMARTER.**
HE EDITED SHMIDT'S DIGITAL PERSONALITY, MADE SURE HIS PSYCHOLOGICAL WEAKNESSES DIDN'T INTERFERE WITH YOUR AMBITIONS.
HE **DID** BUILD A FAIL-SAFE THOUGH--BUT IT WAS NEVER GOING TO BE TRIGGERED FROM DOWN HERE.
ZOLA MADE SURE YOU WERE VULNERABLE TO THE ONE THING HE'D PROTECTED YOU FROM--THE REAL RED SKULL'S **FLAWS.**
WE JUST NEEDED TO GATHER YOU ALL IN ONE PLACE.

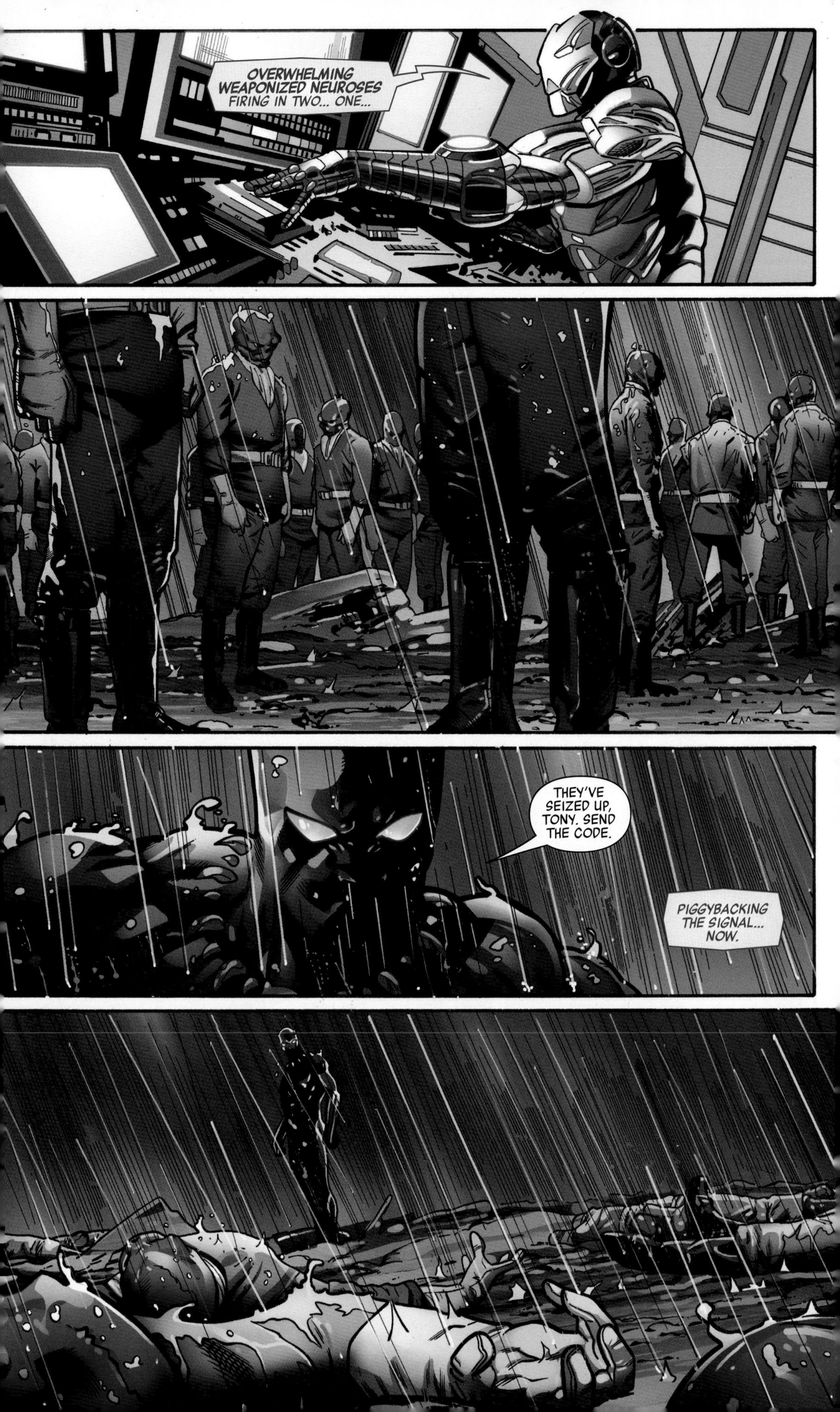
OVERWHELMING WEAPONIZED NEUROSES FIRING IN TWO... ONE...
THEY'VE SEIZED UP, TONY. SEND THE CODE.
PIGGYBACKING THE SIGNAL... NOW.

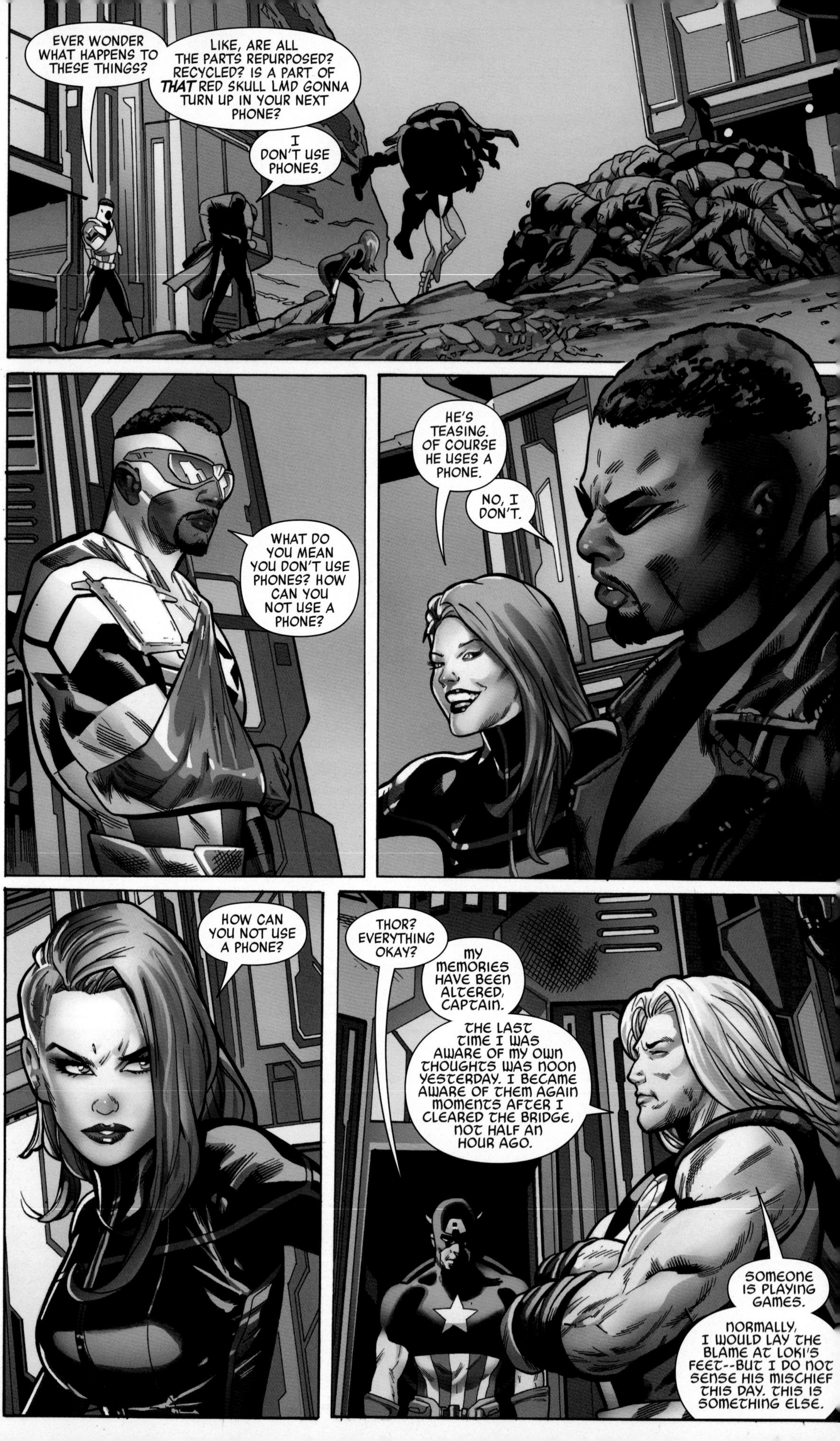

EVER WONDER WHAT HAPPENS TO THESE THINGS?
LIKE, ARE ALL THE PARTS REPURPOSED? RECYCLED? IS A PART OF *THAT* RED SKULL LMD GONNA TURN UP IN YOUR NEXT PHONE?
I DON'T USE PHONES.
WHAT DO YOU MEAN YOU DON'T USE PHONES? HOW CAN YOU NOT USE A PHONE?
HE'S TEASING. OF COURSE HE USES A PHONE.
NO, I DON'T.
HOW CAN YOU NOT USE A PHONE?
THOR? EVERYTHING OKAY?
MY MEMORIES HAVE BEEN ALTERED, CAPTAIN.
THE LAST TIME I WAS AWARE OF MY OWN THOUGHTS WAS NOON YESTERDAY. I BECAME AWARE OF THEM AGAIN MOMENTS AFTER I CLEARED THE BRIDGE, NOT HALF AN HOUR AGO.
SOMEONE IS PLAYING GAMES.
NORMALLY, I WOULD LAY THE BLAME AT LOKI'S FEET--BUT I DO NOT SENSE HIS MISCHIEF THIS DAY. THIS IS SOMETHING ELSE.

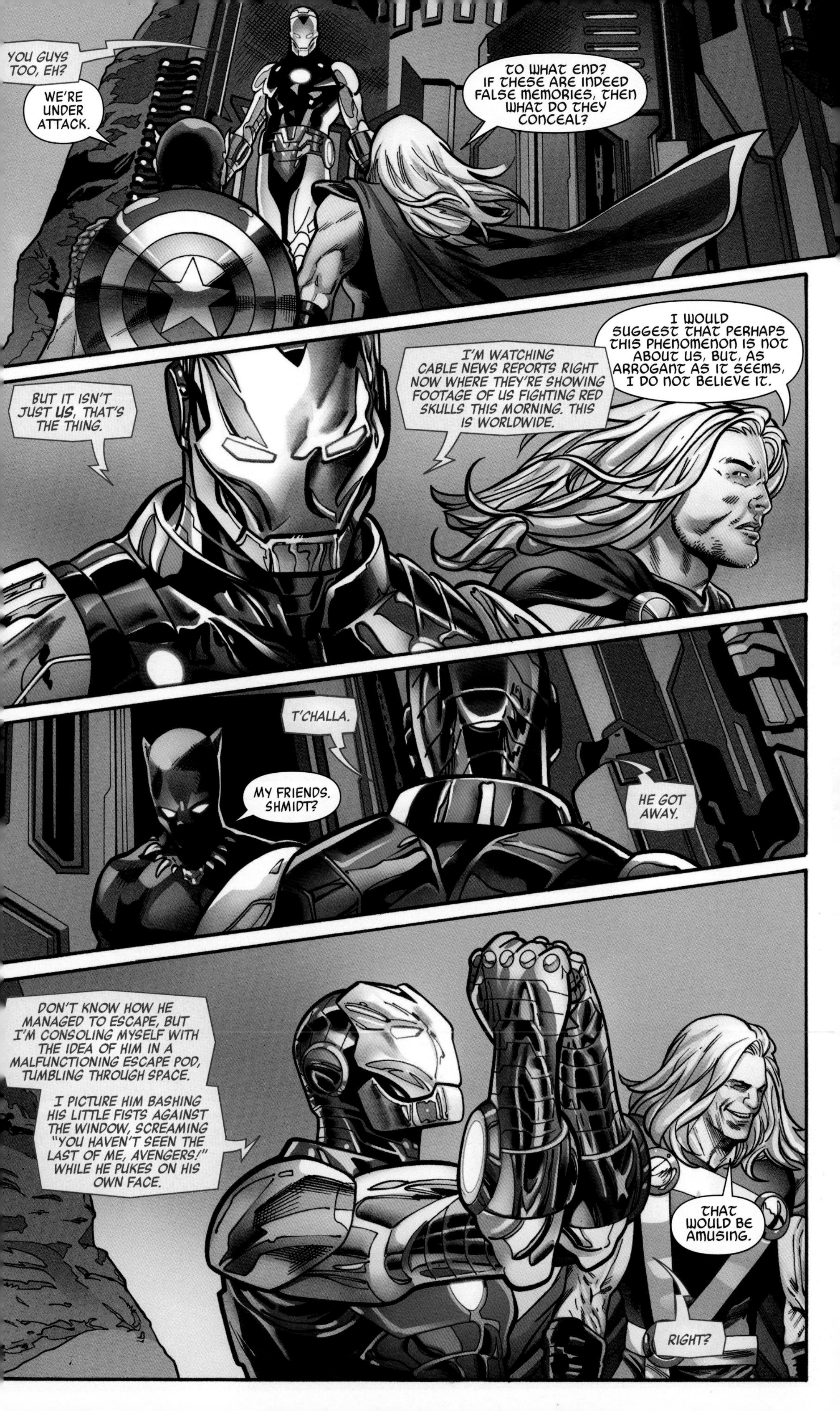

YOU GUYS TOO, EH?
WE'RE UNDER ATTACK.
TO WHAT END? IF THESE ARE INDEED FALSE MEMORIES, THEN WHAT DO THEY CONCEAL?
BUT IT ISN'T JUST US, THAT'S THE THING.
I'M WATCHING CABLE NEWS REPORTS RIGHT NOW WHERE THEY'RE SHOWING FOOTAGE OF US FIGHTING RED SKULLS THIS MORNING. THIS IS WORLDWIDE.
I WOULD SUGGEST THAT PERHAPS THIS PHENOMENON IS NOT ABOUT US, BUT, AS ARROGANT AS IT SEEMS, I DO NOT BELIEVE IT.
T'CHALLA.
MY FRIENDS. SHMIDT?
HE GOT AWAY.
DON'T KNOW HOW HE MANAGED TO ESCAPE, BUT I'M CONSOLING MYSELF WITH THE IDEA OF HIM IN A MALFUNCTIONING ESCAPE POD, TUMBLING THROUGH SPACE.
I PICTURE HIM BASHING HIS LITTLE FISTS AGAINST THE WINDOW, SCREAMING "YOU HAVEN'T SEEN THE LAST OF ME, AVENGERS!" WHILE HE PUKES ON HIS OWN FACE.
THAT WOULD BE AMUSING.
RIGHT?

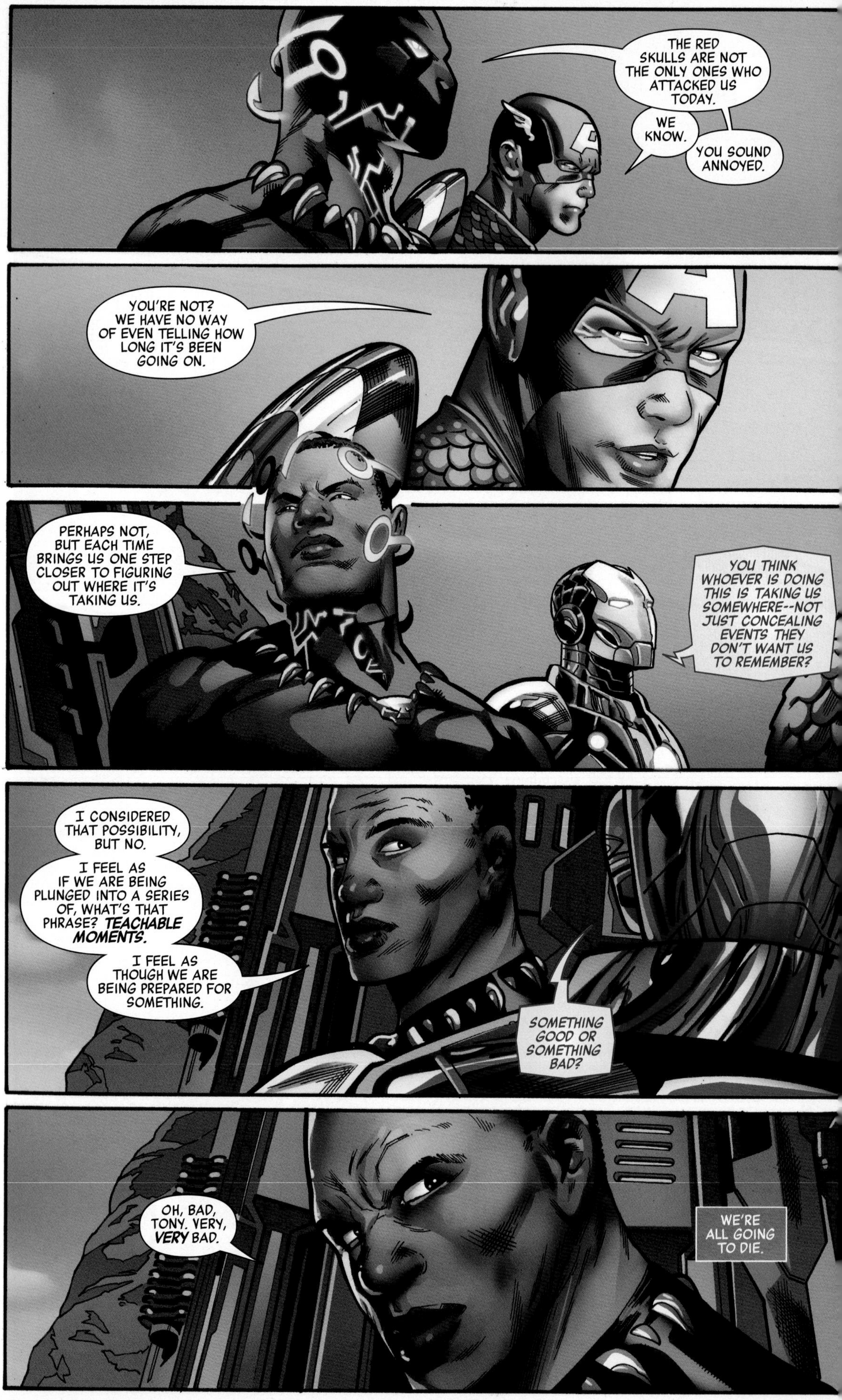
THE RED SKULLS ARE NOT THE ONLY ONES WHO ATTACKED US TODAY.
WE KNOW.
YOU SOUND ANNOYED.
YOU'RE NOT? WE HAVE NO WAY OF EVEN TELLING HOW LONG IT'S BEEN GOING ON.
PERHAPS NOT, BUT EACH TIME BRINGS US ONE STEP CLOSER TO FIGURING OUT WHERE IT'S TAKING US.
YOU THINK WHOEVER IS DOING THIS IS TAKING US SOMEWHERE--NOT JUST CONCEALING EVENTS THEY DON'T WANT US TO REMEMBER?
I CONSIDERED THAT POSSIBILITY, BUT NO.
I FEEL AS IF WE ARE BEING PLUNGED INTO A SERIES OF, WHAT'S THAT PHRASE? ***TEACHABLE MOMENTS.***
I FEEL AS THOUGH WE ARE BEING PREPARED FOR SOMETHING.
SOMETHING GOOD OR SOMETHING BAD?
OH, BAD, TONY. VERY, ***VERY*** BAD.
WE'RE ALL GOING TO DIE.

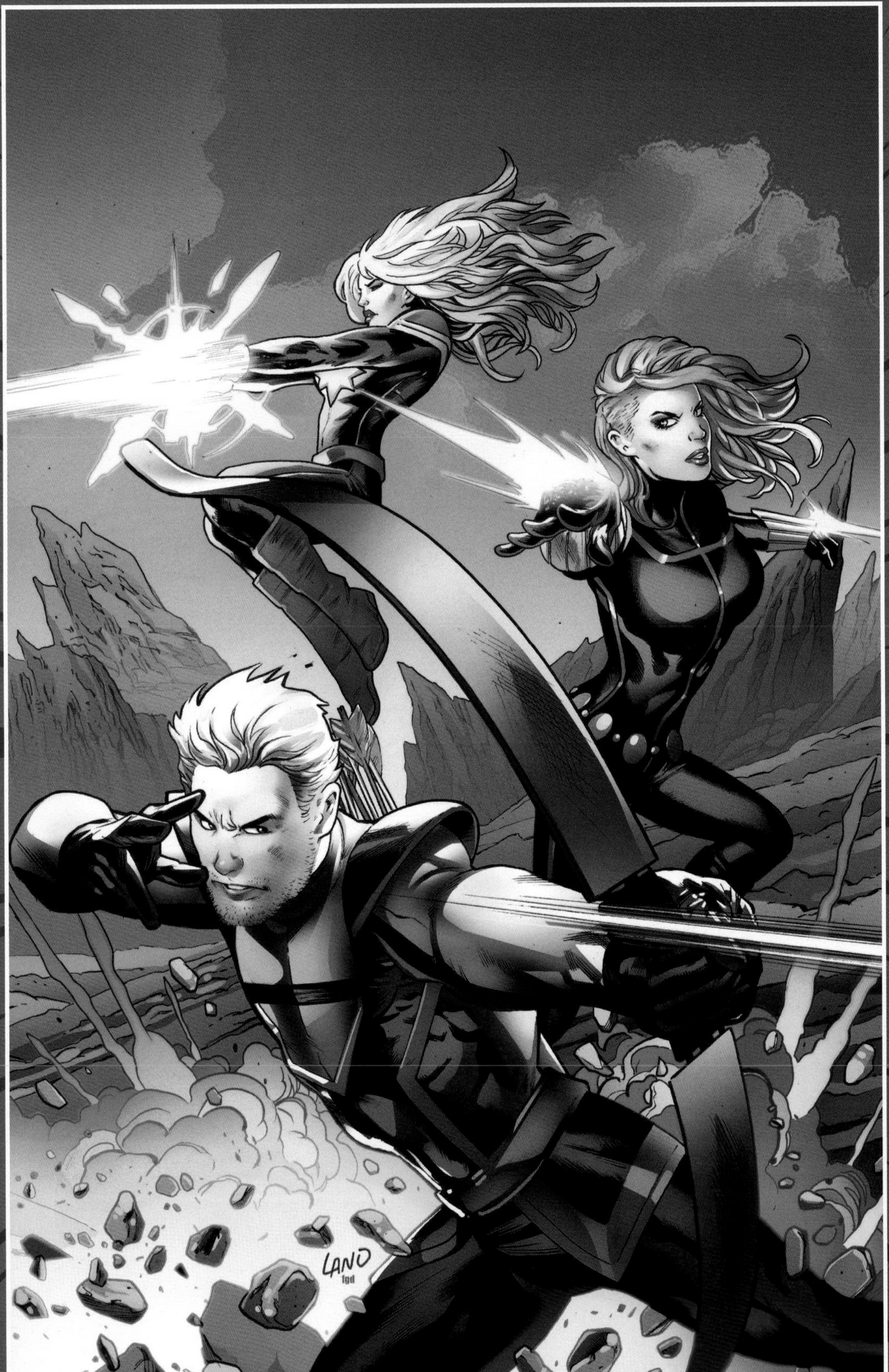
LANO

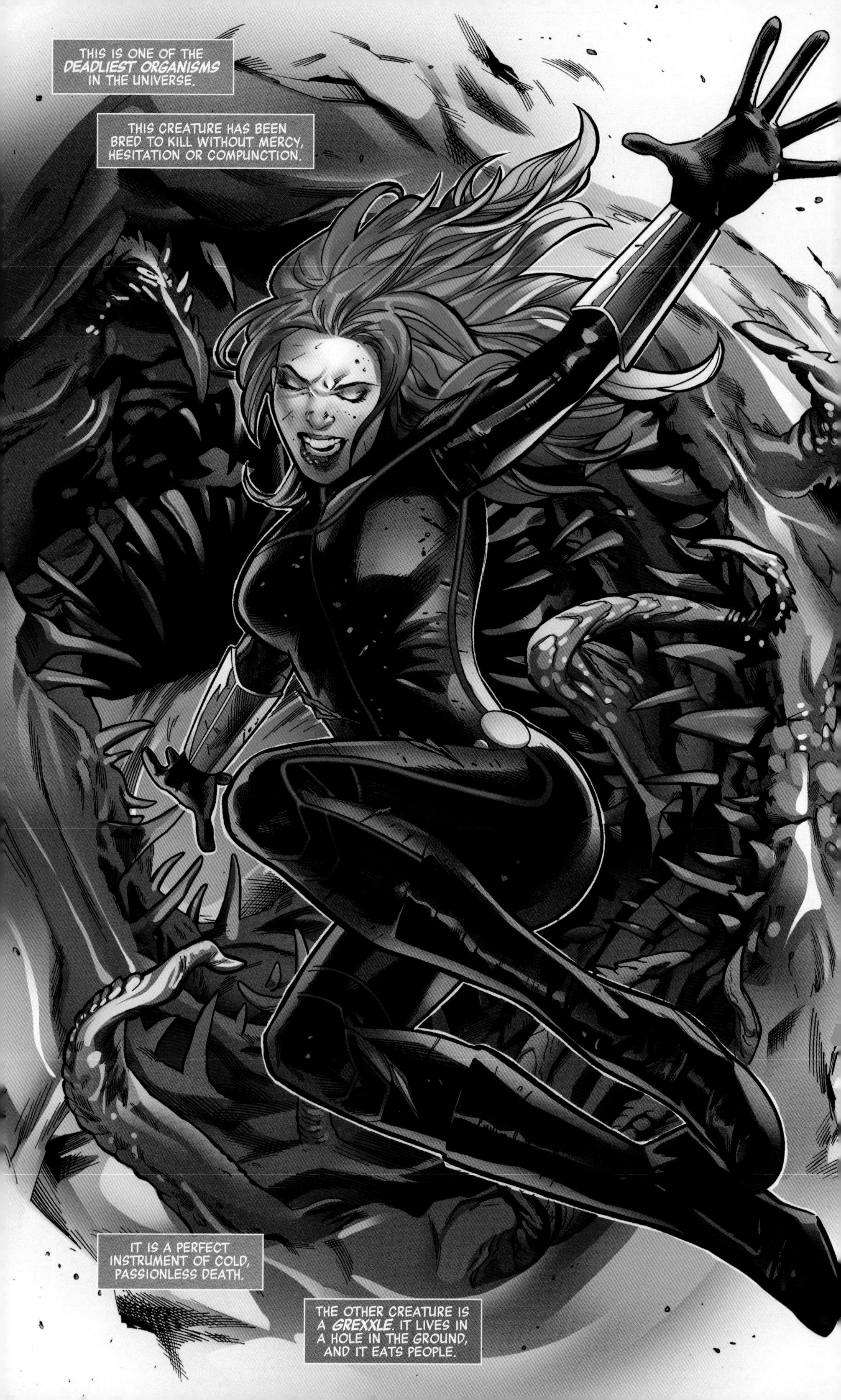

THIS IS ONE OF THE DEADLIEST ORGANISMS IN THE UNIVERSE.
THIS CREATURE HAS BEEN BRED TO KILL WITHOUT MERCY, HESITATION OR COMPUNCTION.
IT IS A PERFECT INSTRUMENT OF COLD, PASSIONLESS DEATH.
THE OTHER CREATURE IS A GREXXLE. IT LIVES IN A HOLE IN THE GROUND, AND IT EATS PEOPLE.

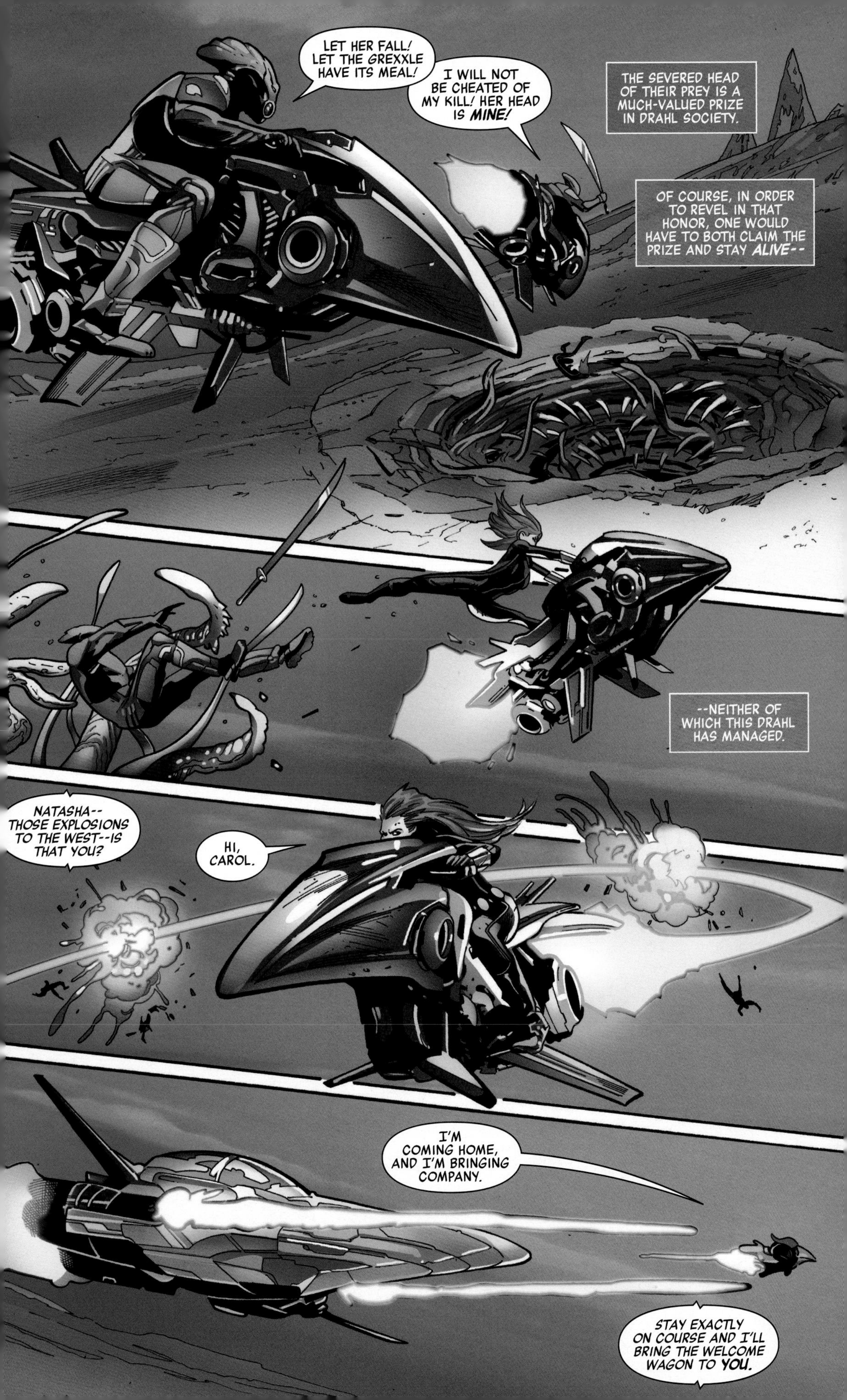
LET HER FALL! LET THE GREXXLE HAVE ITS MEAL!
I WILL NOT BE CHEATED OF MY KILL! HER HEAD IS *MINE!*
THE SEVERED HEAD OF THEIR PREY IS A MUCH-VALUED PRIZE IN DRAHL SOCIETY.
OF COURSE, IN ORDER TO REVEL IN THAT HONOR, ONE WOULD HAVE TO BOTH CLAIM THE PRIZE AND STAY *ALIVE--*
--NEITHER OF WHICH THIS DRAHL HAS MANAGED.
NATASHA-- THOSE EXPLOSIONS TO THE WEST--IS THAT YOU?
HI, CAROL.
I'M COMING HOME, AND I'M BRINGING COMPANY.
STAY EXACTLY ON COURSE AND I'LL BRING THE WELCOME WAGON TO **YOU.**

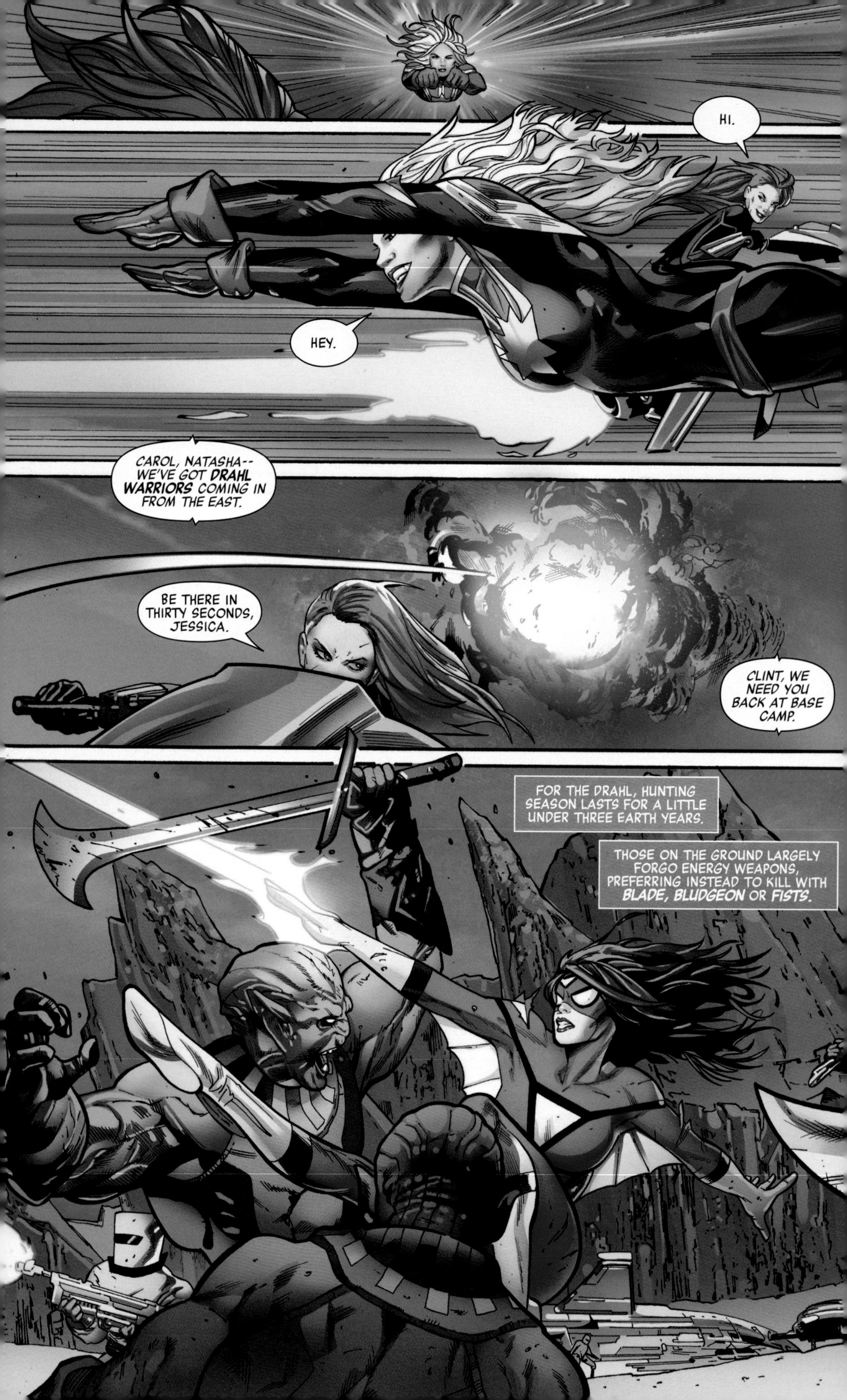

HI.
HEY.
CAROL, NATASHA-- WE'VE GOT DRAHL WARRIORS COMING IN FROM THE EAST.
BE THERE IN THIRTY SECONDS, JESSICA.
CLINT, WE NEED YOU BACK AT BASE CAMP.
FOR THE DRAHL, HUNTING SEASON LASTS FOR A LITTLE UNDER THREE EARTH YEARS.
THOSE ON THE GROUND LARGELY FORGO ENERGY WEAPONS, PREFERRING INSTEAD TO KILL WITH BLADE, BLUDGEON OR FISTS.

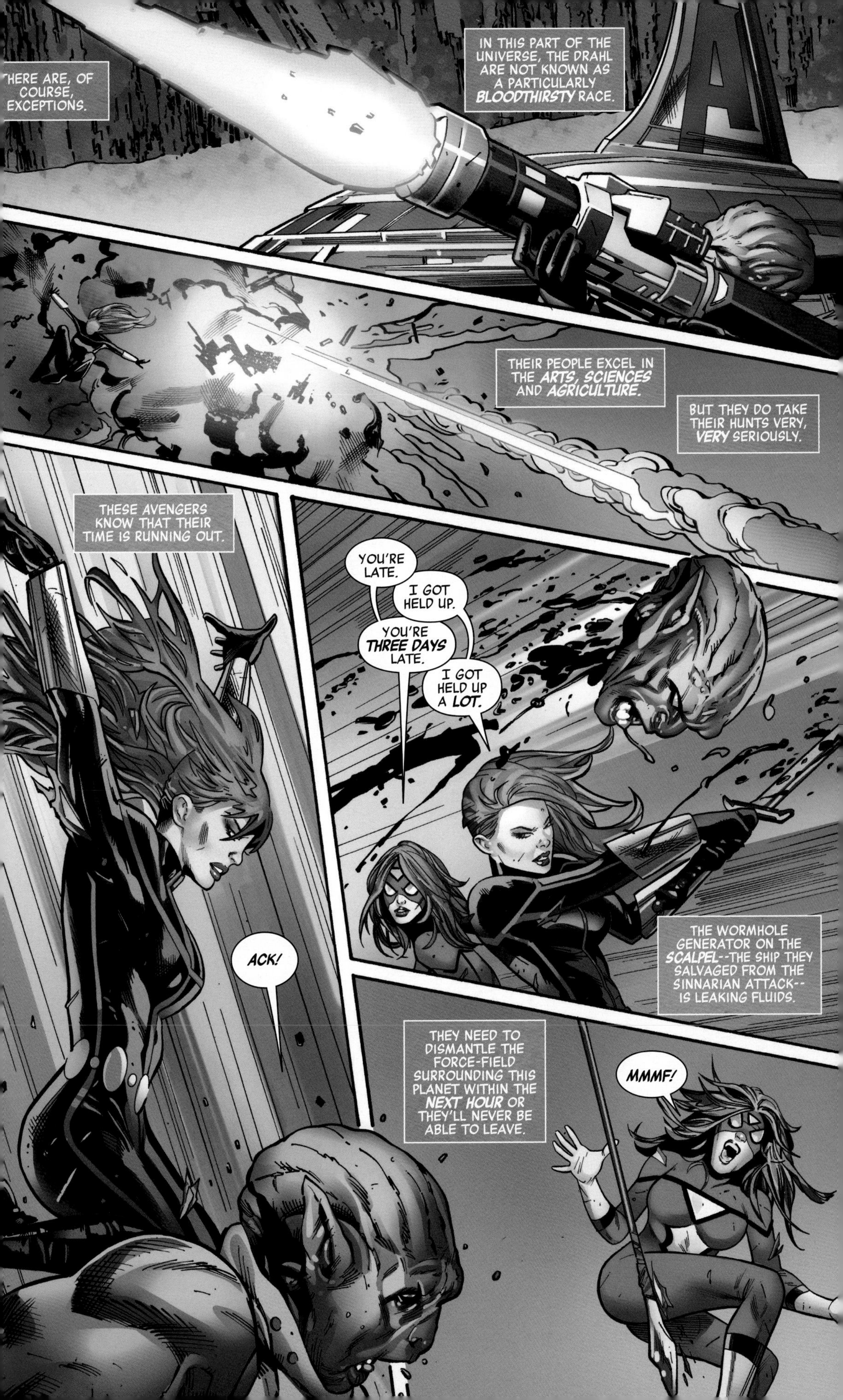

THERE ARE, OF COURSE, EXCEPTIONS.
IN THIS PART OF THE UNIVERSE, THE DRAHL ARE NOT KNOWN AS A PARTICULARLY BLOODTHIRSTY RACE.
THEIR PEOPLE EXCEL IN THE ARTS, SCIENCES AND AGRICULTURE.
BUT THEY DO TAKE THEIR HUNTS VERY, VERY SERIOUSLY.
THESE AVENGERS KNOW THAT THEIR TIME IS RUNNING OUT.
YOU'RE LATE.
I GOT HELD UP.
YOU'RE THREE DAYS LATE.
I GOT HELD UP A LOT.
ACK!
THE WORMHOLE GENERATOR ON THE SCALPEL--THE SHIP THEY SALVAGED FROM THE SINNARIAN ATTACK--IS LEAKING FLUIDS.
THEY NEED TO DISMANTLE THE FORCE-FIELD SURROUNDING THIS PLANET WITHIN THE NEXT HOUR OR THEY'LL NEVER BE ABLE TO LEAVE.
MMMF!

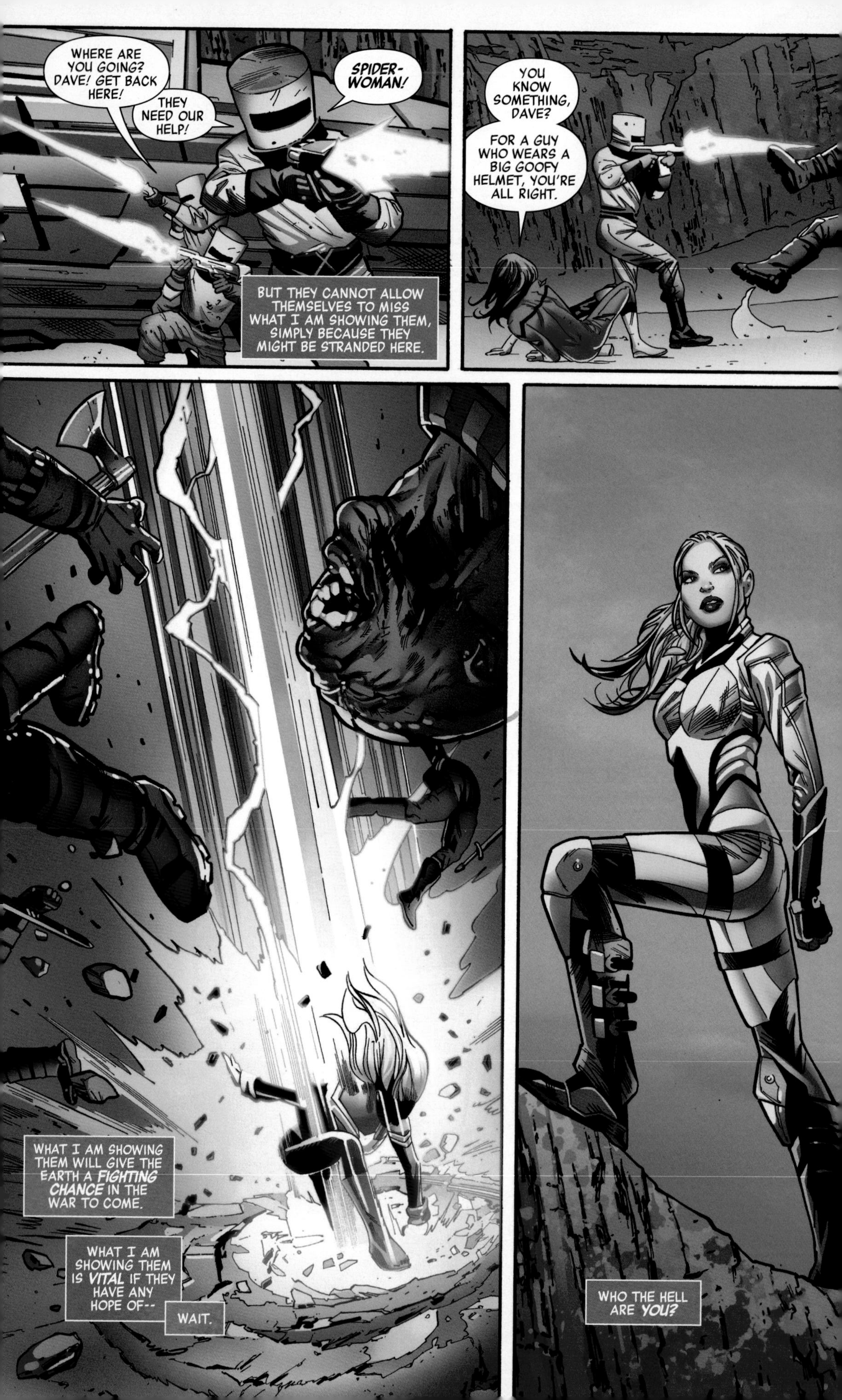

WHERE ARE YOU GOING? DAVE! GET BACK HERE!
THEY NEED OUR HELP!
SPIDER-WOMAN!
BUT THEY CANNOT ALLOW THEMSELVES TO MISS WHAT I AM SHOWING THEM, SIMPLY BECAUSE THEY MIGHT BE STRANDED HERE.
YOU KNOW SOMETHING, DAVE?
FOR A GUY WHO WEARS A BIG GOOFY HELMET, YOU'RE ALL RIGHT.
WHAT I AM SHOWING THEM WILL GIVE THE EARTH A FIGHTING CHANCE IN THE WAR TO COME.
WHAT I AM SHOWING THEM IS VITAL IF THEY HAVE ANY HOPE OF--
WAIT.
WHO THE HELL ARE YOU?

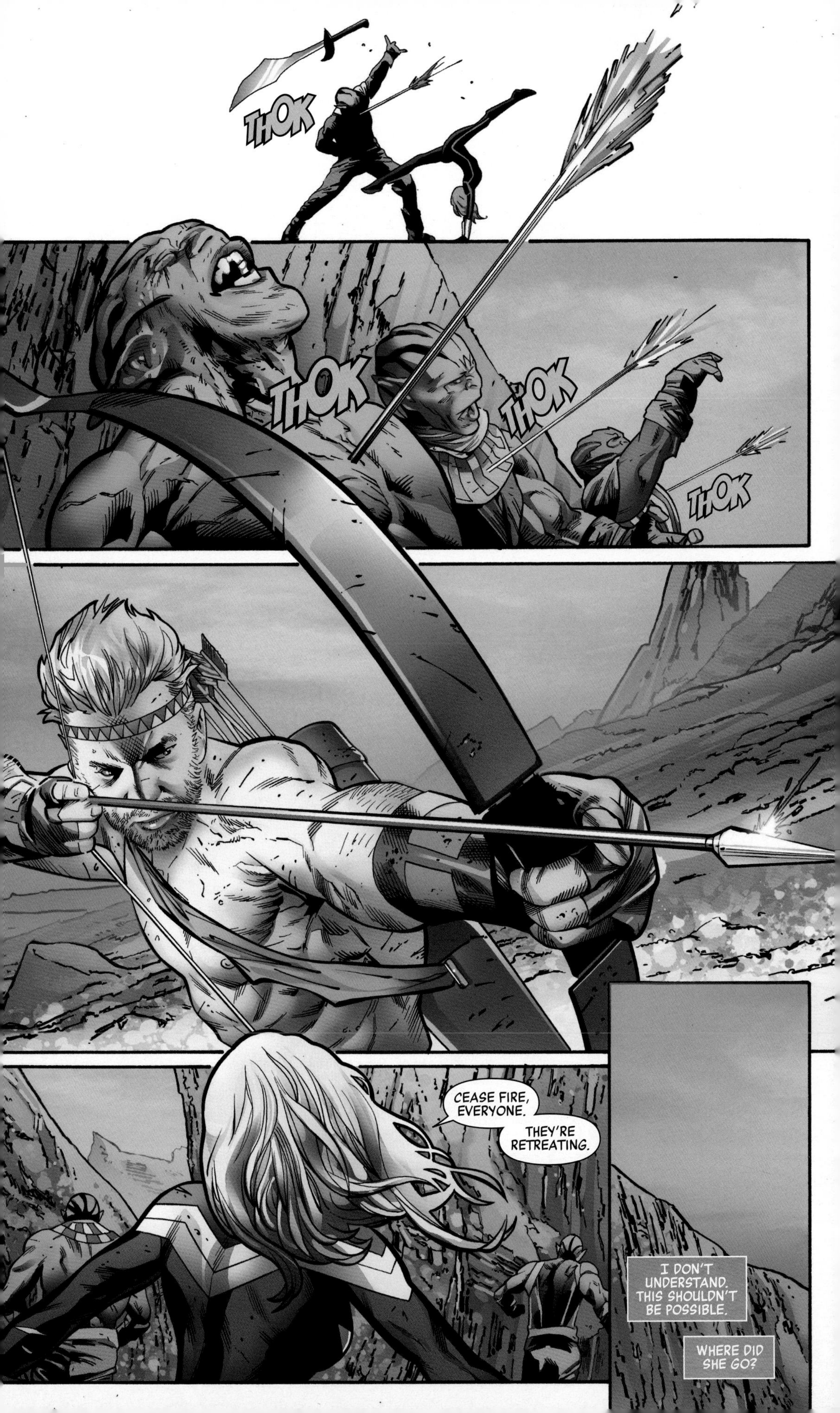
THOK
THOK
THOK
THOK
CEASE FIRE, EVERYONE.
THEY'RE RETREATING.
I DON'T UNDERSTAND. THIS SHOULDN'T BE POSSIBLE.
WHERE DID SHE GO?

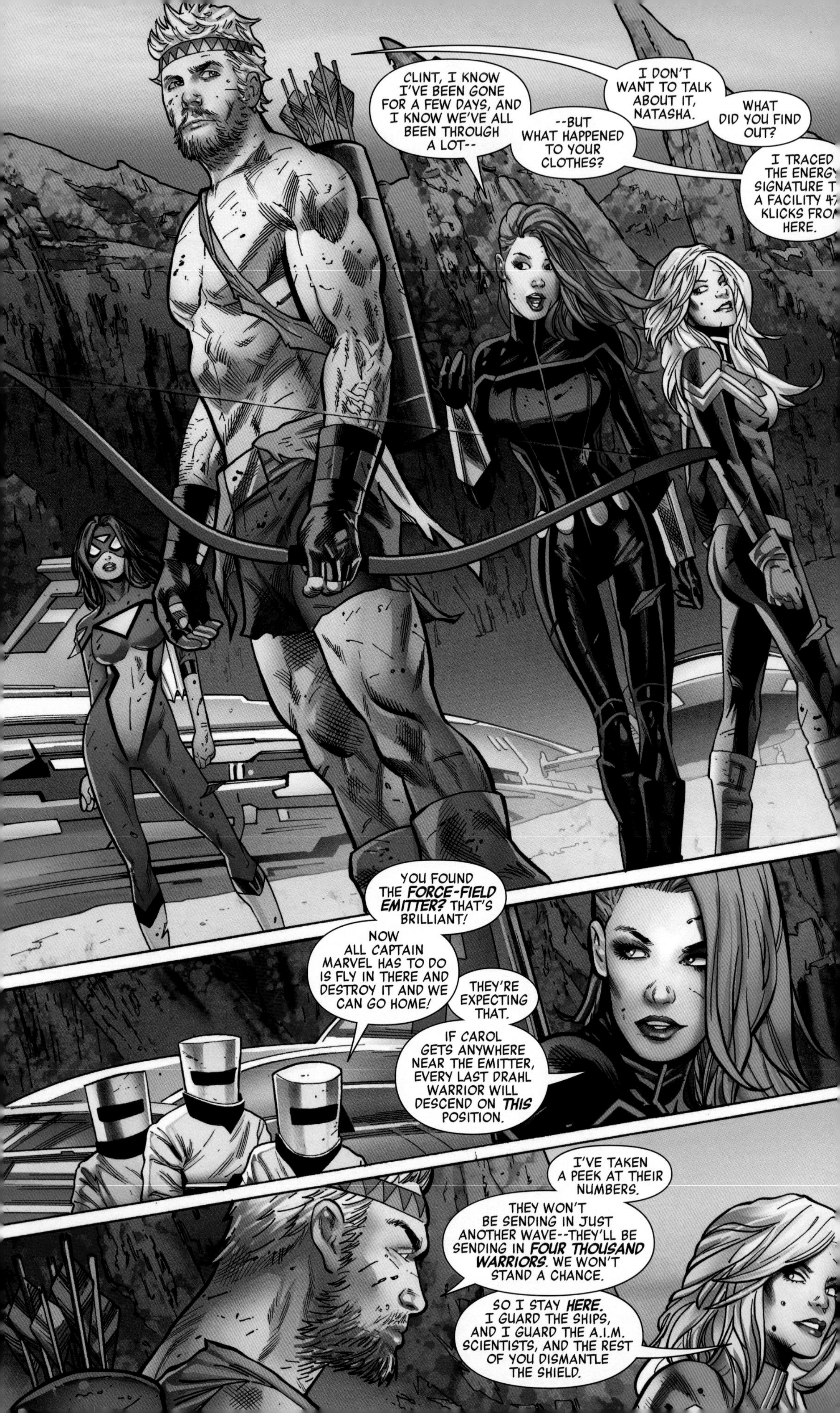
CLINT, I KNOW I'VE BEEN GONE FOR A FEW DAYS, AND I KNOW WE'VE ALL BEEN THROUGH A LOT--
--BUT WHAT HAPPENED TO YOUR CLOTHES?
I DON'T WANT TO TALK ABOUT IT, NATASHA.
WHAT DID YOU FIND OUT?
I TRACED THE ENERGY SIGNATURE T A FACILITY 47 KLICKS FRO HERE.
YOU FOUND THE FORCE-FIELD EMITTER? THAT'S BRILLIANT!
NOW ALL CAPTAIN MARVEL HAS TO DO IS FLY IN THERE AND DESTROY IT AND WE CAN GO HOME!
THEY'RE EXPECTING THAT.
IF CAROL GETS ANYWHERE NEAR THE EMITTER, EVERY LAST DRAHL WARRIOR WILL DESCEND ON THIS POSITION.
I'VE TAKEN A PEEK AT THEIR NUMBERS.
THEY WON'T BE SENDING IN JUST ANOTHER WAVE--THEY'LL BE SENDING IN FOUR THOUSAND WARRIORS. WE WON'T STAND A CHANCE.
SO I STAY HERE. I GUARD THE SHIPS, AND I GUARD THE A.I.M. SCIENTISTS, AND THE REST OF YOU DISMANTLE THE SHIELD.

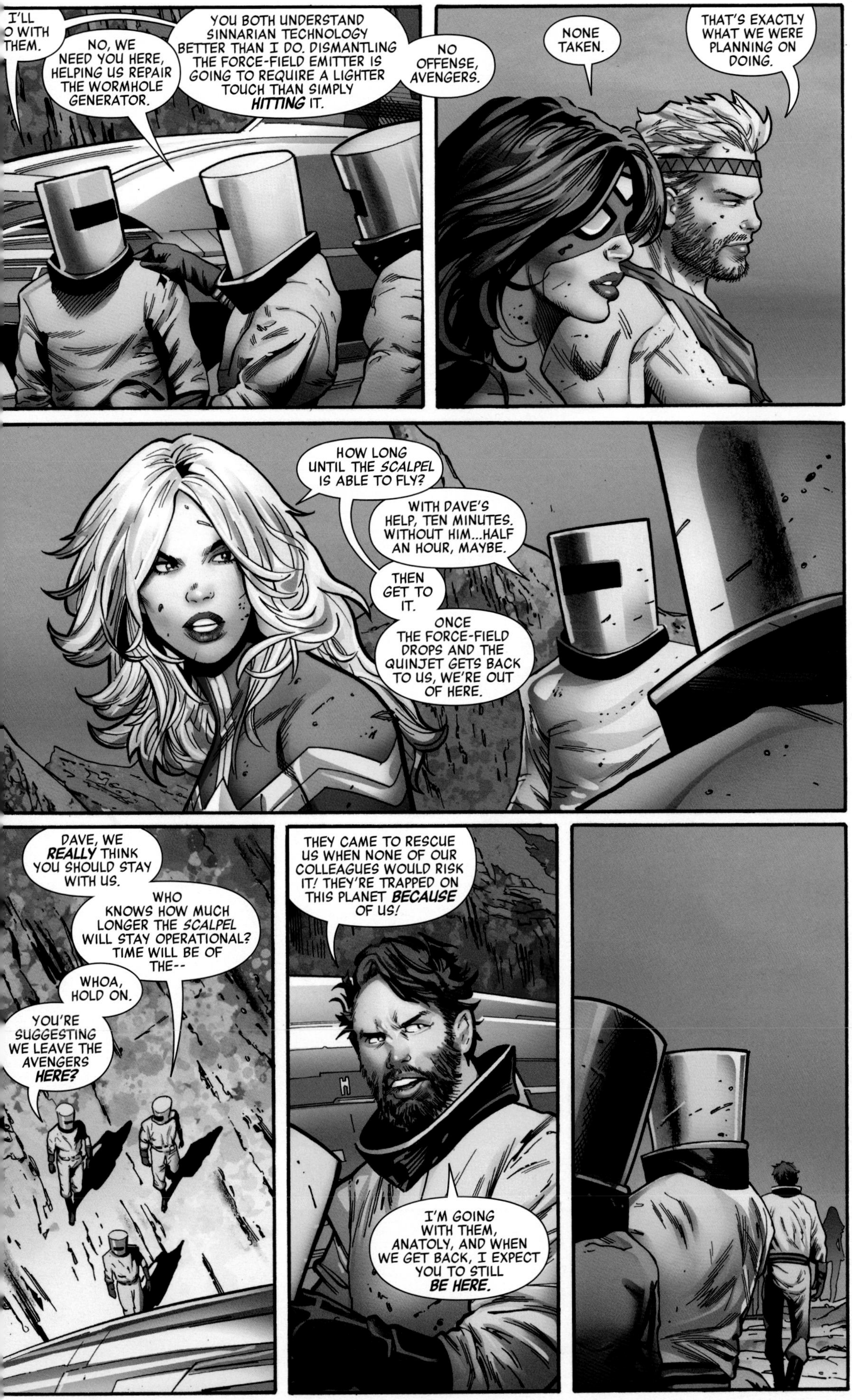

I'LL
O WITH
THEM.
NO, WE NEED YOU HERE, HELPING US REPAIR THE WORMHOLE GENERATOR.
YOU BOTH UNDERSTAND SINNARIAN TECHNOLOGY BETTER THAN I DO. DISMANTLING THE FORCE-FIELD EMITTER IS GOING TO REQUIRE A LIGHTER TOUCH THAN SIMPLY HITTING IT.
NO OFFENSE, AVENGERS.
NONE TAKEN.
THAT'S EXACTLY WHAT WE WERE PLANNING ON DOING.
HOW LONG UNTIL THE SCALPEL IS ABLE TO FLY?
WITH DAVE'S HELP, TEN MINUTES. WITHOUT HIM...HALF AN HOUR, MAYBE.
THEN GET TO IT.
ONCE THE FORCE-FIELD DROPS AND THE QUINJET GETS BACK TO US, WE'RE OUT OF HERE.
DAVE, WE REALLY THINK YOU SHOULD STAY WITH US.
WHO KNOWS HOW MUCH LONGER THE SCALPEL WILL STAY OPERATIONAL? TIME WILL BE OF THE--
WHOA, HOLD ON.
YOU'RE SUGGESTING WE LEAVE THE AVENGERS HERE?
THEY CAME TO RESCUE US WHEN NONE OF OUR COLLEAGUES WOULD RISK IT! THEY'RE TRAPPED ON THIS PLANET BECAUSE OF US!
I'M GOING WITH THEM, ANATOLY, AND WHEN WE GET BACK, I EXPECT YOU TO STILL BE HERE.

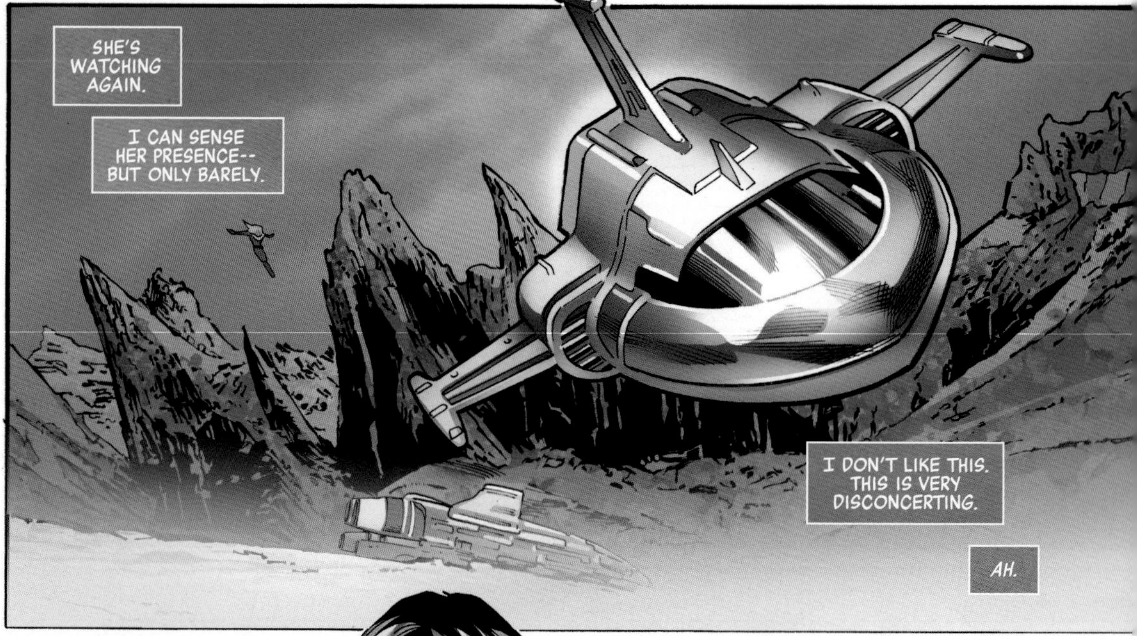
SHE'S WATCHING AGAIN.
I CAN SENSE HER PRESENCE-- BUT ONLY BARELY.
I DON'T LIKE THIS. THIS IS VERY DISCONCERTING.
AH.

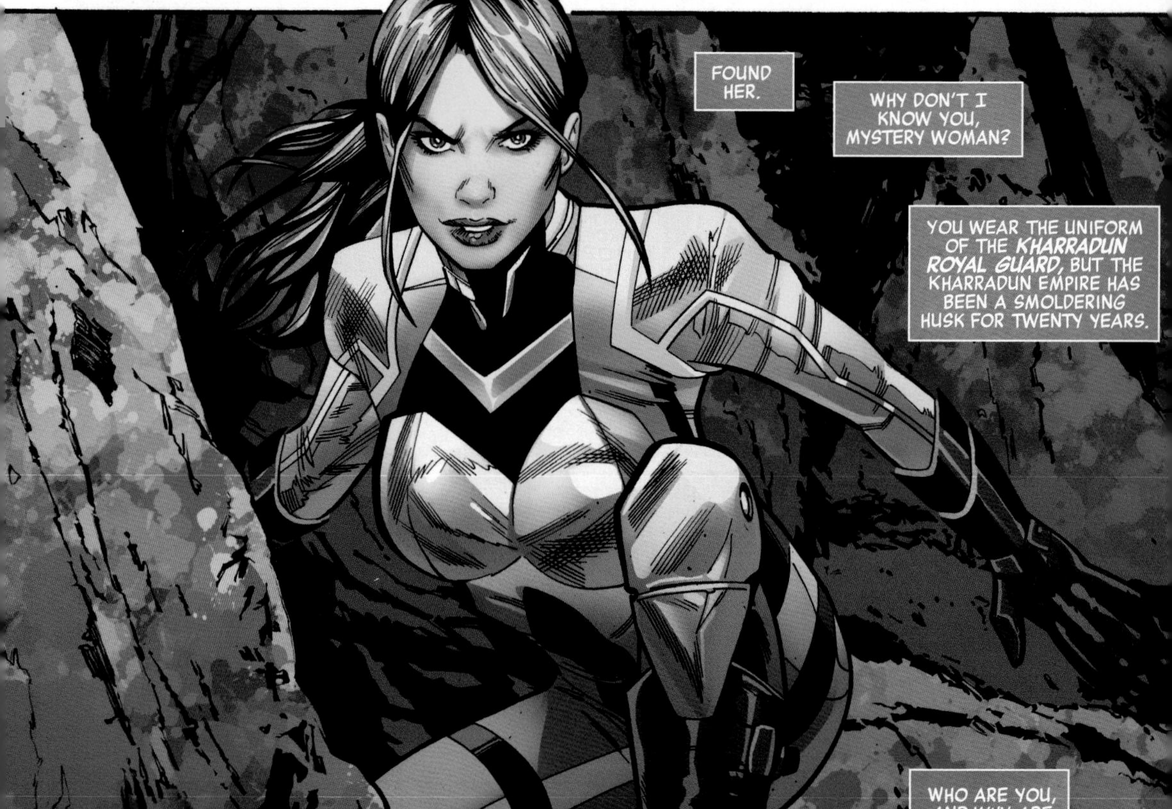
FOUND HER.
WHY DON'T I KNOW YOU, MYSTERY WOMAN?
YOU WEAR THE UNIFORM OF THE ***KHARRADUN ROYAL GUARD***, BUT THE KHARRADUN EMPIRE HAS BEEN A SMOLDERING HUSK FOR TWENTY YEARS.
WHO ARE YOU, AND WHY ARE YOU HERE?

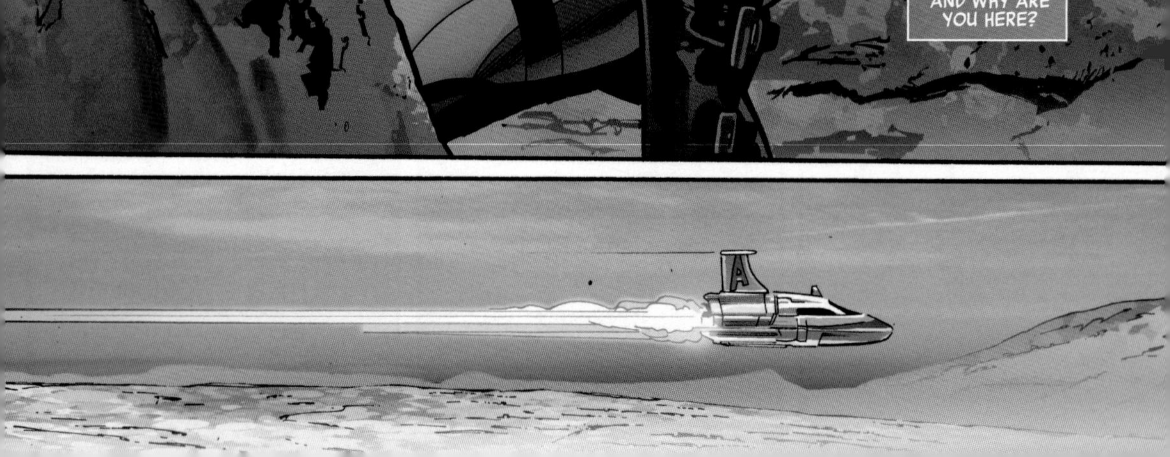

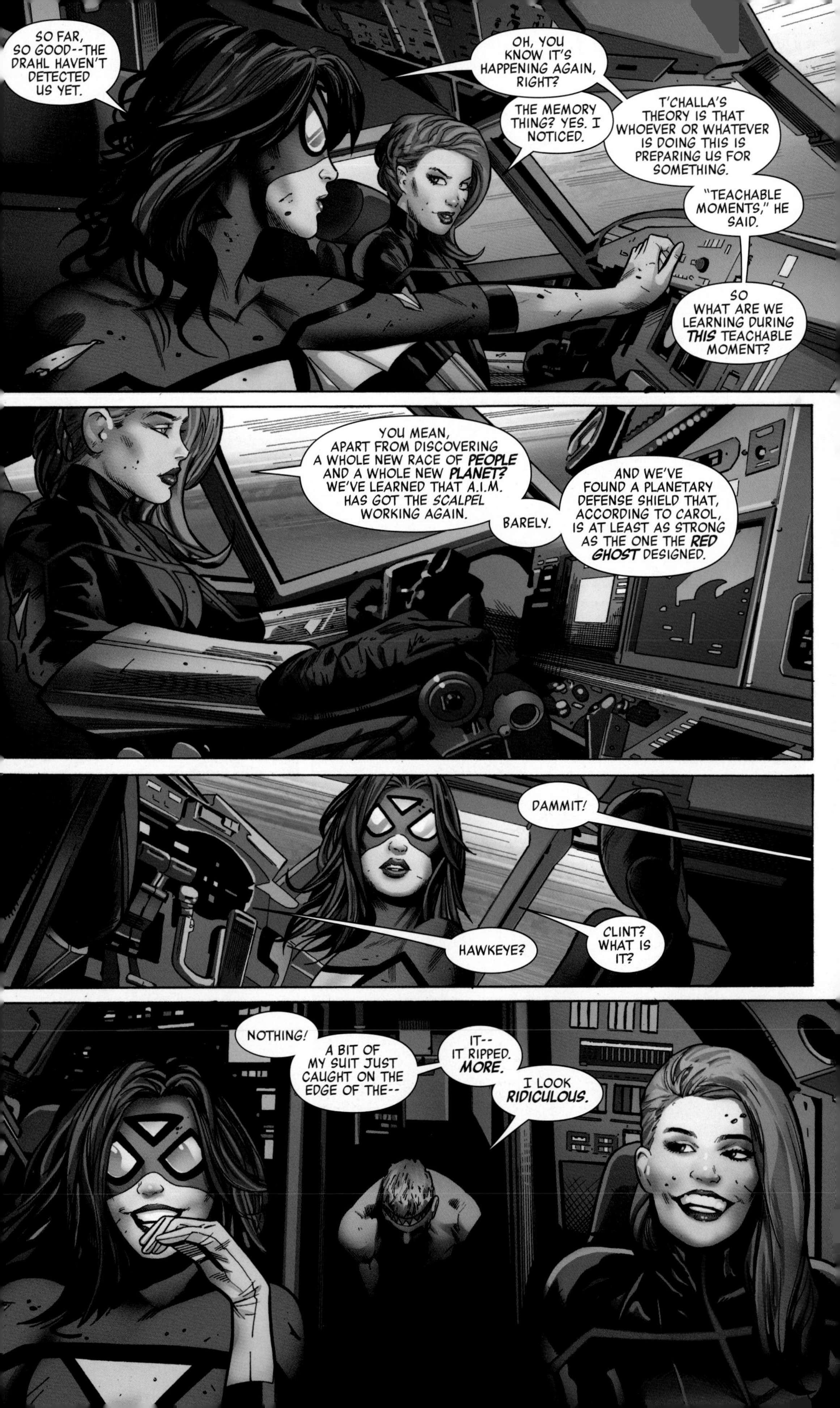
SO FAR, SO GOOD--THE DRAHL HAVEN'T DETECTED US YET.
OH, YOU KNOW IT'S HAPPENING AGAIN, RIGHT?
THE MEMORY THING? YES. I NOTICED.
T'CHALLA'S THEORY IS THAT WHOEVER OR WHATEVER IS DOING THIS IS PREPARING US FOR SOMETHING.
"TEACHABLE MOMENTS," HE SAID.
SO WHAT ARE WE LEARNING DURING THIS TEACHABLE MOMENT?
YOU MEAN, APART FROM DISCOVERING A WHOLE NEW RACE OF PEOPLE AND A WHOLE NEW PLANET? WE'VE LEARNED THAT A.I.M. HAS GOT THE SCALPEL WORKING AGAIN.
BARELY.
AND WE'VE FOUND A PLANETARY DEFENSE SHIELD THAT, ACCORDING TO CAROL, IS AT LEAST AS STRONG AS THE ONE THE RED GHOST DESIGNED.
DAMMIT!
HAWKEYE?
CLINT? WHAT IS IT?
NOTHING!
A BIT OF MY SUIT JUST CAUGHT ON THE EDGE OF THE--
IT-- IT RIPPED. MORE.
I LOOK RIDICULOUS.

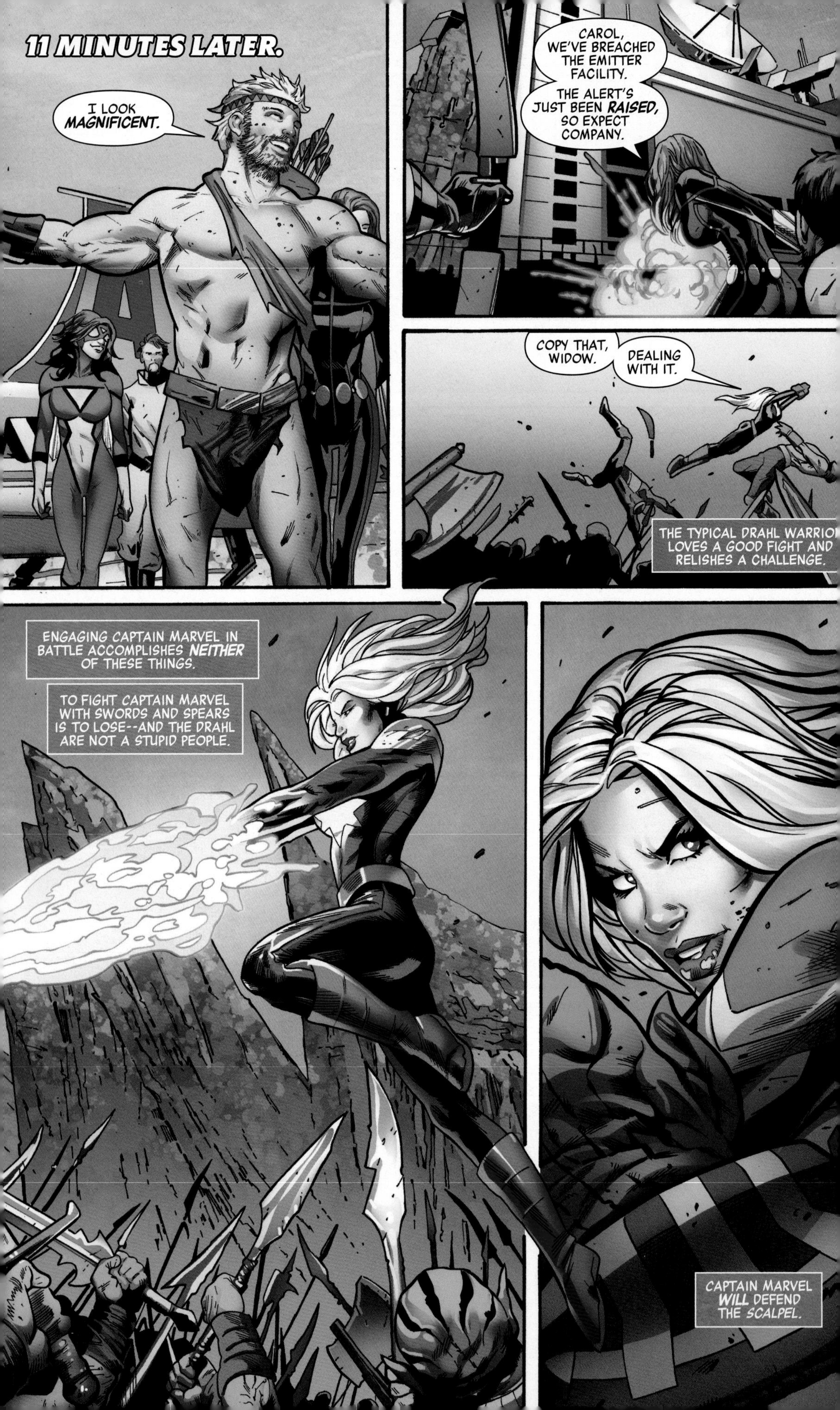
11 MINUTES LATER.
I LOOK MAGNIFICENT.
CAROL, WE'VE BREACHED THE EMITTER FACILITY.
THE ALERT'S JUST BEEN RAISED, SO EXPECT COMPANY.
COPY THAT, WIDOW.
DEALING WITH IT.
THE TYPICAL DRAHL WARRIO LOVES A GOOD FIGHT AND RELISHES A CHALLENGE.
ENGAGING CAPTAIN MARVEL IN BATTLE ACCOMPLISHES NEITHER OF THESE THINGS.
TO FIGHT CAPTAIN MARVEL WITH SWORDS AND SPEARS IS TO LOSE--AND THE DRAHL ARE NOT A STUPID PEOPLE.
CAPTAIN MARVEL WILL DEFEND THE SCALPEL.

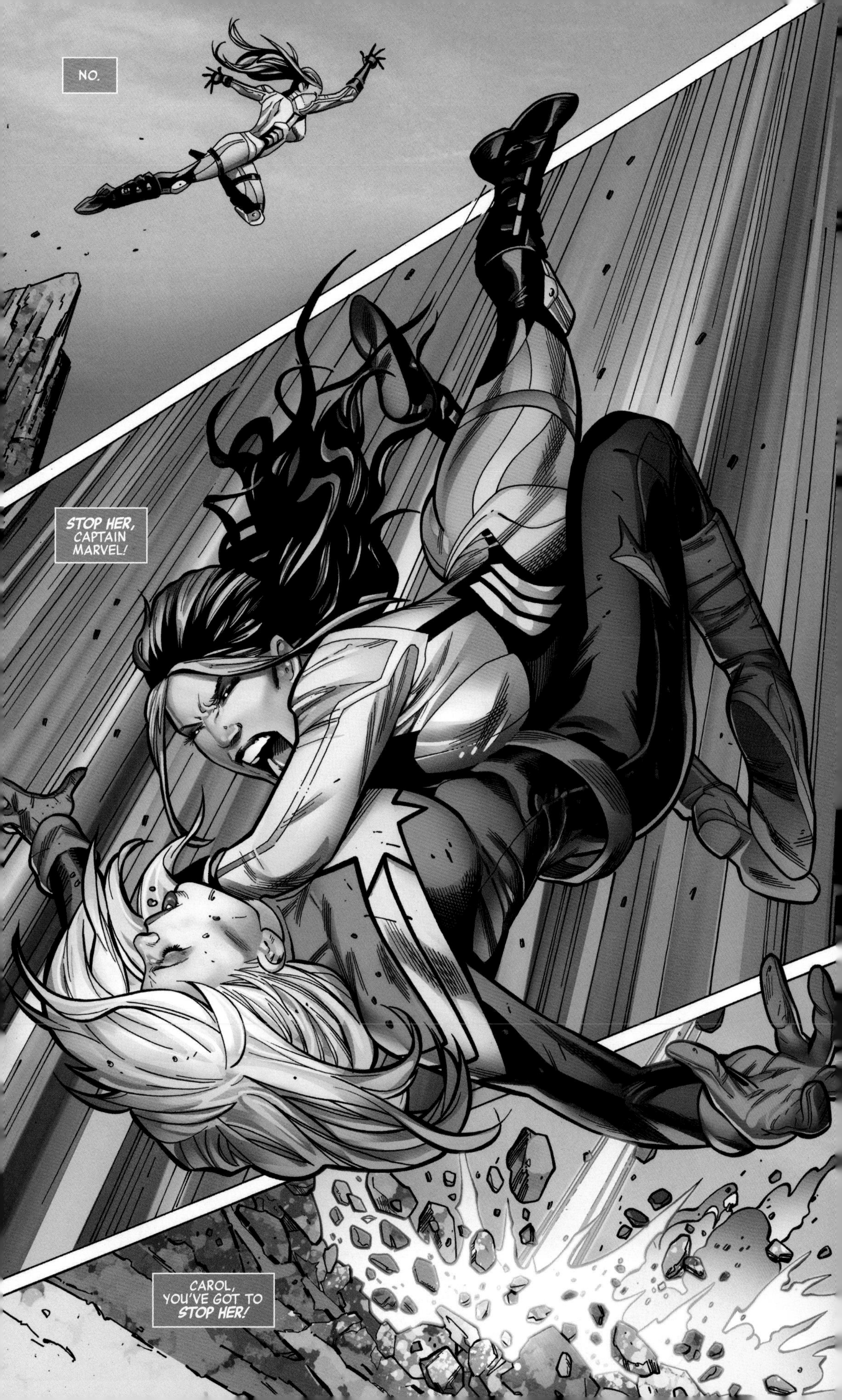
NO.
STOP HER, CAPTAIN MARVEL!
CAROL, YOU'VE GOT TO STOP HER!

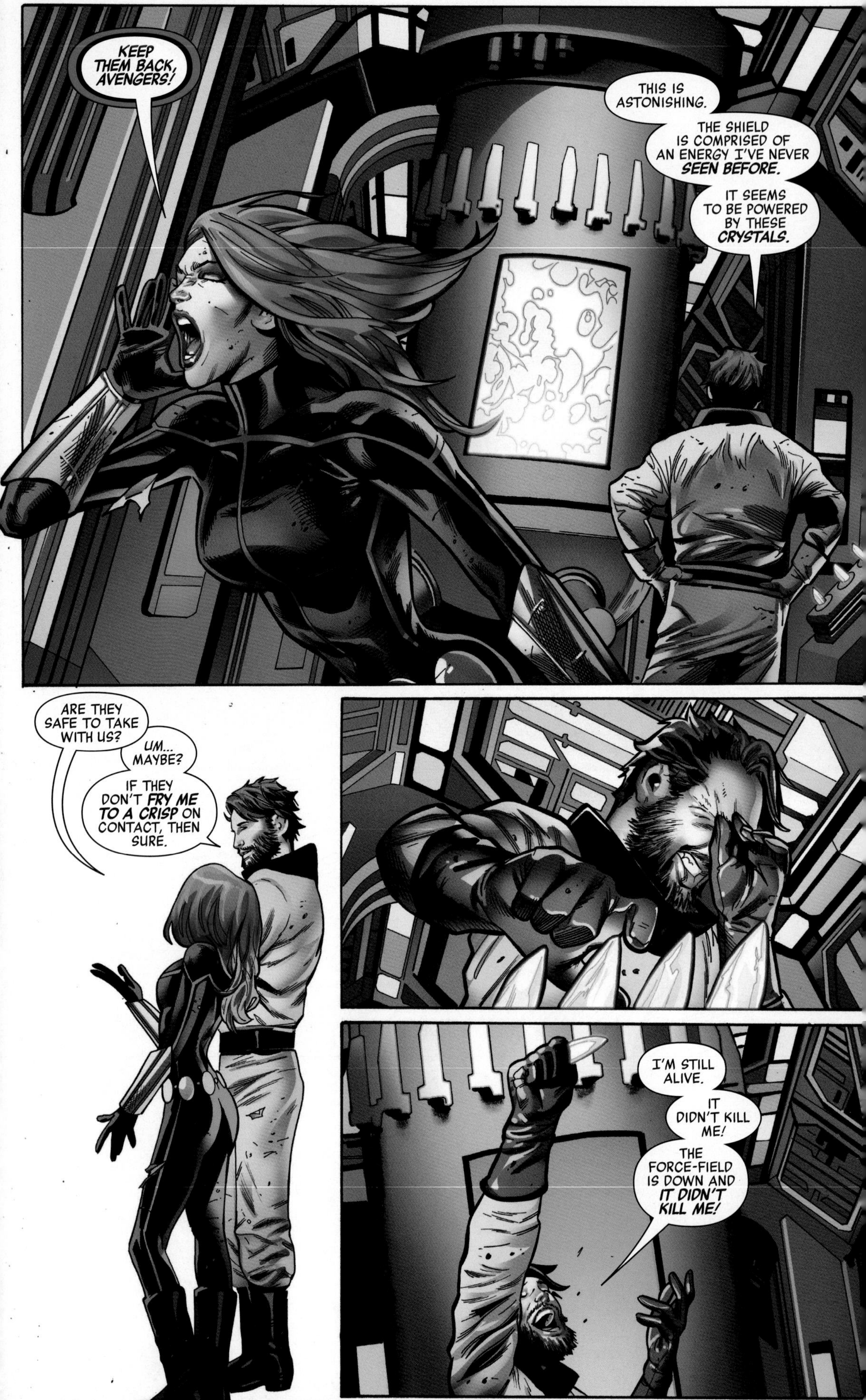

KEEP THEM BACK, AVENGERS!
THIS IS ASTONISHING.
THE SHIELD IS COMPRISED OF AN ENERGY I'VE NEVER SEEN BEFORE.
IT SEEMS TO BE POWERED BY THESE CRYSTALS.
ARE THEY SAFE TO TAKE WITH US?
UM... MAYBE?
IF THEY DON'T FRY ME TO A CRISP ON CONTACT, THEN SURE.
I'M STILL ALIVE.
IT DIDN'T KILL ME!
THE FORCE-FIELD IS DOWN AND IT DIDN'T KILL ME!

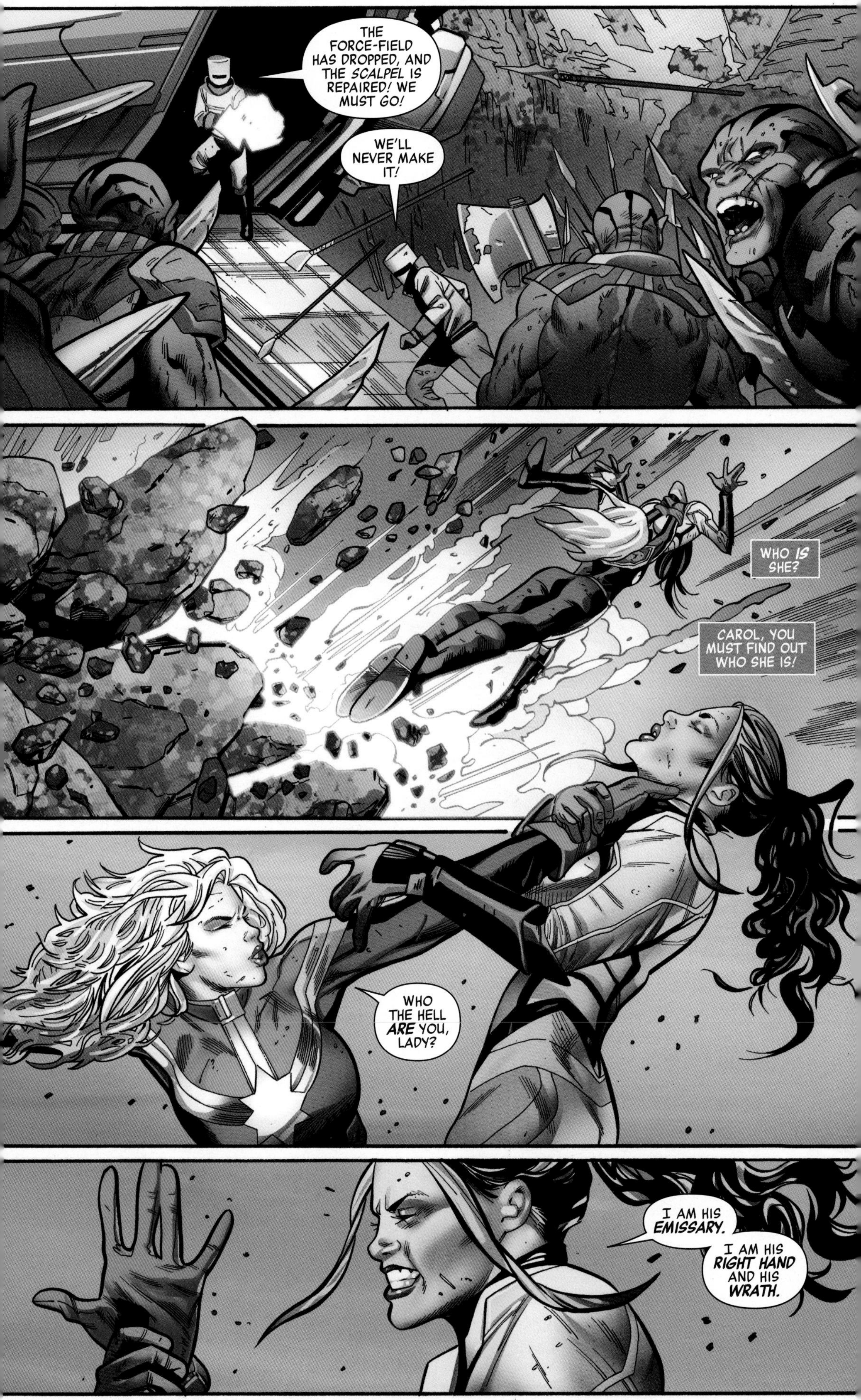
THE FORCE-FIELD HAS DROPPED, AND THE *SCALPEL* IS REPAIRED! WE MUST GO!
WE'LL NEVER MAKE IT!
WHO *IS* SHE?
CAROL, YOU MUST FIND OUT WHO SHE IS!
WHO THE HELL ***ARE*** YOU, LADY?
I AM HIS ***EMISSARY.***
I AM HIS ***RIGHT HAND*** AND HIS ***WRATH.***

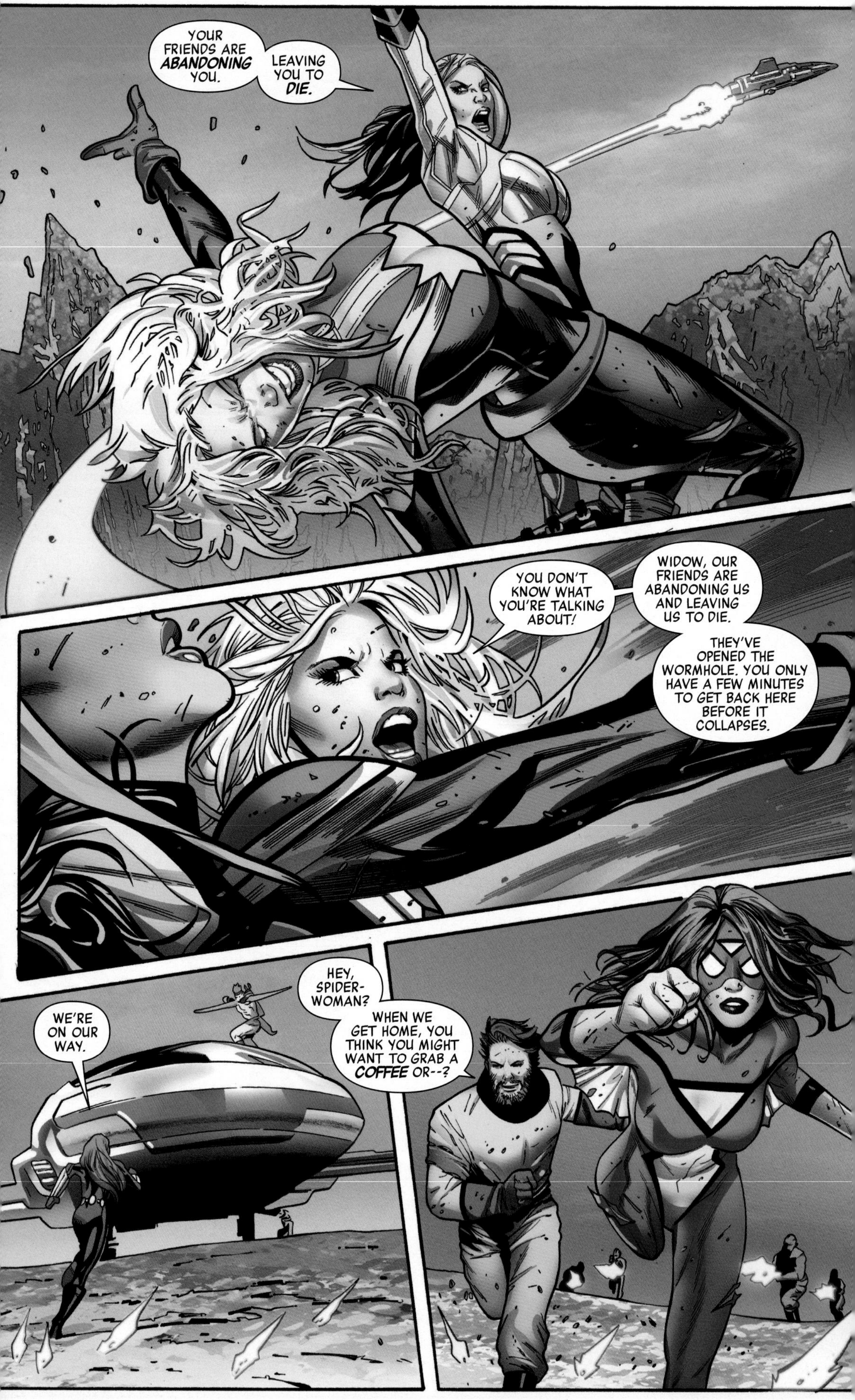
YOUR FRIENDS ARE ABANDONING YOU.
LEAVING YOU TO DIE.
YOU DON'T KNOW WHAT YOU'RE TALKING ABOUT!
WIDOW, OUR FRIENDS ARE ABANDONING US AND LEAVING US TO DIE.
THEY'VE OPENED THE WORMHOLE. YOU ONLY HAVE A FEW MINUTES TO GET BACK HERE BEFORE IT COLLAPSES.
WE'RE ON OUR WAY.
HEY, SPIDER-WOMAN?
WHEN WE GET HOME, YOU THINK YOU MIGHT WANT TO GRAB A COFFEE OR--?

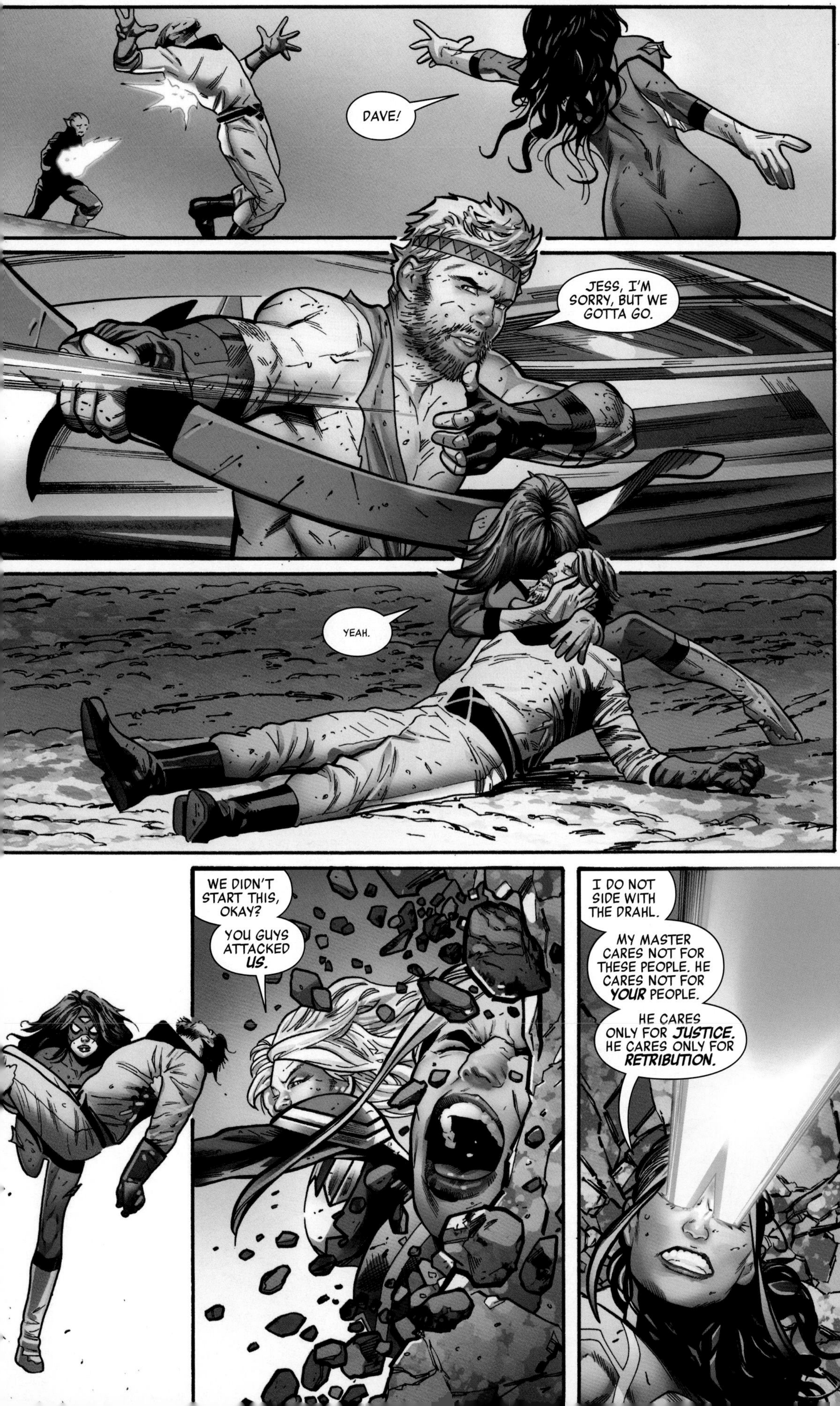
DAVE!
JESS, I'M SORRY, BUT WE GOTTA GO.
YEAH.
WE DIDN'T START THIS, OKAY?
YOU GUYS ATTACKED *US*.
I DO NOT SIDE WITH THE DRAHL.
MY MASTER CARES NOT FOR THESE PEOPLE. HE CARES NOT FOR *YOUR* PEOPLE.
HE CARES ONLY FOR *JUSTICE*. HE CARES ONLY FOR *RETRIBUTION*.

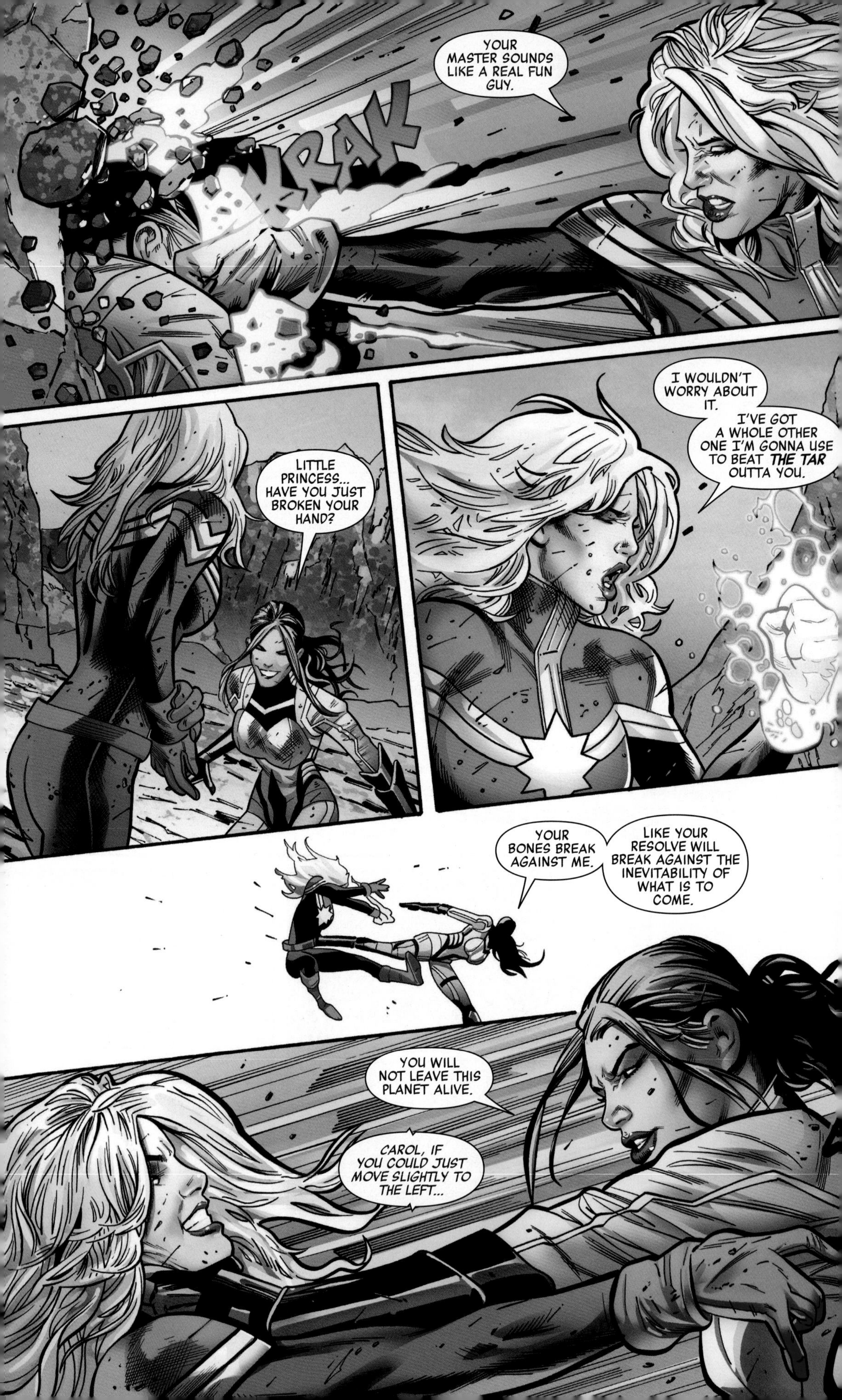
YOUR MASTER SOUNDS LIKE A REAL FUN GUY.
KRAK
LITTLE PRINCESS... HAVE YOU JUST BROKEN YOUR HAND?
I WOULDN'T WORRY ABOUT IT.
I'VE GOT A WHOLE OTHER ONE I'M GONNA USE TO BEAT THE TAR OUTTA YOU.
YOUR BONES BREAK AGAINST ME.
LIKE YOUR RESOLVE WILL BREAK AGAINST THE INEVITABILITY OF WHAT IS TO COME.
YOU WILL NOT LEAVE THIS PLANET ALIVE.
CAROL, IF YOU COULD JUST MOVE SLIGHTLY TO THE LEFT...

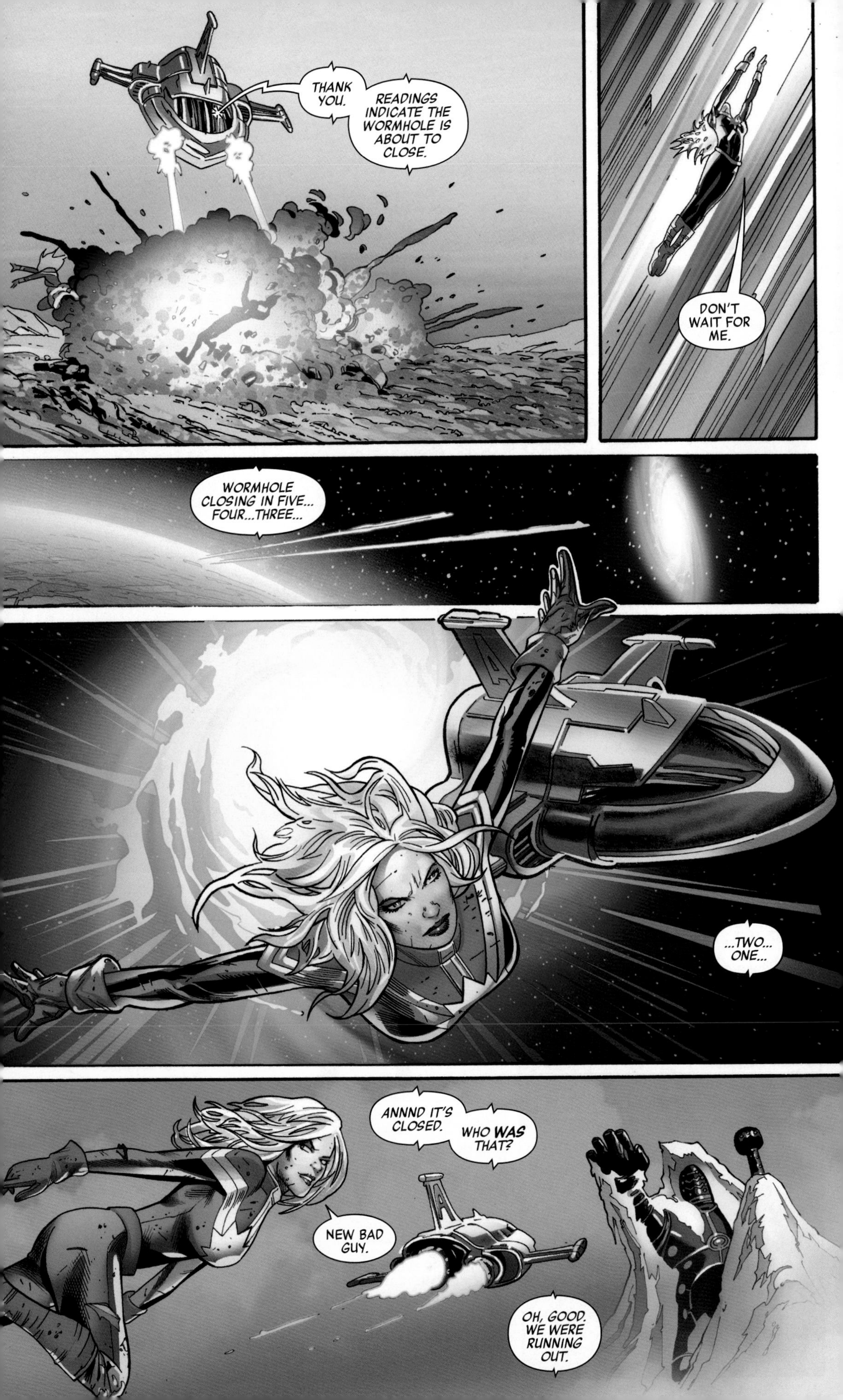
THANK YOU.
READINGS INDICATE THE WORMHOLE IS ABOUT TO CLOSE.
DON'T WAIT FOR ME.
WORMHOLE CLOSING IN FIVE... FOUR...THREE...
...TWO... ONE...
ANNND IT'S CLOSED.
WHO **WAS** THAT?
NEW BAD GUY.
OH, GOOD. WE WERE RUNNING OUT.

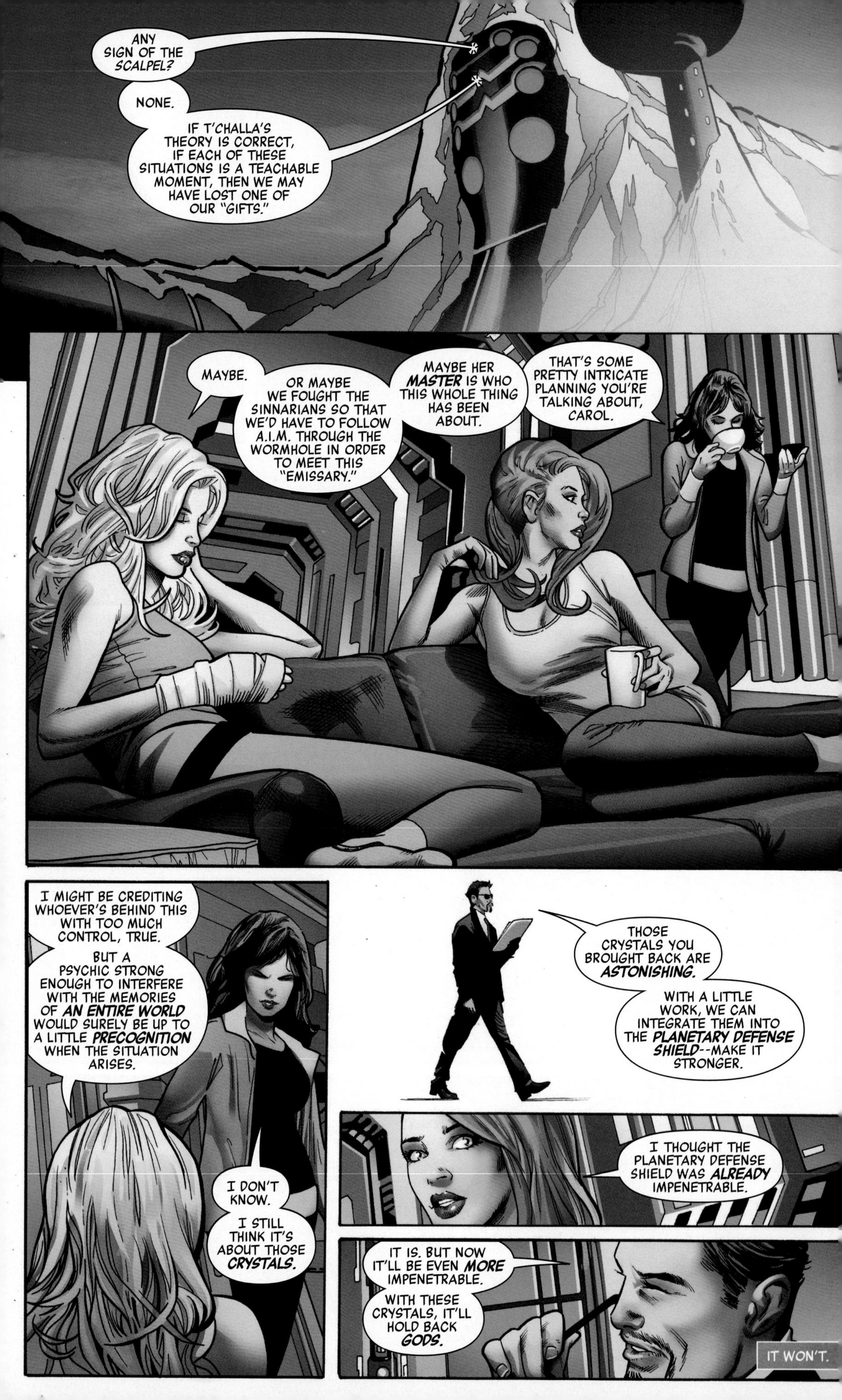

ANY SIGN OF THE SCALPEL?
NONE.
IF T'CHALLA'S THEORY IS CORRECT, IF EACH OF THESE SITUATIONS IS A TEACHABLE MOMENT, THEN WE MAY HAVE LOST ONE OF OUR "GIFTS."
MAYBE.
OR MAYBE WE FOUGHT THE SINNARIANS SO THAT WE'D HAVE TO FOLLOW A.I.M. THROUGH THE WORMHOLE IN ORDER TO MEET THIS "EMISSARY."
MAYBE HER **MASTER** IS WHO THIS WHOLE THING HAS BEEN ABOUT.
THAT'S SOME PRETTY INTRICATE PLANNING YOU'RE TALKING ABOUT, CAROL.
I MIGHT BE CREDITING WHOEVER'S BEHIND THIS WITH TOO MUCH CONTROL, TRUE.
BUT A PSYCHIC STRONG ENOUGH TO INTERFERE WITH THE MEMORIES OF **AN ENTIRE WORLD** WOULD SURELY BE UP TO A LITTLE **PRECOGNITION** WHEN THE SITUATION ARISES.
I DON'T KNOW.
I STILL THINK IT'S ABOUT THOSE **CRYSTALS.**
THOSE CRYSTALS YOU BROUGHT BACK ARE **ASTONISHING.**
WITH A LITTLE WORK, WE CAN INTEGRATE THEM INTO THE **PLANETARY DEFENSE SHIELD**--MAKE IT STRONGER.
I THOUGHT THE PLANETARY DEFENSE SHIELD WAS **ALREADY** IMPENETRABLE.
IT IS. BUT NOW IT'LL BE EVEN **MORE** IMPENETRABLE.
WITH THESE CRYSTALS, IT'LL HOLD BACK **GODS.**
IT WON'T.

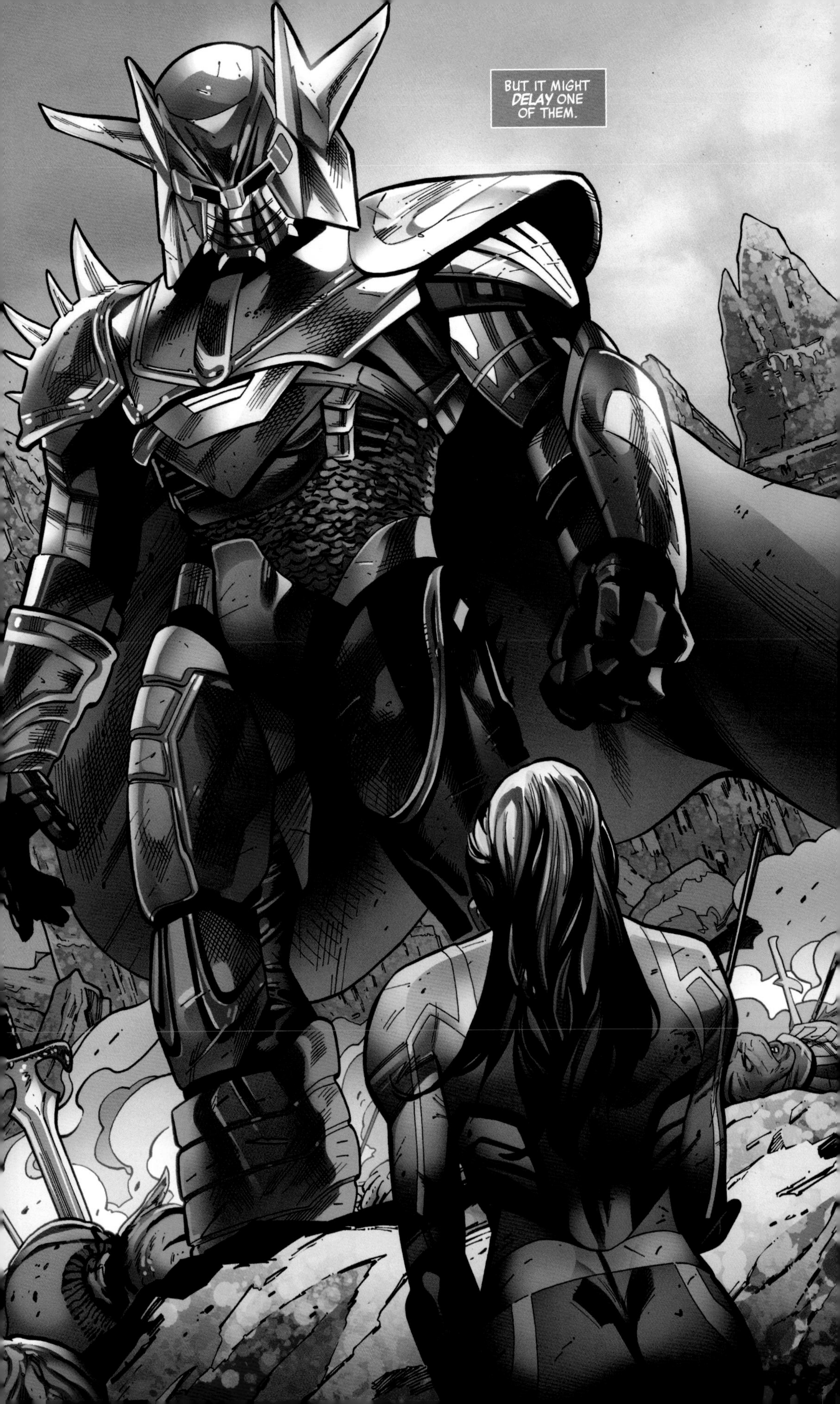
BUT IT MIGHT *DELAY* ONE OF THEM.

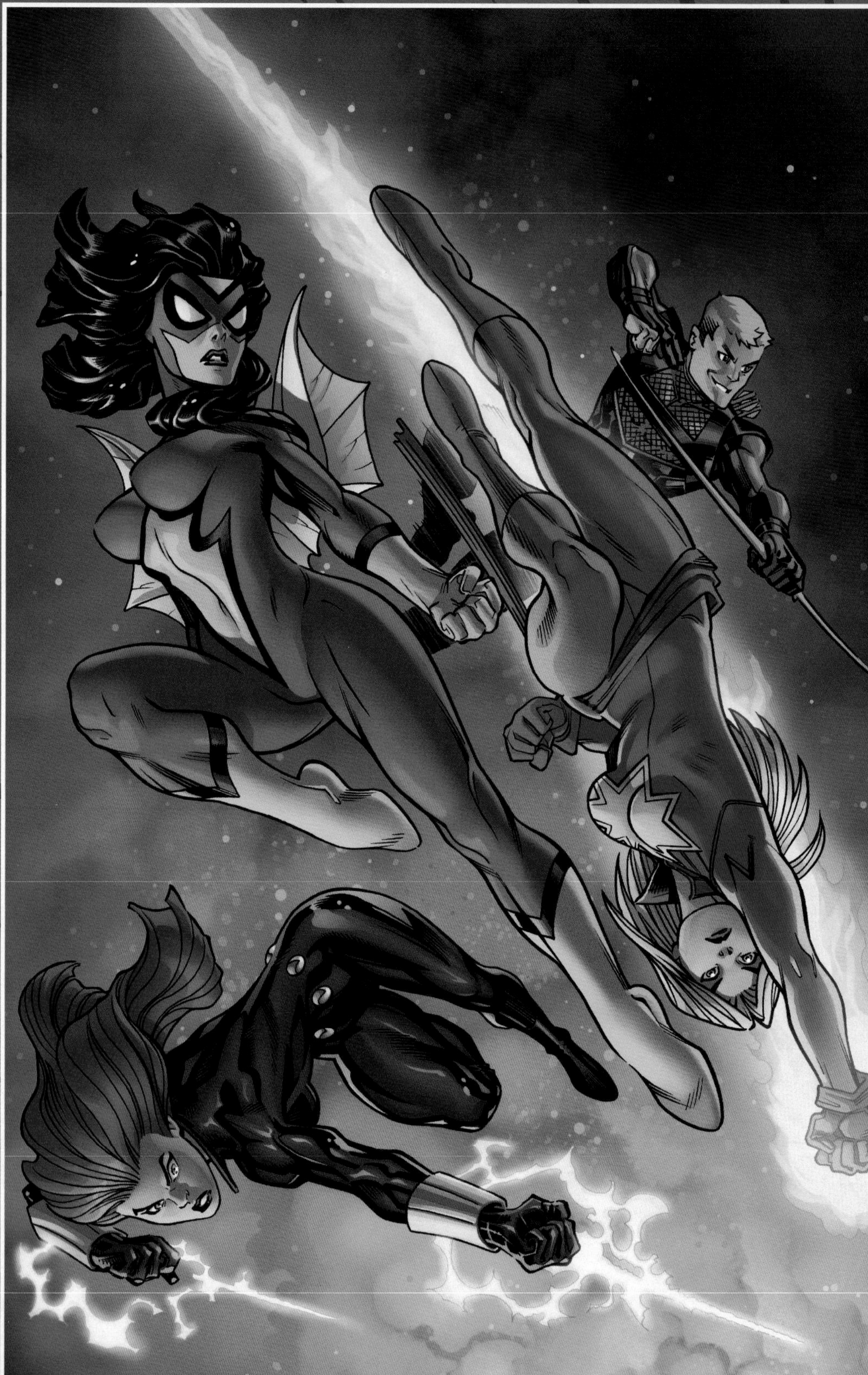
eMcG'22! laura

ED McGUINNESS & **LAURA MARTIN**
#4 VARIANT

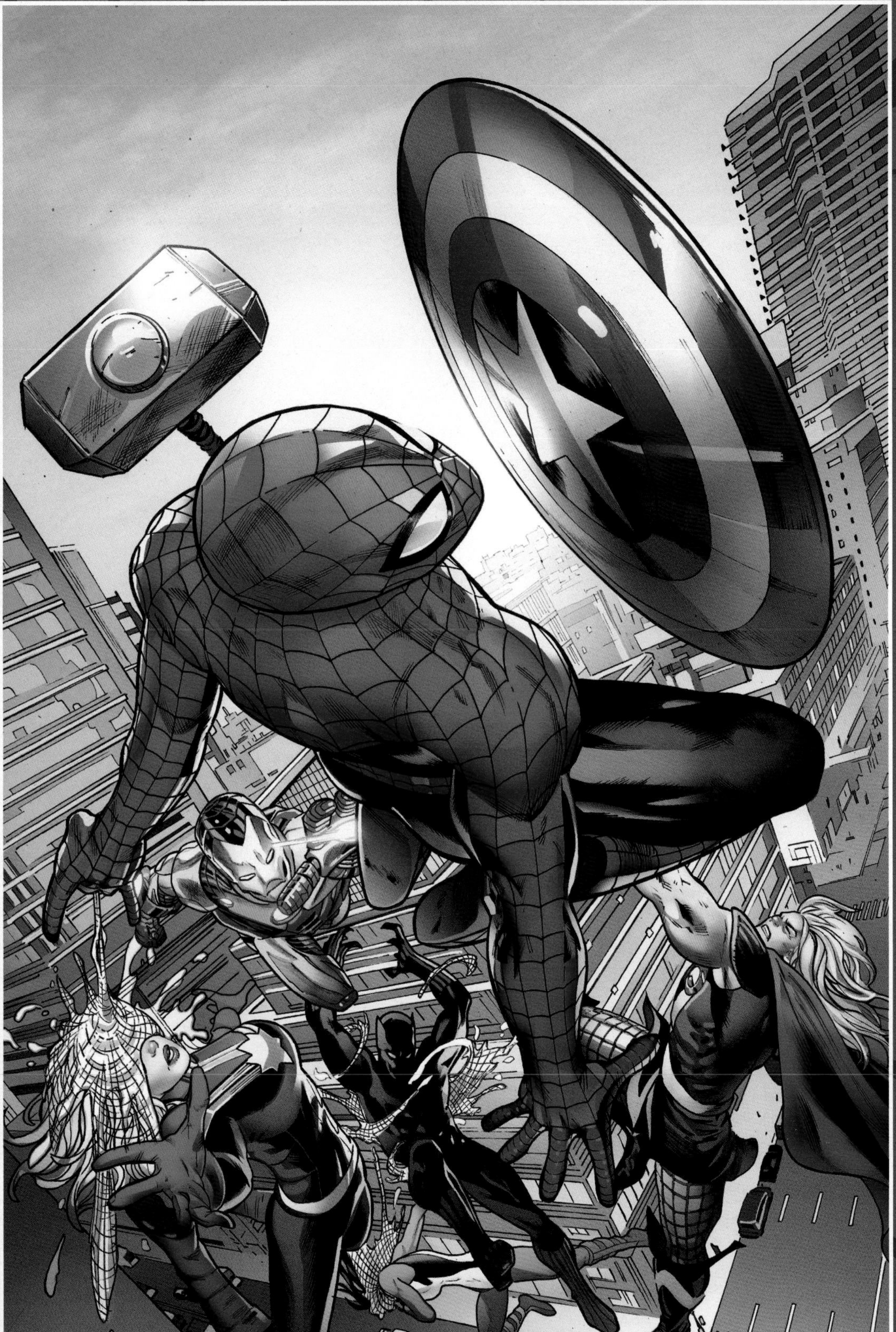
LAND

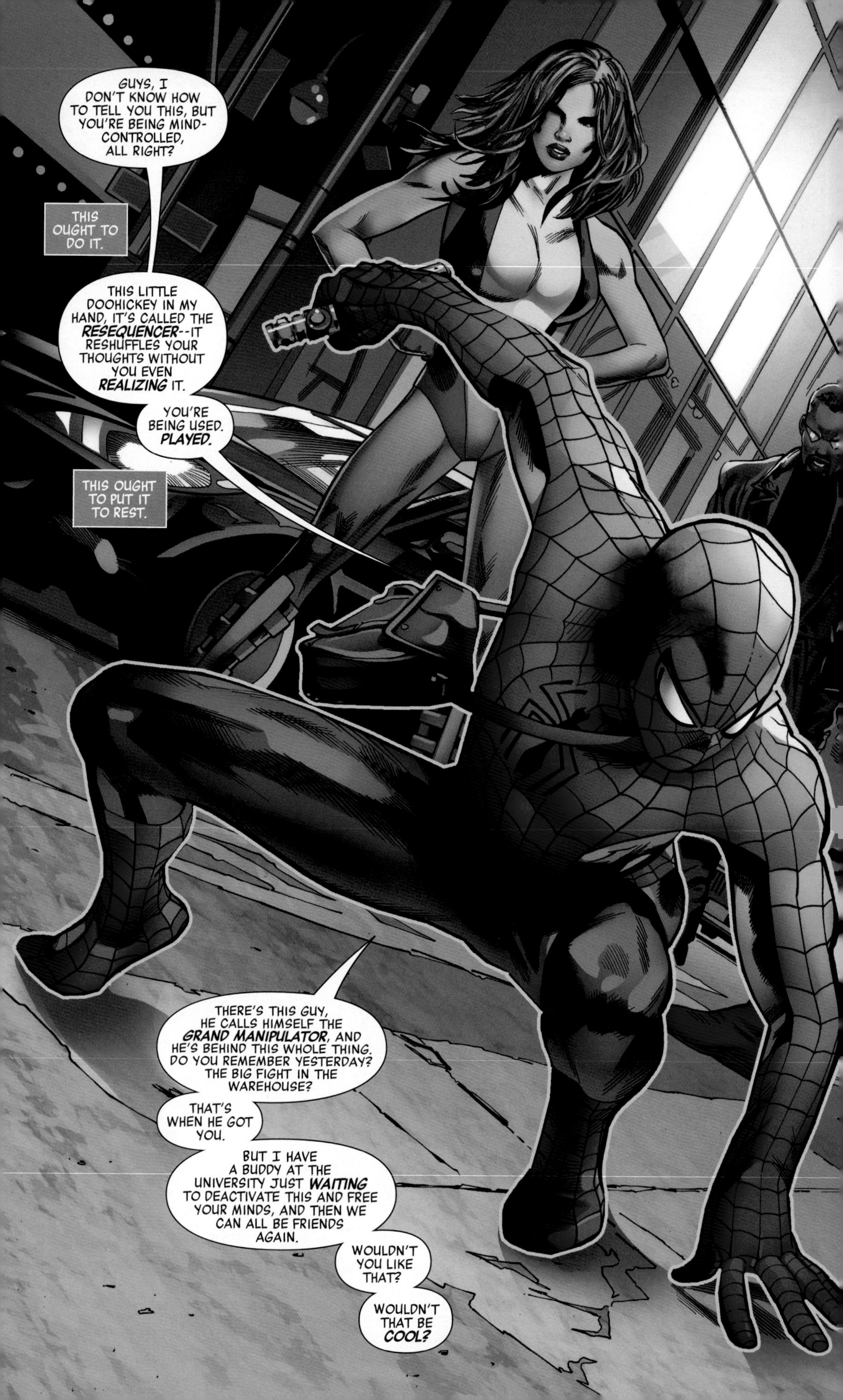
GUYS, I DON'T KNOW HOW TO TELL YOU THIS, BUT YOU'RE BEING MIND-CONTROLLED, ALL RIGHT?
THIS OUGHT TO DO IT.
THIS LITTLE DOOHICKEY IN MY HAND, IT'S CALLED THE RESEQUENCER--IT RESHUFFLES YOUR THOUGHTS WITHOUT YOU EVEN REALIZING IT.
YOU'RE BEING USED. PLAYED.
THIS OUGHT TO PUT IT TO REST.
THERE'S THIS GUY, HE CALLS HIMSELF THE GRAND MANIPULATOR, AND HE'S BEHIND THIS WHOLE THING. DO YOU REMEMBER YESTERDAY? THE BIG FIGHT IN THE WAREHOUSE?
THAT'S WHEN HE GOT YOU.
BUT I HAVE A BUDDY AT THE UNIVERSITY JUST WAITING TO DEACTIVATE THIS AND FREE YOUR MINDS, AND THEN WE CAN ALL BE FRIENDS AGAIN.
WOULDN'T YOU LIKE THAT?
WOULDN'T THAT BE COOL?

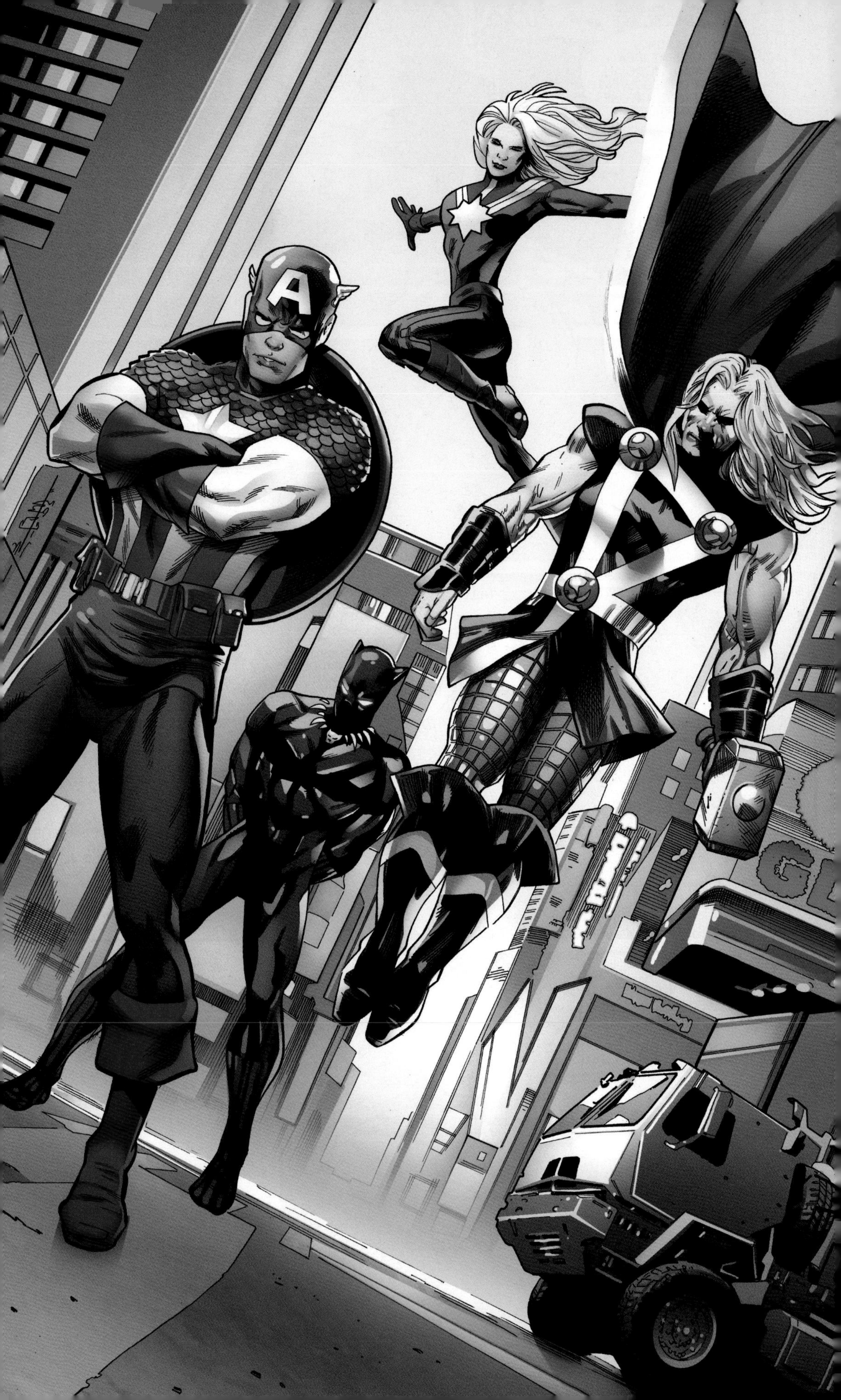

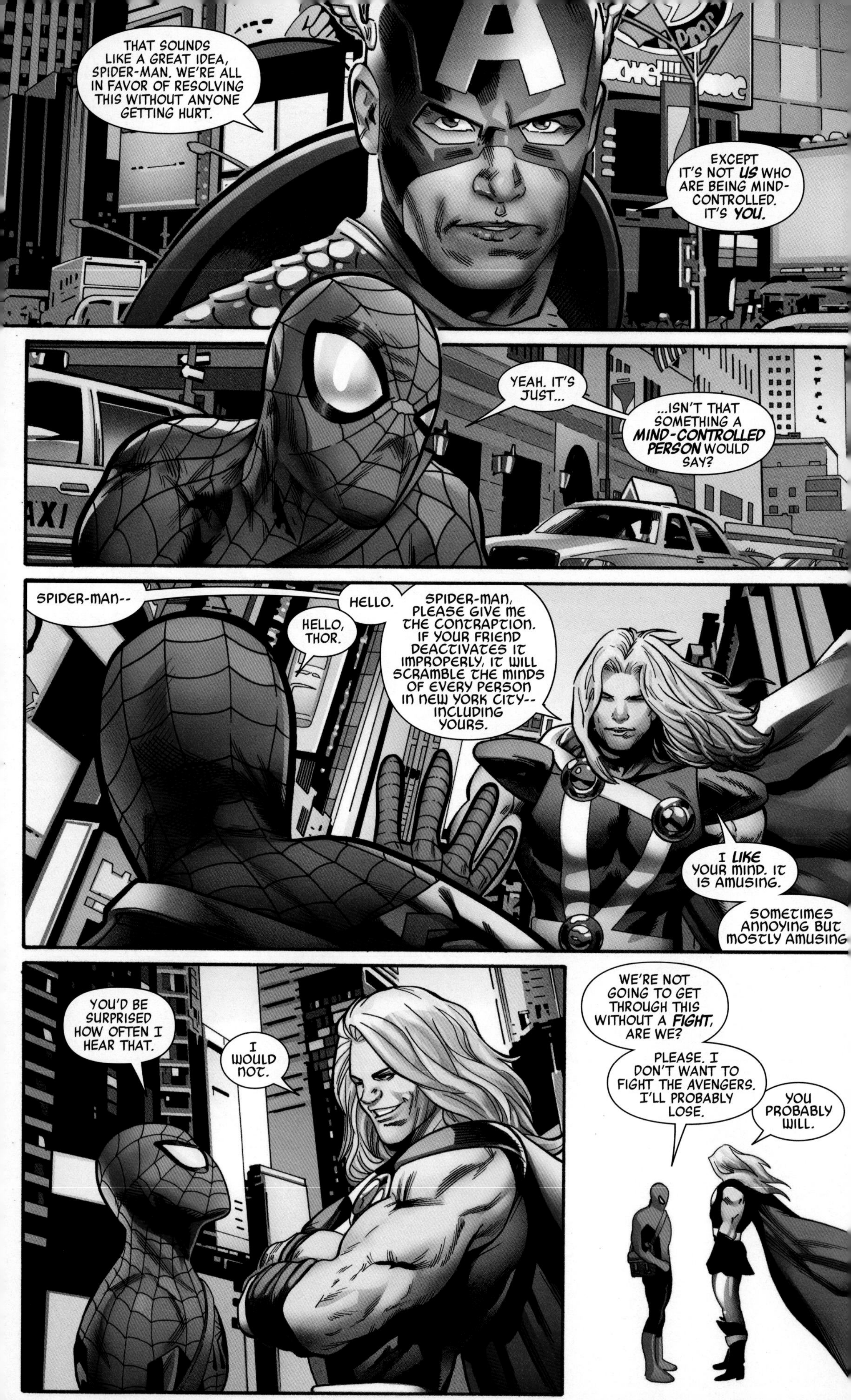

THAT SOUNDS LIKE A GREAT IDEA, SPIDER-MAN. WE'RE ALL IN FAVOR OF RESOLVING THIS WITHOUT ANYONE GETTING HURT.
EXCEPT IT'S NOT *US* WHO ARE BEING MIND-CONTROLLED. IT'S *YOU.*
YEAH. IT'S JUST...
...ISN'T THAT SOMETHING A *MIND-CONTROLLED PERSON* WOULD SAY?
SPIDER-MAN--
HELLO.
HELLO, THOR.
SPIDER-MAN, PLEASE GIVE ME THE CONTRAPTION. IF YOUR FRIEND DEACTIVATES IT IMPROPERLY, IT WILL SCRAMBLE THE MINDS OF EVERY PERSON IN NEW YORK CITY--INCLUDING YOURS.
I *LIKE* YOUR MIND. IT IS AMUSING.
SOMETIMES ANNOYING BUT MOSTLY AMUSING
YOU'D BE SURPRISED HOW OFTEN I HEAR THAT.
I WOULD NOT.
WE'RE NOT GOING TO GET THROUGH THIS WITHOUT A *FIGHT,* ARE WE?
PLEASE. I DON'T WANT TO FIGHT THE AVENGERS. I'LL PROBABLY LOSE.
YOU PROBABLY WILL.

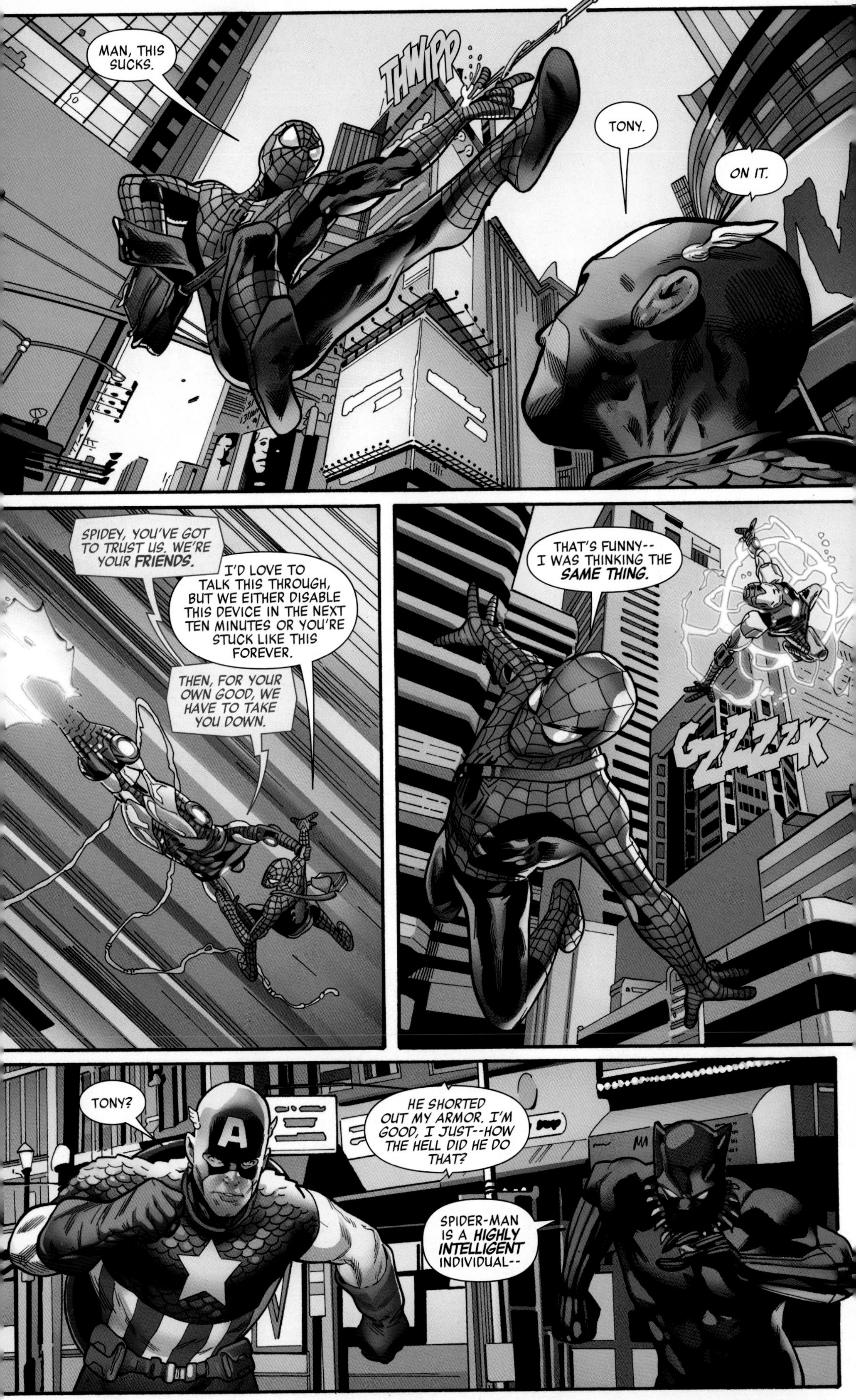
MAN, THIS SUCKS.
THWIPP
TONY.
ON IT.
SPIDEY, YOU'VE GOT TO TRUST US. WE'RE YOUR FRIENDS.
I'D LOVE TO TALK THIS THROUGH, BUT WE EITHER DISABLE THIS DEVICE IN THE NEXT TEN MINUTES OR YOU'RE STUCK LIKE THIS FOREVER.
THEN, FOR YOUR OWN GOOD, WE HAVE TO TAKE YOU DOWN.
THAT'S FUNNY-- I WAS THINKING THE SAME THING.
GZZZZK
TONY?
HE SHORTED OUT MY ARMOR. I'M GOOD, I JUST--HOW THE HELL DID HE DO THAT?
SPIDER-MAN IS A HIGHLY INTELLIGENT INDIVIDUAL--

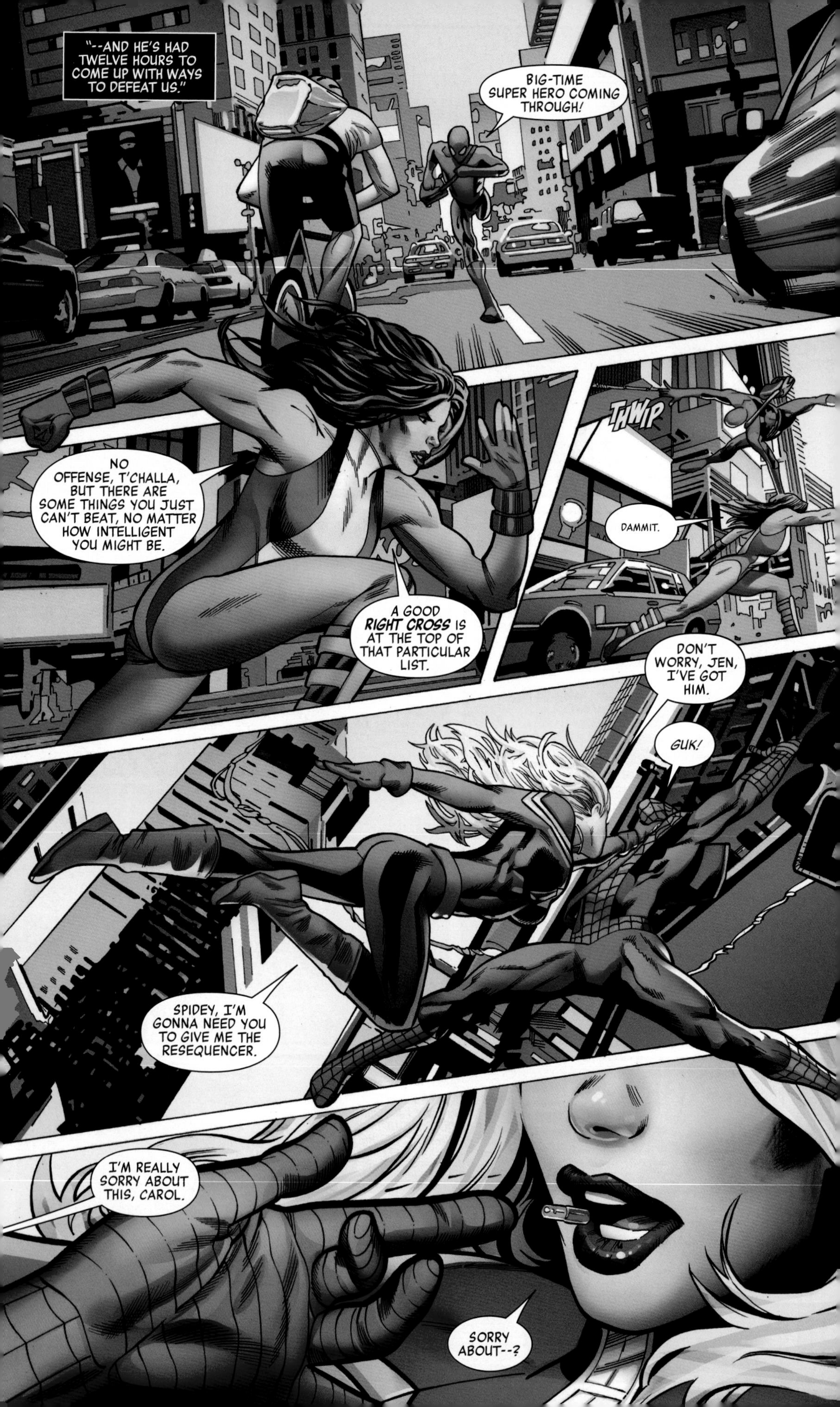
"--AND HE'S HAD TWELVE HOURS TO COME UP WITH WAYS TO DEFEAT US."
BIG-TIME SUPER HERO COMING THROUGH!
NO OFFENSE, T'CHALLA, BUT THERE ARE SOME THINGS YOU JUST CAN'T BEAT, NO MATTER HOW INTELLIGENT YOU MIGHT BE.
A GOOD RIGHT CROSS IS AT THE TOP OF THAT PARTICULAR LIST.
THWIP
DAMMIT.
DON'T WORRY, JEN, I'VE GOT HIM.
GUK!
SPIDEY, I'M GONNA NEED YOU TO GIVE ME THE RESEQUENCER.
I'M REALLY SORRY ABOUT THIS, CAROL.
SORRY ABOUT--?

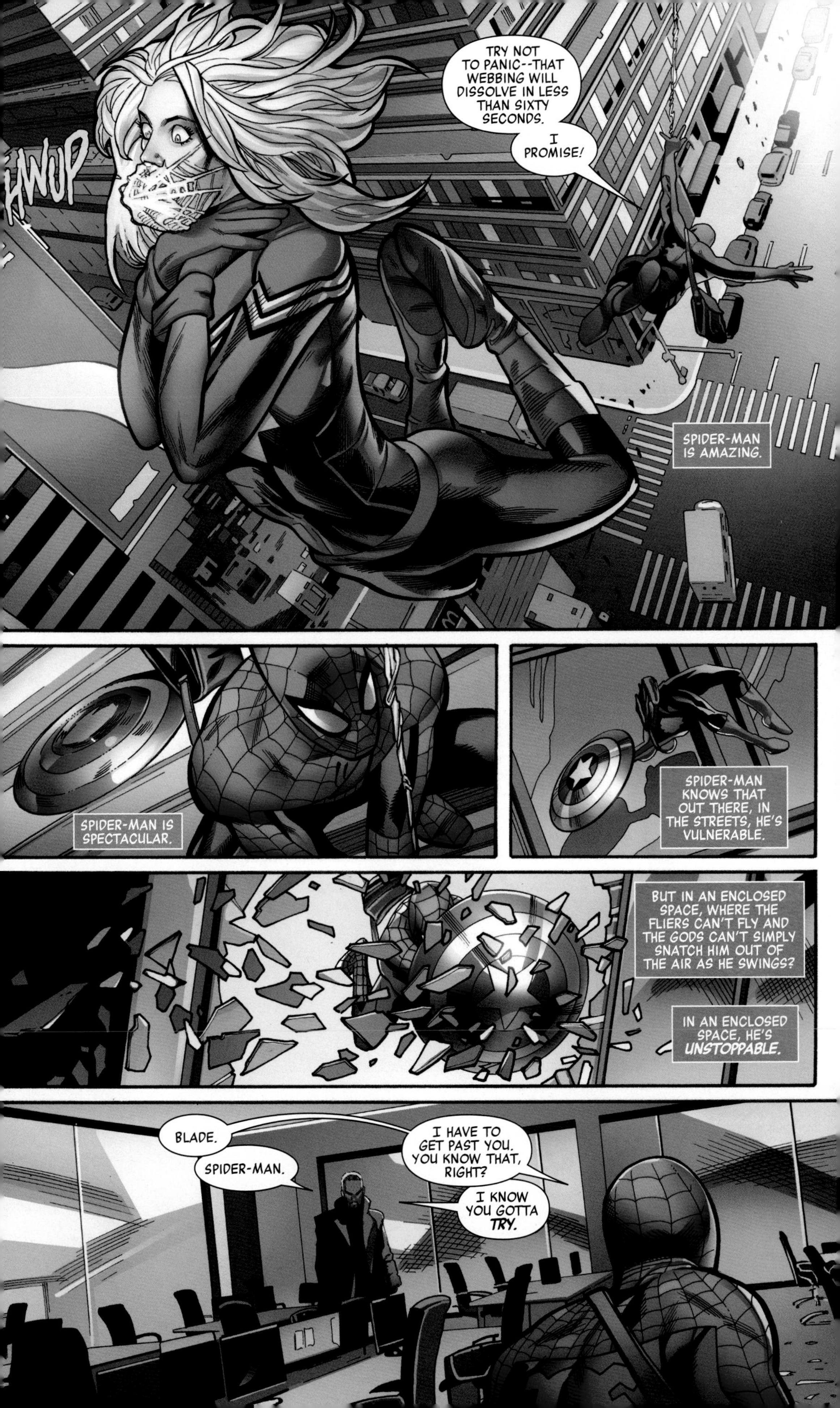
THWUP
TRY NOT TO PANIC--THAT WEBBING WILL DISSOLVE IN LESS THAN SIXTY SECONDS.
I PROMISE!
SPIDER-MAN IS AMAZING.
SPIDER-MAN IS SPECTACULAR.
SPIDER-MAN KNOWS THAT OUT THERE, IN THE STREETS, HE'S VULNERABLE.
BUT IN AN ENCLOSED SPACE, WHERE THE FLIERS CAN'T FLY AND THE GODS CAN'T SIMPLY SNATCH HIM OUT OF THE AIR AS HE SWINGS?
IN AN ENCLOSED SPACE, HE'S *UNSTOPPABLE.*
BLADE.
SPIDER-MAN.
I HAVE TO GET PAST YOU. YOU KNOW THAT, RIGHT?
I KNOW YOU GOTTA *TRY.*

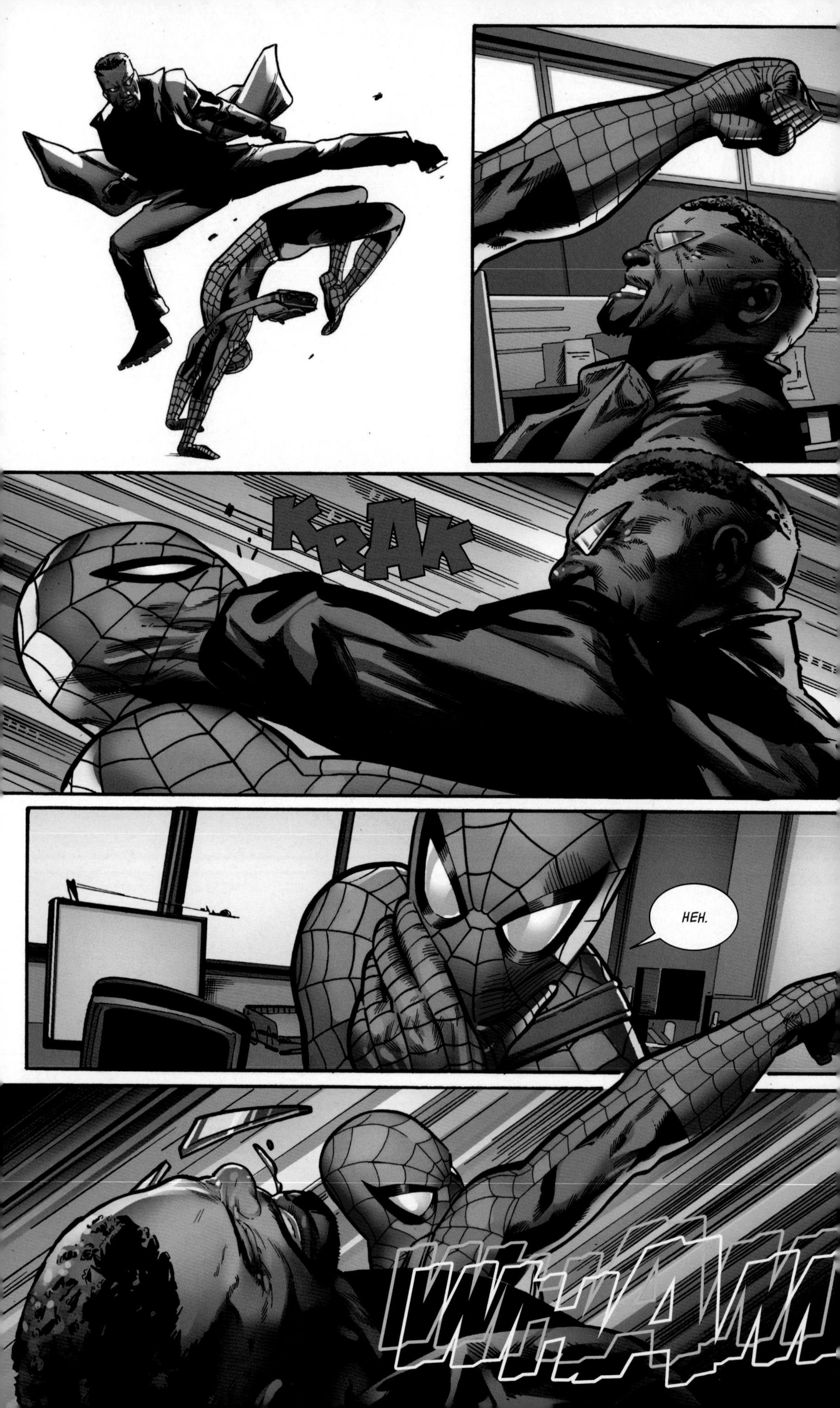
KRAK
HEH.

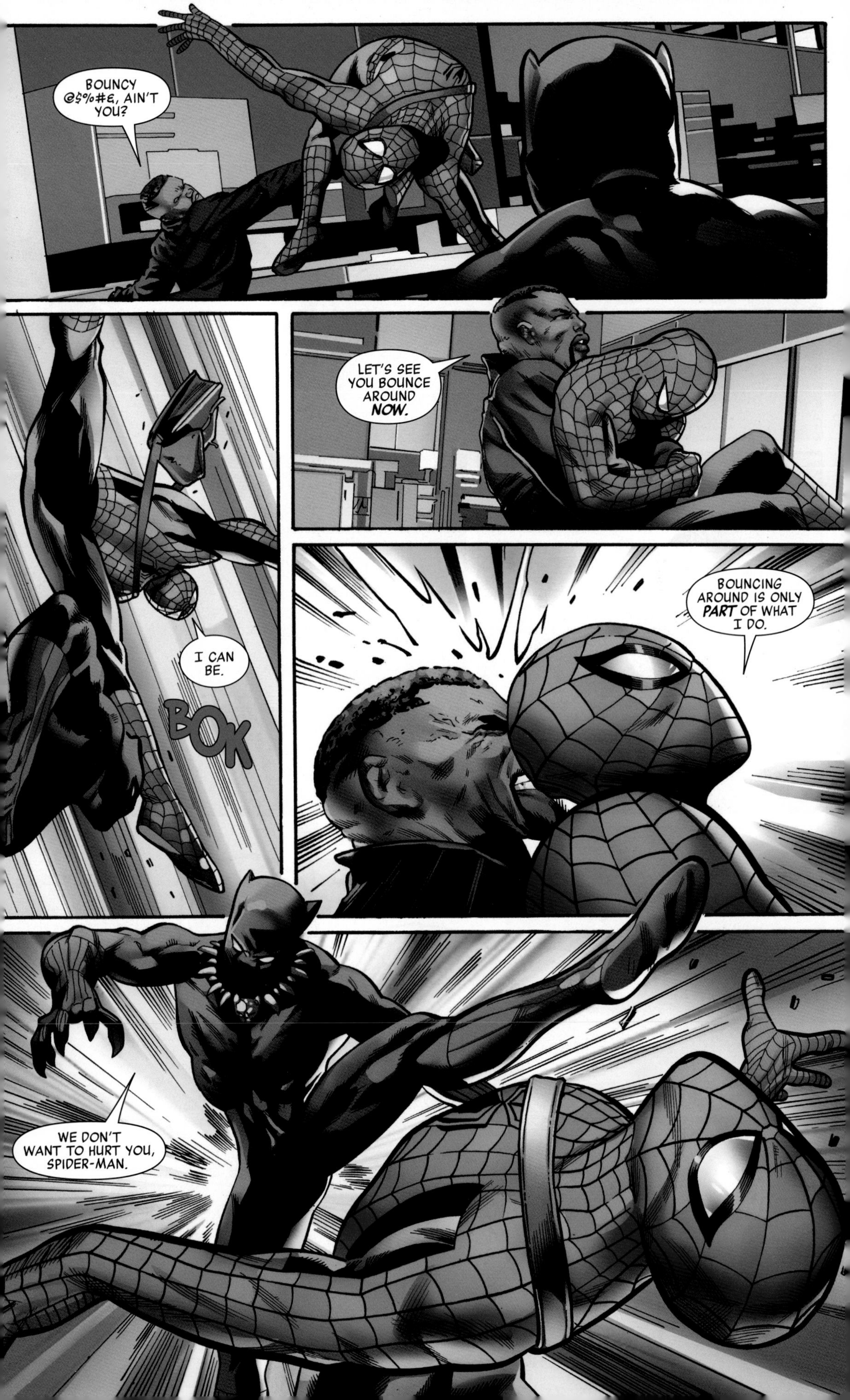
BOUNCY @$%#&, AIN'T YOU?
I CAN BE.
BOK
LET'S SEE YOU BOUNCE AROUND NOW.
BOUNCING AROUND IS ONLY PART OF WHAT I DO.
WE DON'T WANT TO HURT YOU, SPIDER-MAN.

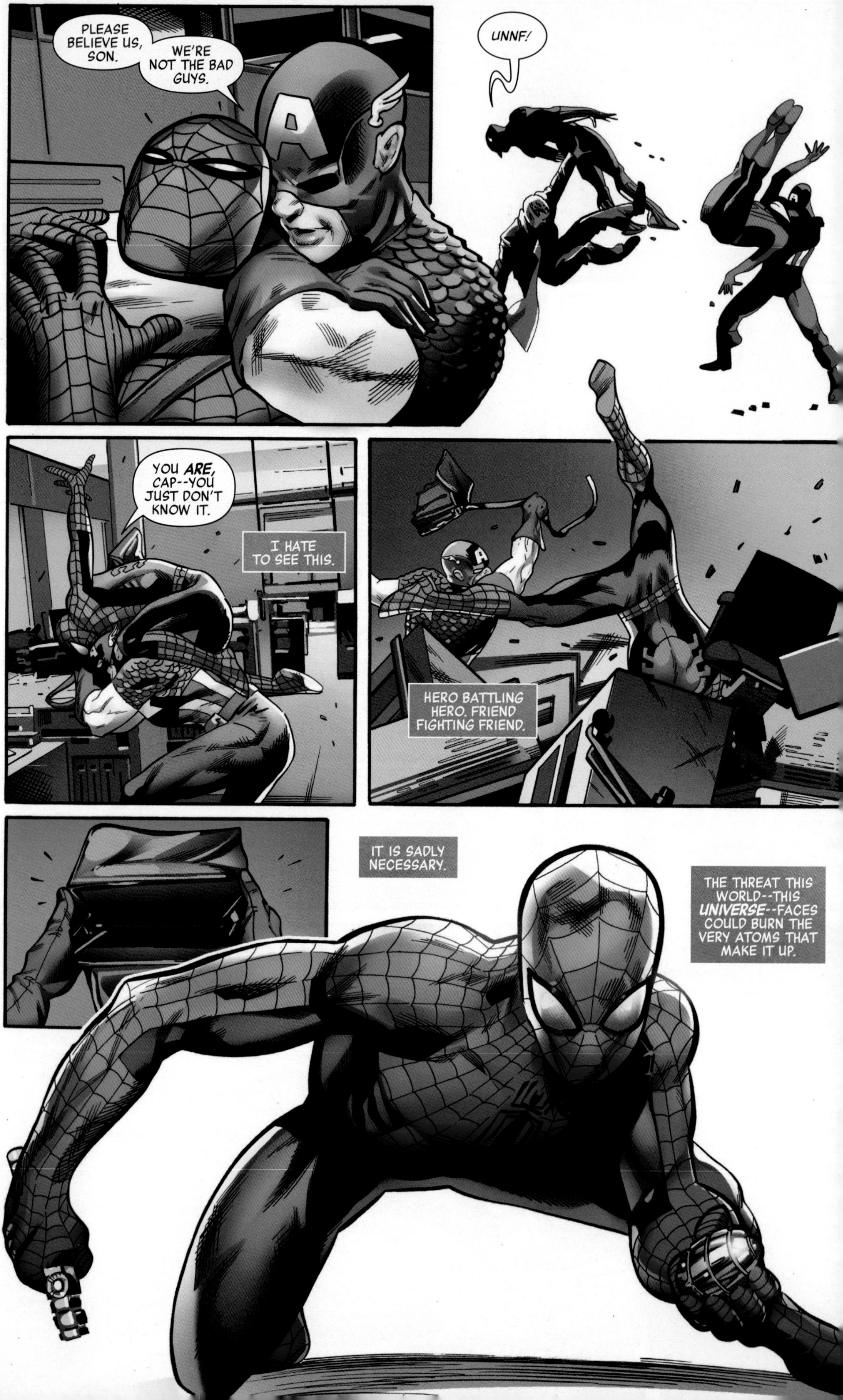
PLEASE BELIEVE US, SON.
WE'RE NOT THE BAD GUYS.
UNNF!
YOU **ARE,** CAP--YOU JUST DON'T KNOW IT.
I HATE TO SEE THIS.
HERO BATTLING HERO. FRIEND FIGHTING FRIEND.
IT IS SADLY NECESSARY.
THE THREAT THIS WORLD--THIS ***UNIVERSE***--FACES COULD BURN THE VERY ATOMS THAT MAKE IT UP.

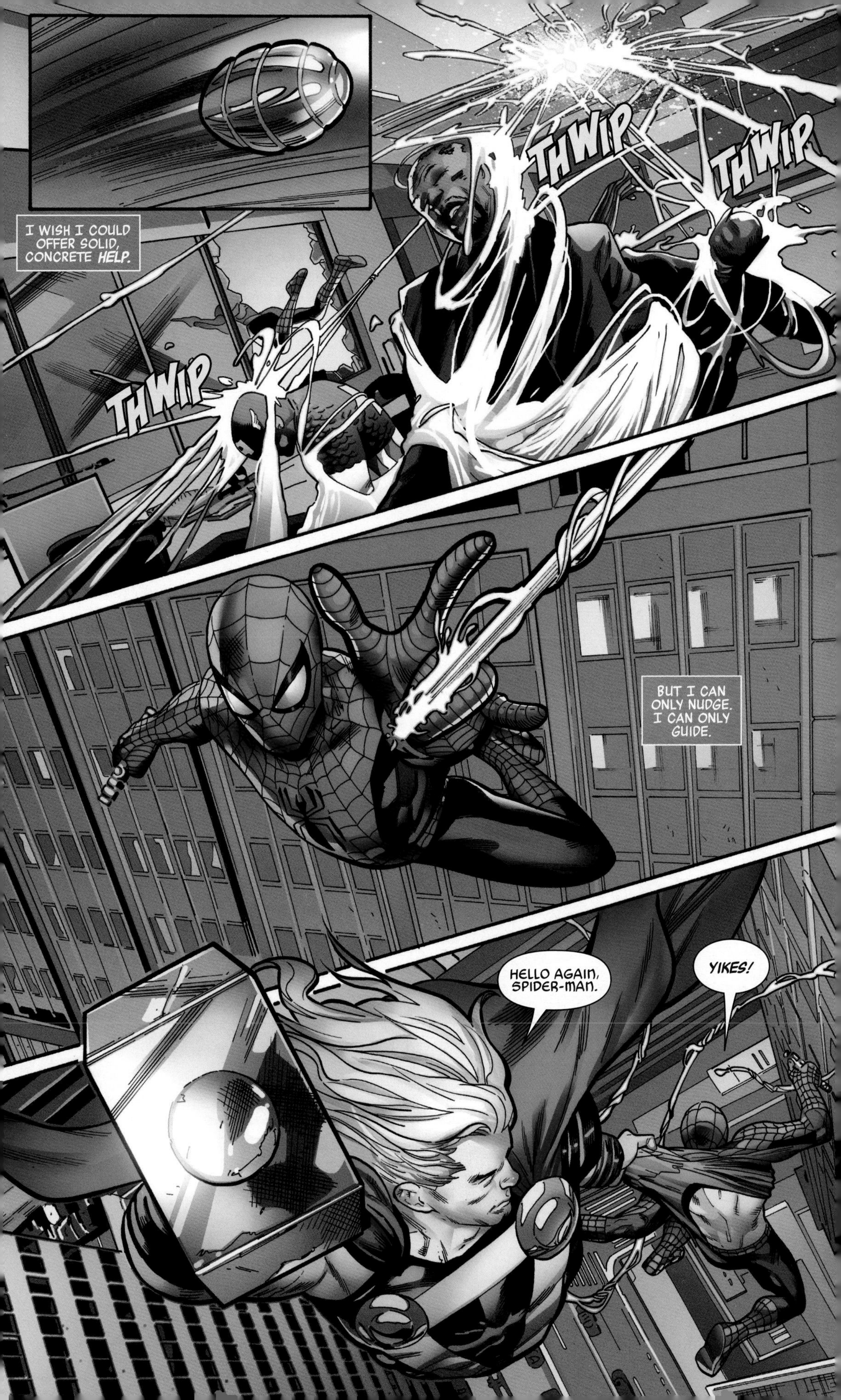
I WISH I COULD OFFER SOLID, CONCRETE HELP.
THWIP
THWIP
THWIP
BUT I CAN ONLY NUDGE. I CAN ONLY GUIDE.
HELLO AGAIN, SPIDER-MAN.
YIKES!

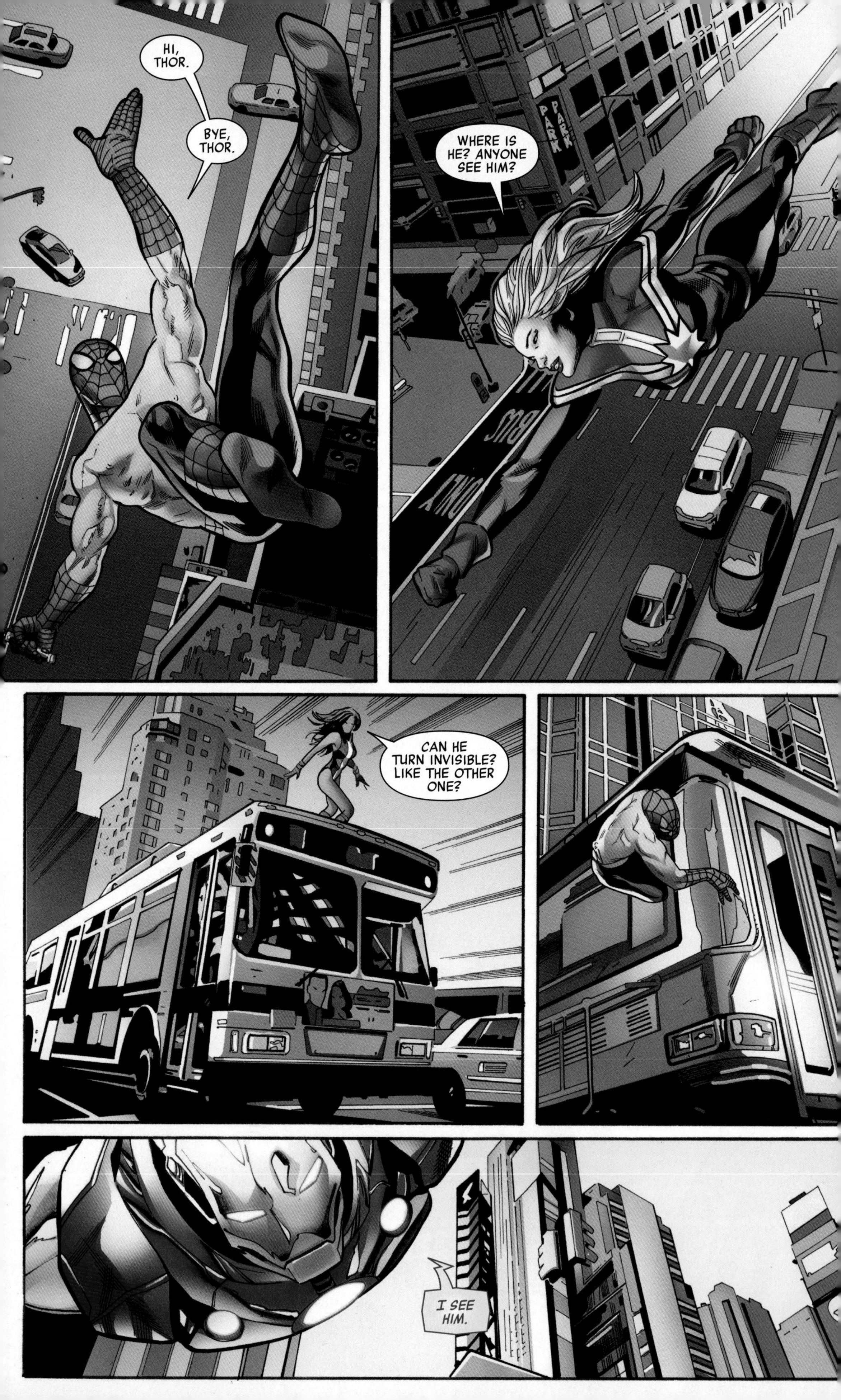
HI, THOR.
BYE, THOR.
WHERE IS HE? ANYONE SEE HIM?
PARK
CAN HE TURN INVISIBLE? LIKE THE OTHER ONE?
I SEE HIM.

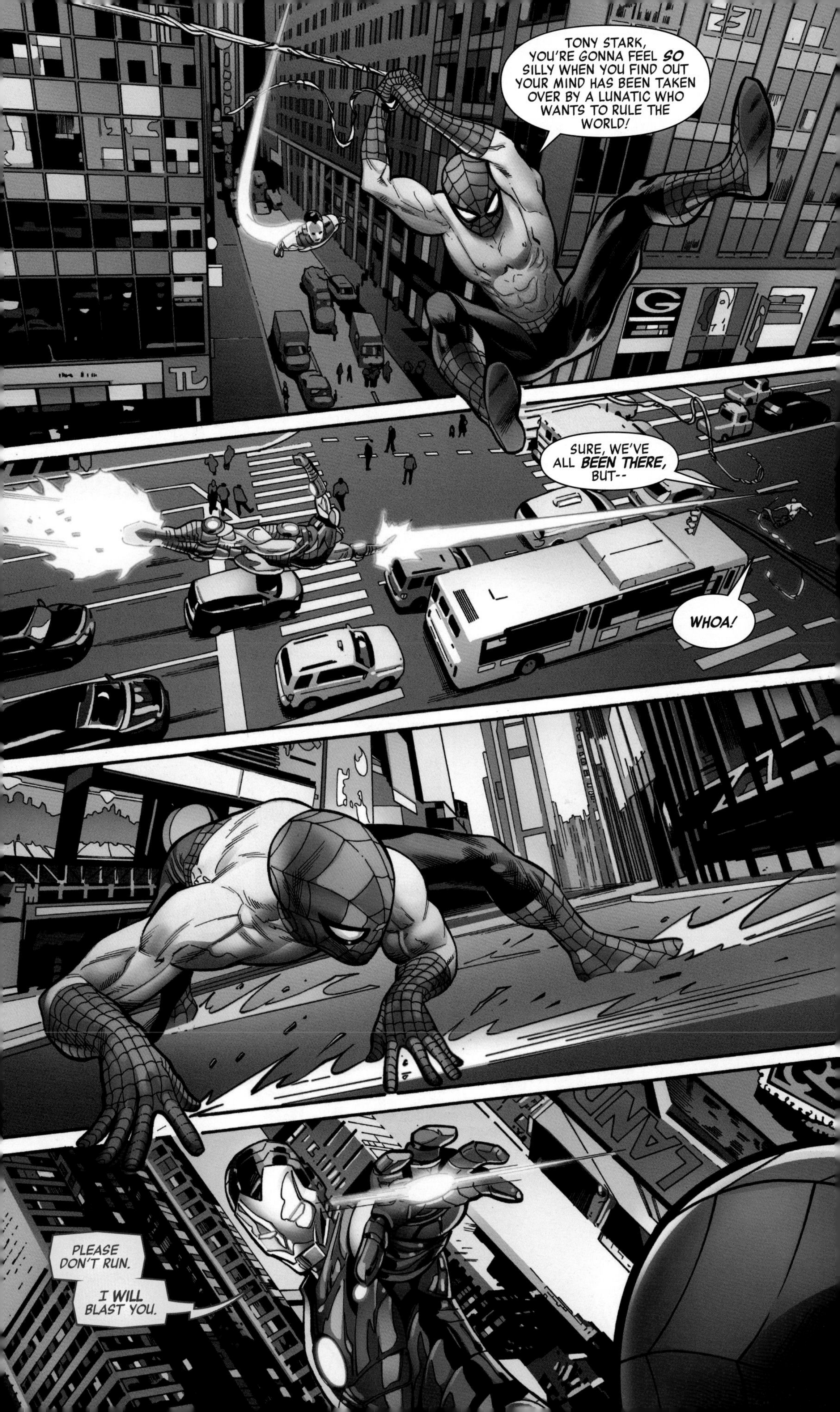
TONY STARK, YOU'RE GONNA FEEL SO SILLY WHEN YOU FIND OUT YOUR MIND HAS BEEN TAKEN OVER BY A LUNATIC WHO WANTS TO RULE THE WORLD!
SURE, WE'VE ALL BEEN THERE, BUT--
WHOA!
PLEASE DON'T RUN.
I WILL BLAST YOU.

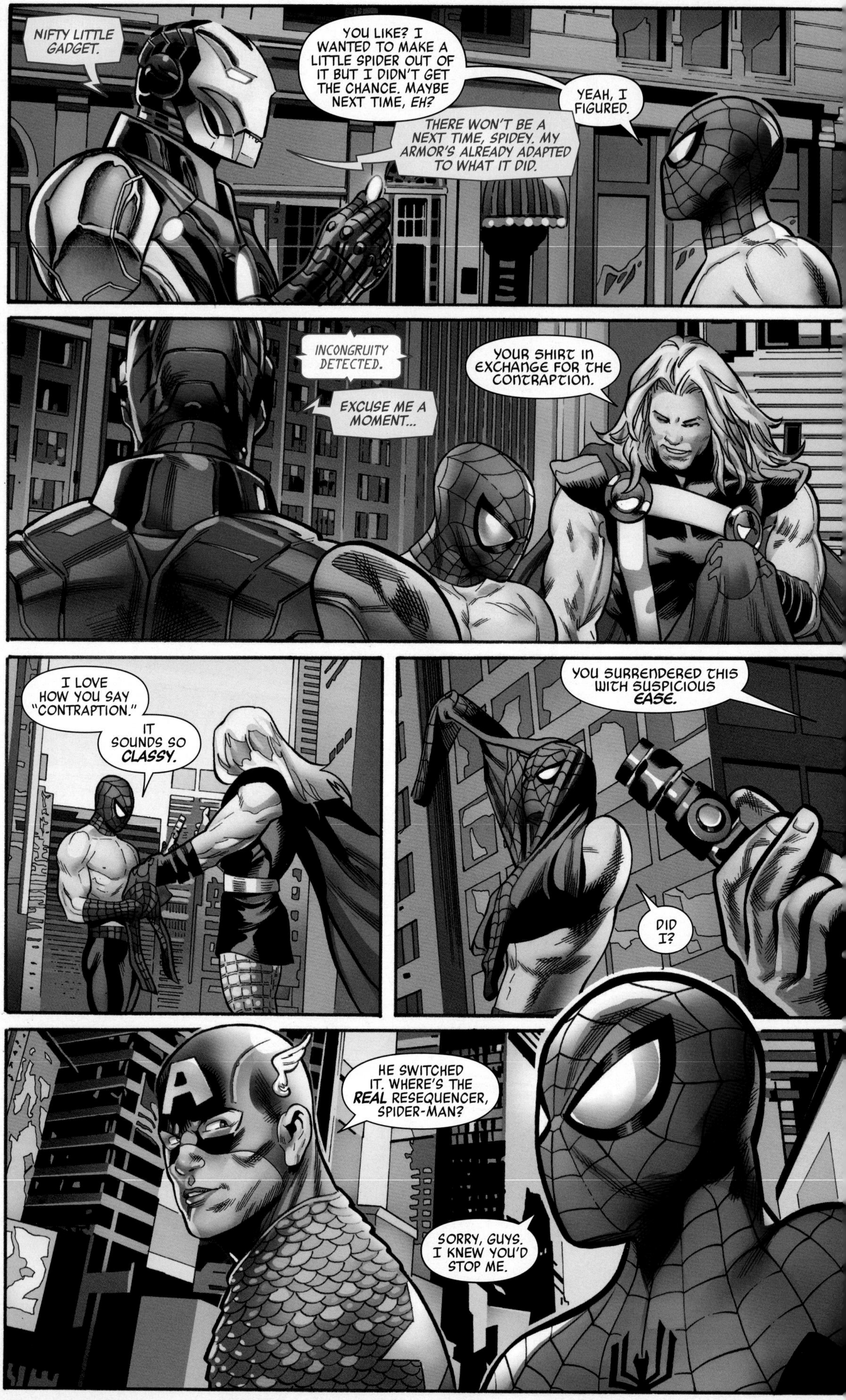
NIFTY LITTLE GADGET.
YOU LIKE? I WANTED TO MAKE A LITTLE SPIDER OUT OF IT BUT I DIDN'T GET THE CHANCE. MAYBE NEXT TIME, *EH?*
YEAH, I FIGURED.
THERE WON'T BE A NEXT TIME, SPIDEY. MY ARMOR'S ALREADY ADAPTED TO WHAT IT DID.
INCONGRUITY DETECTED.
EXCUSE ME A MOMENT...
YOUR SHIRT IN EXCHANGE FOR THE CONTRAPTION.
I LOVE HOW YOU SAY "CONTRAPTION."
IT SOUNDS SO ***CLASSY.***
YOU SURRENDERED THIS WITH SUSPICIOUS ***EASE.***
DID I?
HE SWITCHED IT. WHERE'S THE ***REAL*** RESEQUENCER, SPIDER-MAN?
SORRY, GUYS. I KNEW YOU'D STOP ME.

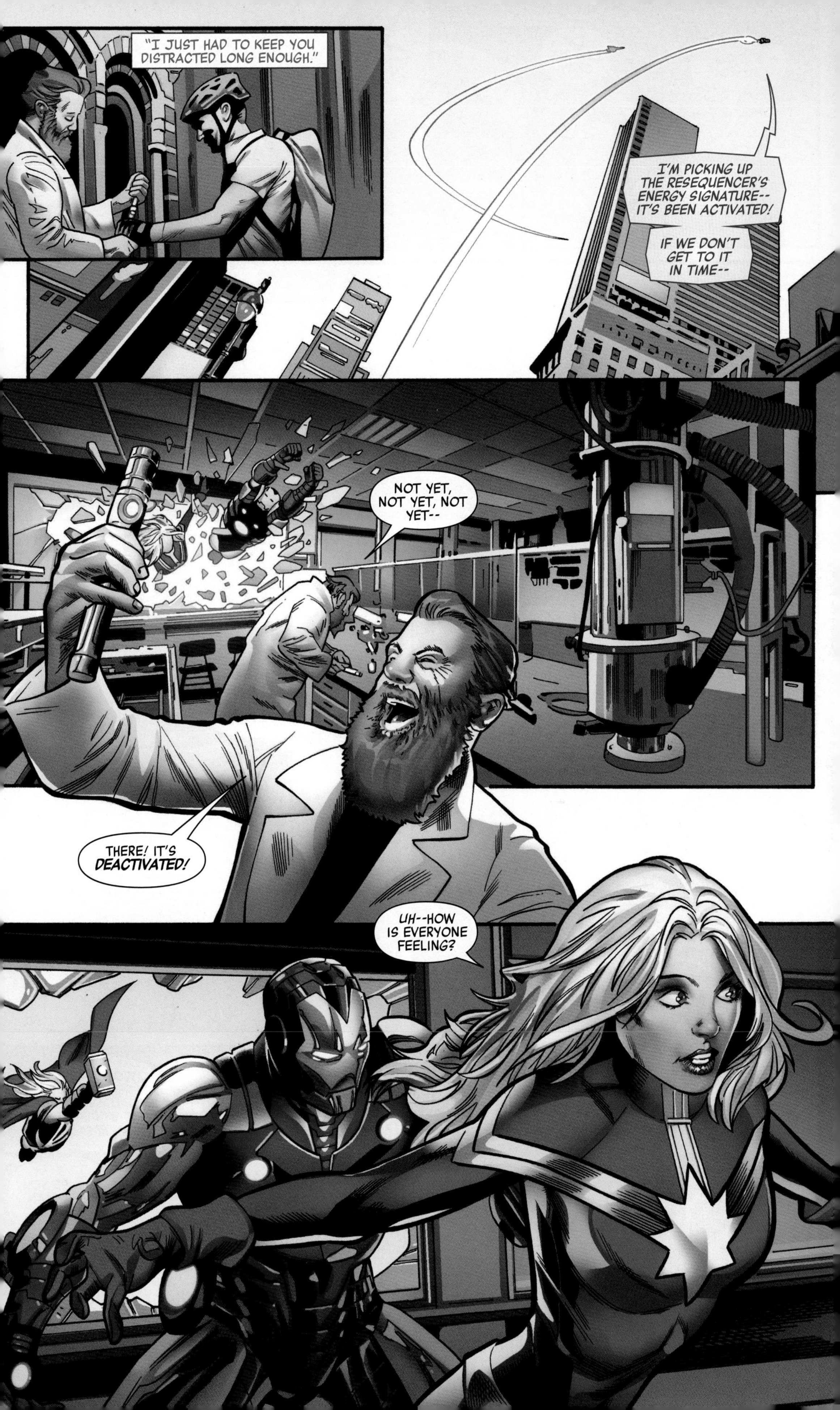
"I JUST HAD TO KEEP YOU DISTRACTED LONG ENOUGH."
I'M PICKING UP THE RESEQUENCER'S ENERGY SIGNATURE-- IT'S BEEN ACTIVATED!
IF WE DON'T GET TO IT IN TIME--
NOT YET, NOT YET, NOT YET--
THERE! IT'S DEACTIVATED!
UH--HOW IS EVERYONE FEELING?

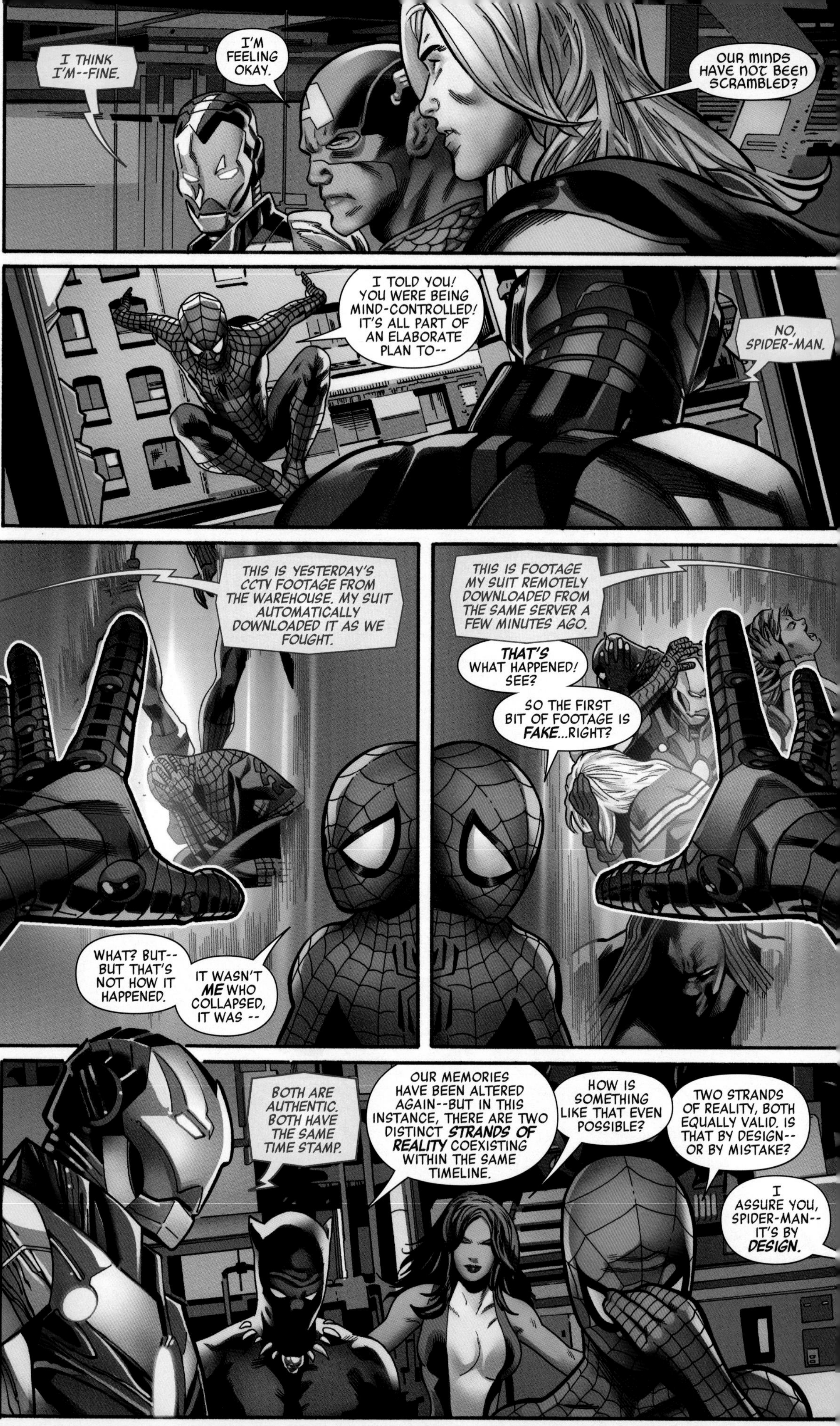
I THINK I'M--FINE.
I'M FEELING OKAY.
OUR MINDS HAVE NOT BEEN SCRAMBLED?
I TOLD YOU! YOU WERE BEING MIND-CONTROLLED! IT'S ALL PART OF AN ELABORATE PLAN TO--
NO, SPIDER-MAN.
THIS IS YESTERDAY'S CCTV FOOTAGE FROM THE WAREHOUSE. MY SUIT AUTOMATICALLY DOWNLOADED IT AS WE FOUGHT.
WHAT? BUT-- BUT THAT'S NOT HOW IT HAPPENED.
IT WASN'T ME WHO COLLAPSED, IT WAS --
THIS IS FOOTAGE MY SUIT REMOTELY DOWNLOADED FROM THE SAME SERVER A FEW MINUTES AGO.
THAT'S WHAT HAPPENED! SEE?
SO THE FIRST BIT OF FOOTAGE IS FAKE...RIGHT?
BOTH ARE AUTHENTIC. BOTH HAVE THE SAME TIME STAMP.
OUR MEMORIES HAVE BEEN ALTERED AGAIN--BUT IN THIS INSTANCE, THERE ARE TWO DISTINCT STRANDS OF REALITY COEXISTING WITHIN THE SAME TIMELINE.
HOW IS SOMETHING LIKE THAT EVEN POSSIBLE?
TWO STRANDS OF REALITY, BOTH EQUALLY VALID. IS THAT BY DESIGN-- OR BY MISTAKE?
I ASSURE YOU, SPIDER-MAN-- IT'S BY DESIGN.

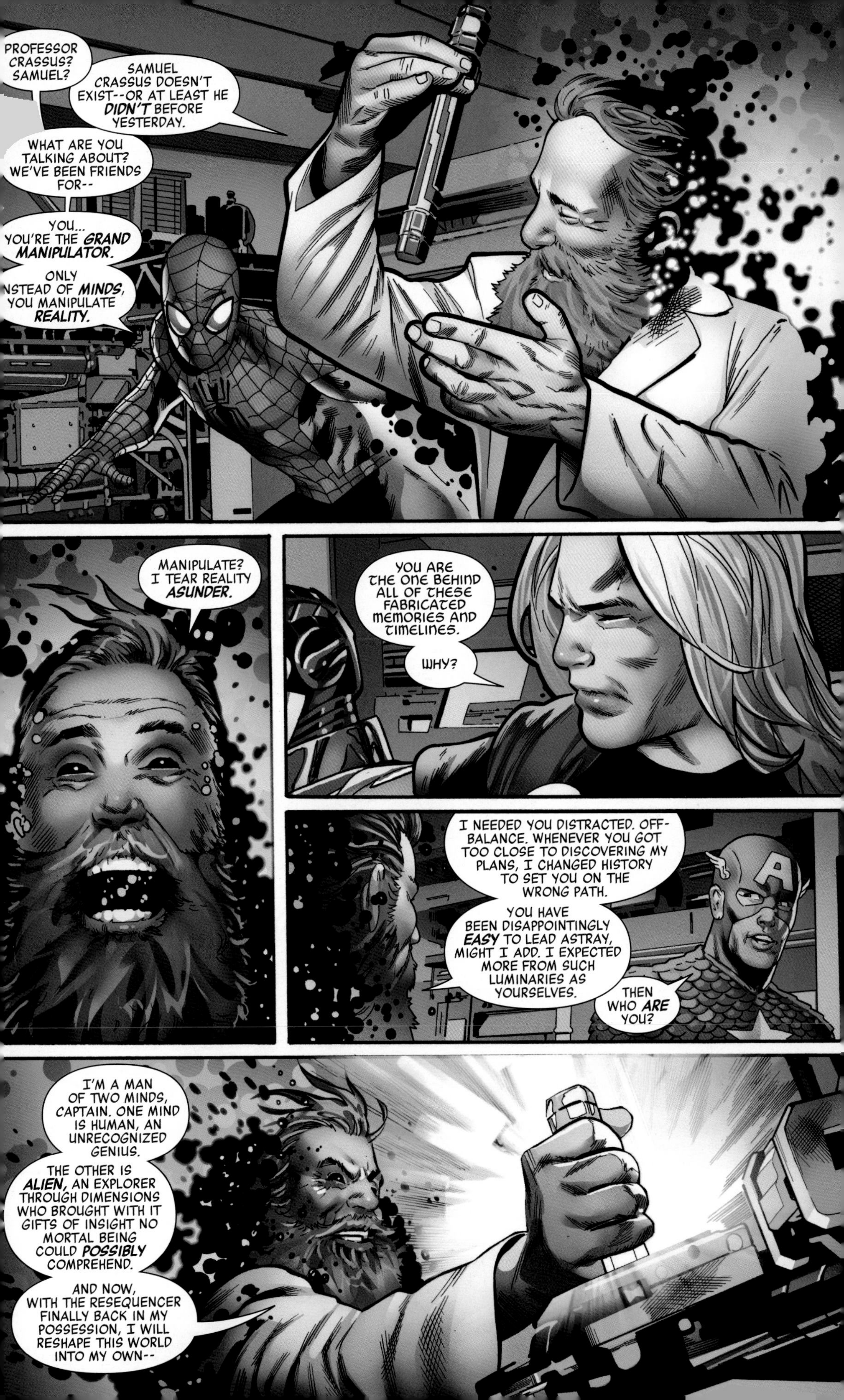
PROFESSOR CRASSUS? SAMUEL?
SAMUEL CRASSUS DOESN'T EXIST--OR AT LEAST HE DIDN'T BEFORE YESTERDAY.
WHAT ARE YOU TALKING ABOUT? WE'VE BEEN FRIENDS FOR--
YOU... YOU'RE THE GRAND MANIPULATOR.
ONLY NSTEAD OF MINDS, YOU MANIPULATE REALITY.
MANIPULATE? I TEAR REALITY ASUNDER.
YOU ARE THE ONE BEHIND ALL OF THESE FABRICATED MEMORIES AND TIMELINES.
WHY?
I NEEDED YOU DISTRACTED. OFF-BALANCE. WHENEVER YOU GOT TOO CLOSE TO DISCOVERING MY PLANS, I CHANGED HISTORY TO SET YOU ON THE WRONG PATH.
YOU HAVE BEEN DISAPPOINTINGLY EASY TO LEAD ASTRAY, MIGHT I ADD. I EXPECTED MORE FROM SUCH LUMINARIES AS YOURSELVES.
THEN WHO ARE YOU?
I'M A MAN OF TWO MINDS, CAPTAIN. ONE MIND IS HUMAN, AN UNRECOGNIZED GENIUS.
THE OTHER IS ALIEN, AN EXPLORER THROUGH DIMENSIONS WHO BROUGHT WITH IT GIFTS OF INSIGHT NO MORTAL BEING COULD POSSIBLY COMPREHEND.
AND NOW, WITH THE RESEQUENCER FINALLY BACK IN MY POSSESSION, I WILL RESHAPE THIS WORLD INTO MY OWN--

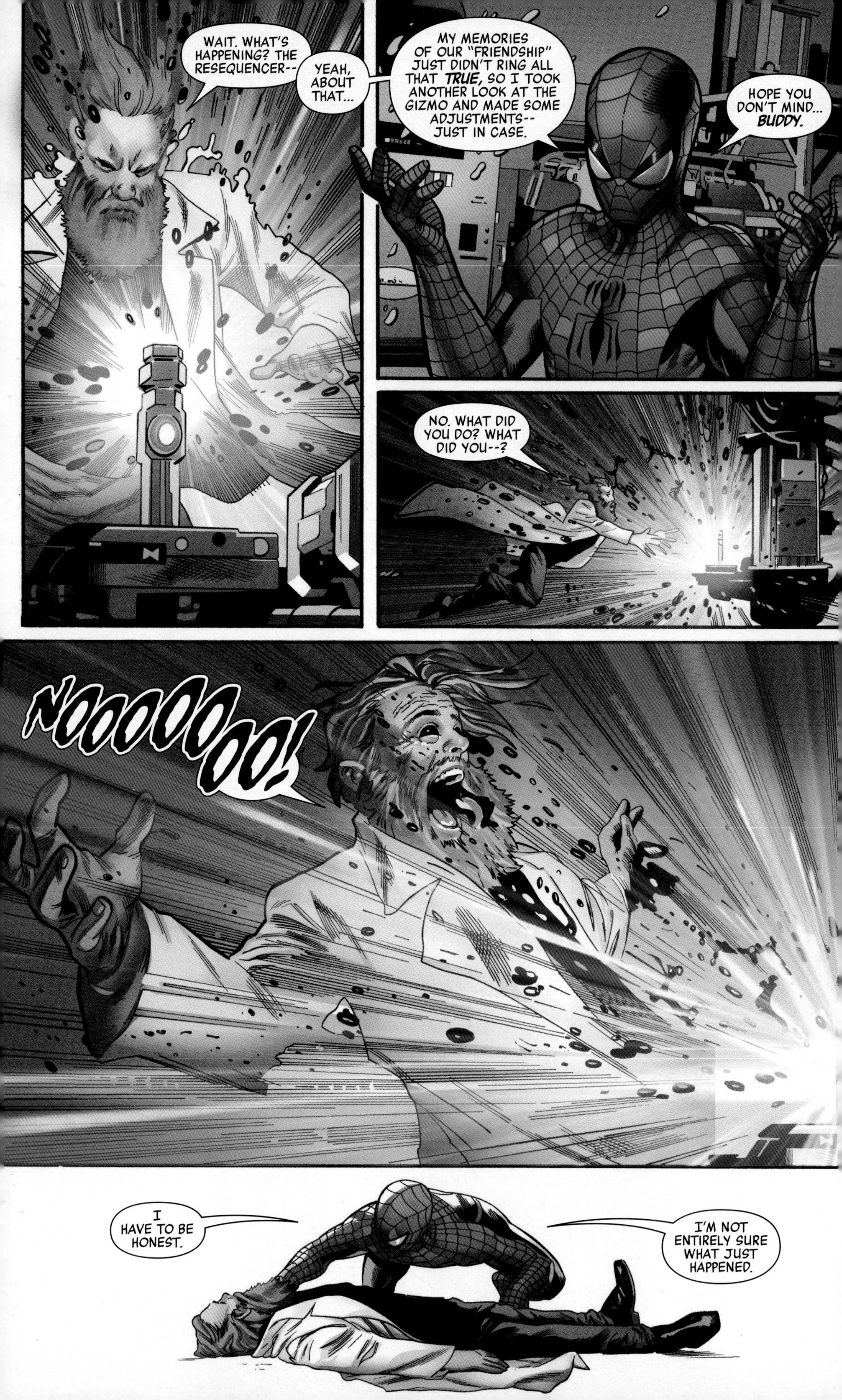
WAIT. WHAT'S HAPPENING? THE RESEQUENCER--
YEAH, ABOUT THAT...
MY MEMORIES OF OUR "FRIENDSHIP" JUST DIDN'T RING ALL THAT TRUE, SO I TOOK ANOTHER LOOK AT THE GIZMO AND MADE SOME ADJUSTMENTS-- JUST IN CASE.
HOPE YOU DON'T MIND... BUDDY.
NO. WHAT DID YOU DO? WHAT DID YOU--?
NOOOOOOO!
I HAVE TO BE HONEST.
I'M NOT ENTIRELY SURE WHAT JUST HAPPENED.

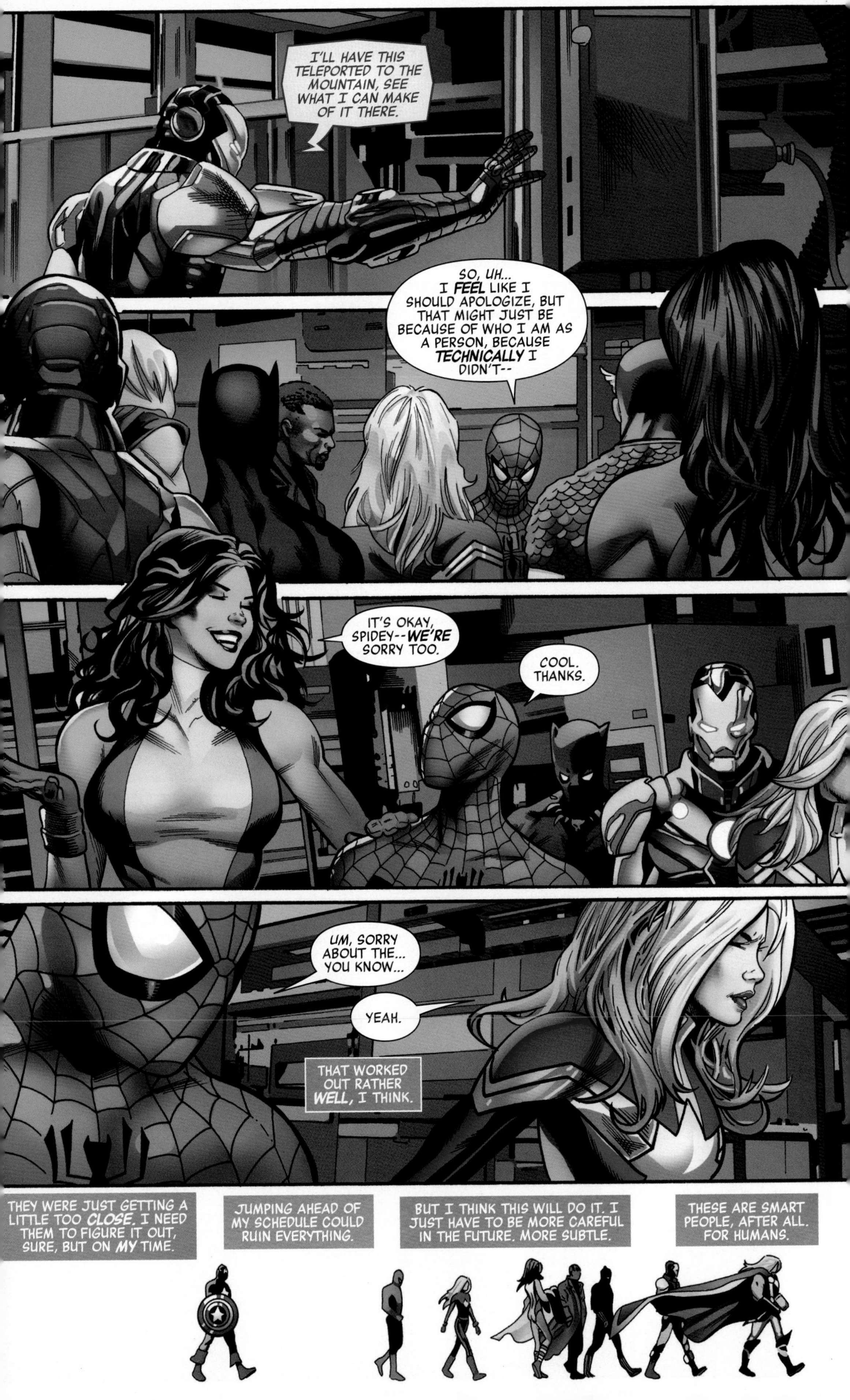

I'LL HAVE THIS TELEPORTED TO THE MOUNTAIN, SEE WHAT I CAN MAKE OF IT THERE.
SO, UH... I FEEL LIKE I SHOULD APOLOGIZE, BUT THAT MIGHT JUST BE BECAUSE OF WHO I AM AS A PERSON, BECAUSE TECHNICALLY I DIDN'T--
IT'S OKAY, SPIDEY--WE'RE SORRY TOO.
COOL. THANKS.
UM, SORRY ABOUT THE... YOU KNOW...
YEAH.
THAT WORKED OUT RATHER WELL, I THINK.
THEY WERE JUST GETTING A LITTLE TOO CLOSE. I NEED THEM TO FIGURE IT OUT, SURE, BUT ON MY TIME.
JUMPING AHEAD OF MY SCHEDULE COULD RUIN EVERYTHING.
BUT I THINK THIS WILL DO IT. I JUST HAVE TO BE MORE CAREFUL IN THE FUTURE. MORE SUBTLE.
THESE ARE SMART PEOPLE, AFTER ALL. FOR HUMANS.

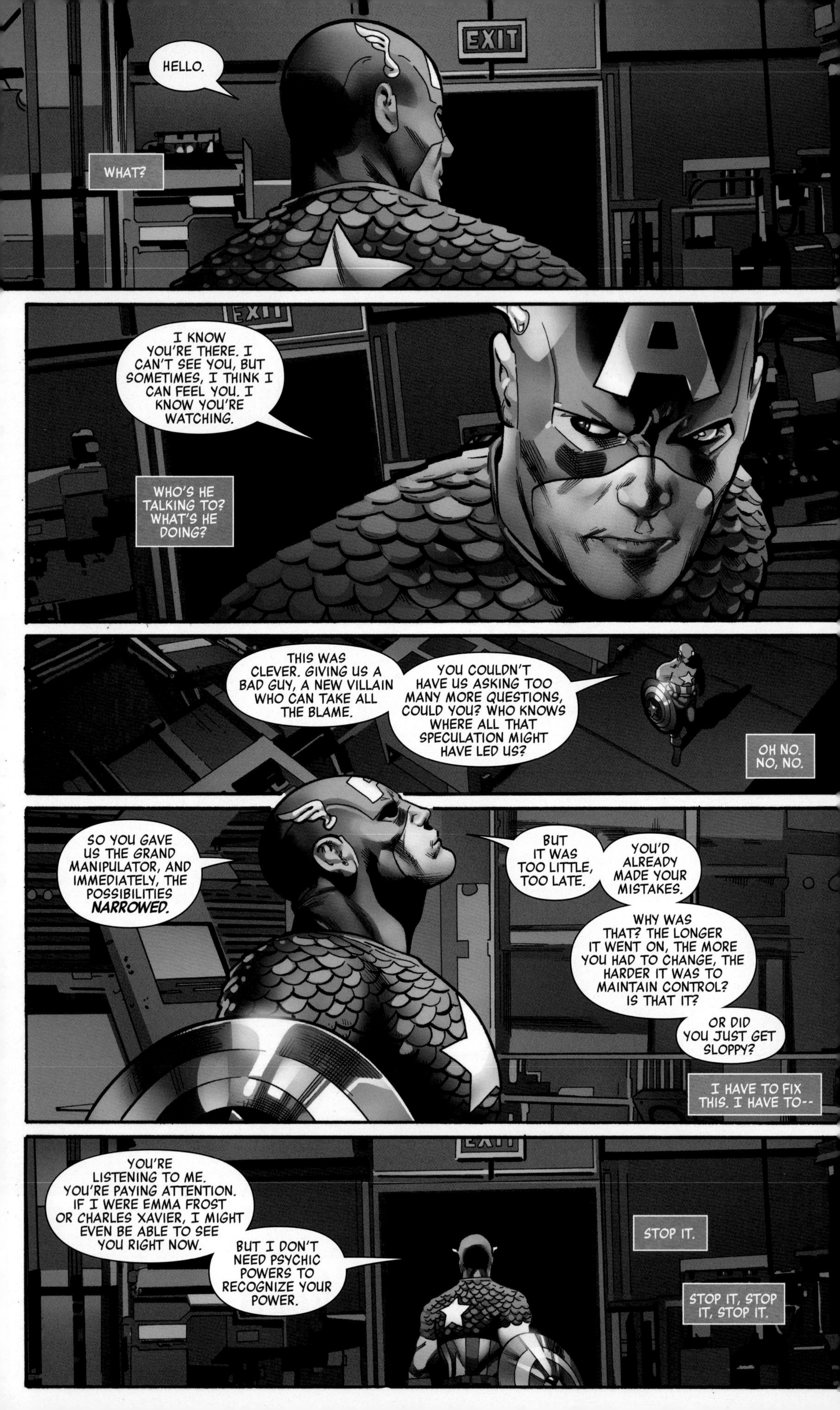

EXIT
HELLO.
WHAT?
I KNOW YOU'RE THERE. I CAN'T SEE YOU, BUT SOMETIMES, I THINK I CAN FEEL YOU. I KNOW YOU'RE WATCHING.
WHO'S HE TALKING TO? WHAT'S HE DOING?
THIS WAS CLEVER. GIVING US A BAD GUY, A NEW VILLAIN WHO CAN TAKE ALL THE BLAME.
YOU COULDN'T HAVE US ASKING TOO MANY MORE QUESTIONS, COULD YOU? WHO KNOWS WHERE ALL THAT SPECULATION MIGHT HAVE LED US?
OH NO. NO, NO.
SO YOU GAVE US THE GRAND MANIPULATOR, AND IMMEDIATELY, THE POSSIBILITIES ***NARROWED.***
BUT IT WAS TOO LITTLE, TOO LATE.
YOU'D ALREADY MADE YOUR MISTAKES.
WHY WAS THAT? THE LONGER IT WENT ON, THE MORE YOU HAD TO CHANGE, THE HARDER IT WAS TO MAINTAIN CONTROL? IS THAT IT?
OR DID YOU JUST GET SLOPPY?
I HAVE TO FIX THIS. I HAVE TO--
YOU'RE LISTENING TO ME. YOU'RE PAYING ATTENTION. IF I WERE EMMA FROST OR CHARLES XAVIER, I MIGHT EVEN BE ABLE TO SEE YOU RIGHT NOW.
BUT I DON'T NEED PSYCHIC POWERS TO RECOGNIZE YOUR POWER.
STOP IT.
STOP IT, STOP IT, STOP IT.

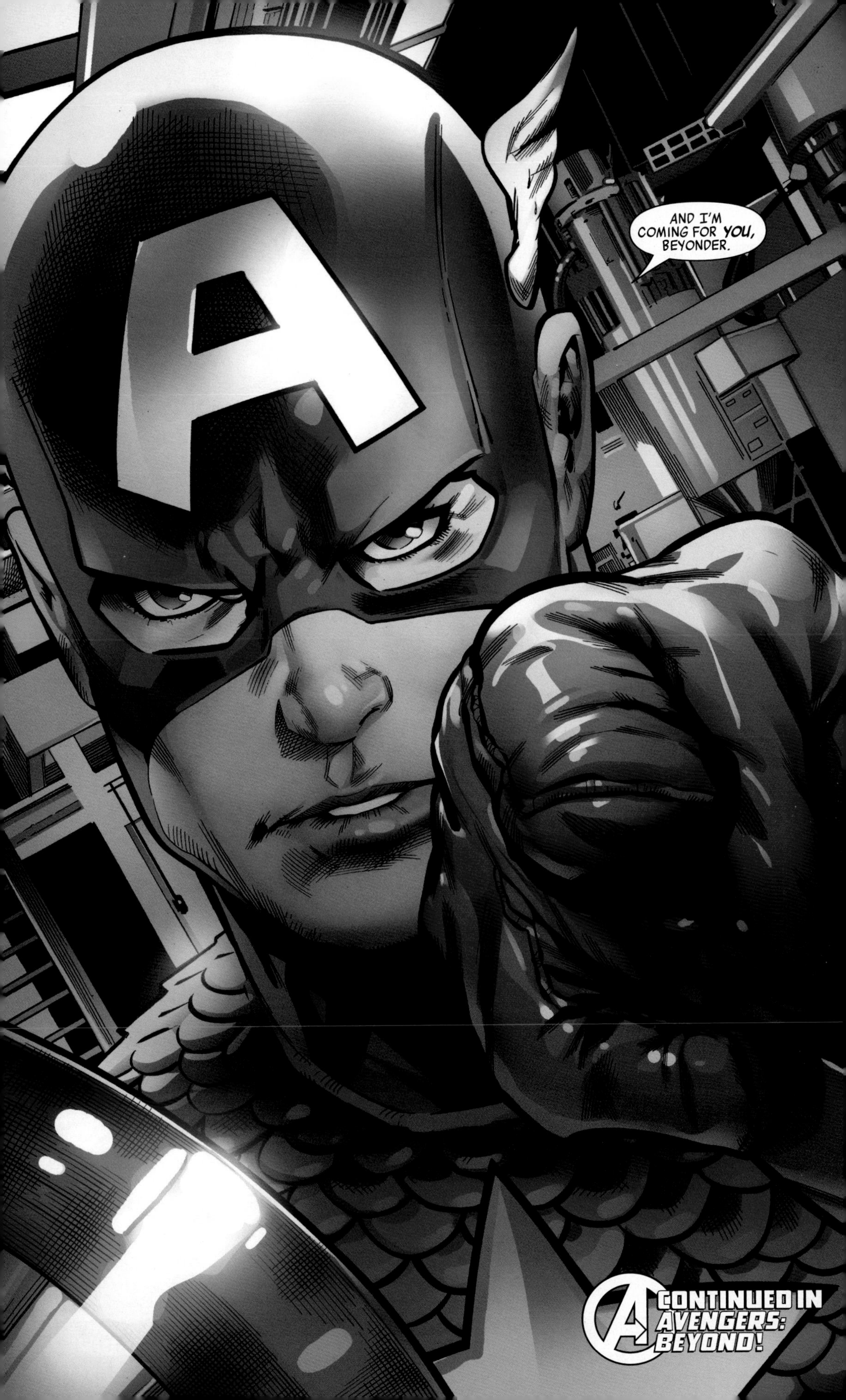
AND I'M COMING FOR YOU, BEYONDER.
CONTINUED IN AVENGERS: BEYOND!

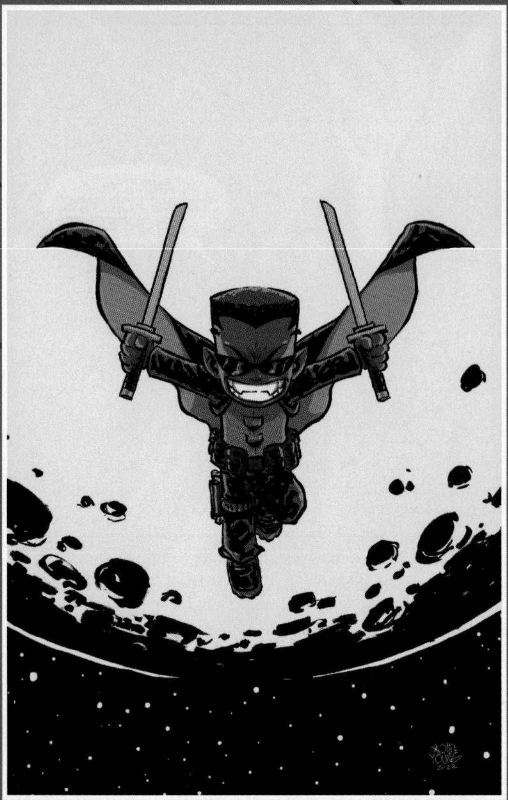

SKOTTIE YOUNG
#1 VARIANT

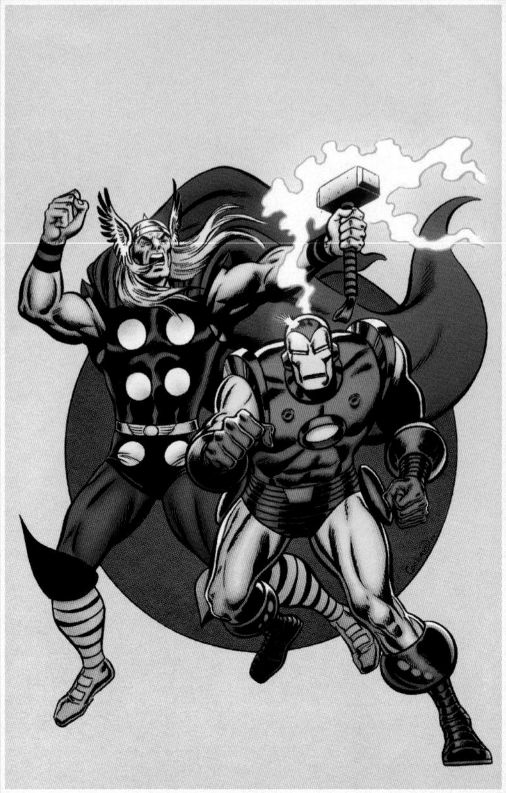

DAVE COCKRUM & MORRY HOLLOWE
#1 HIDDEN GEM VARIANT

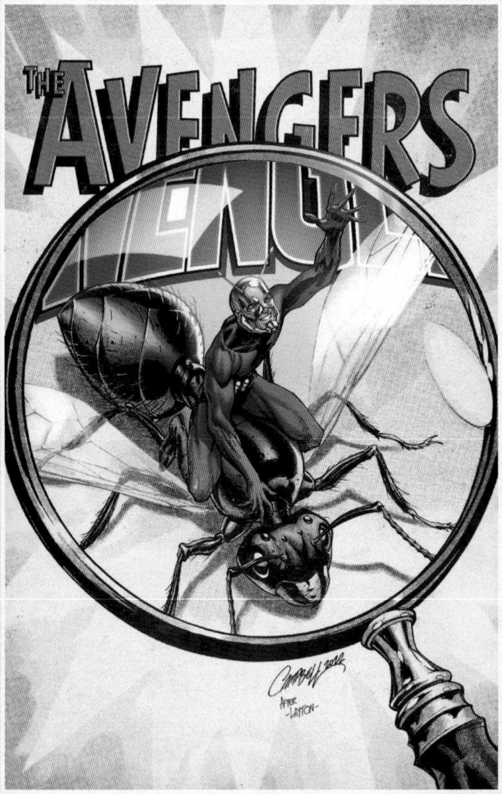
THE AVENGERS

J. SCOTT CAMPBELL & SABINE RICH
#1 ANNIVERSARY VARIANT

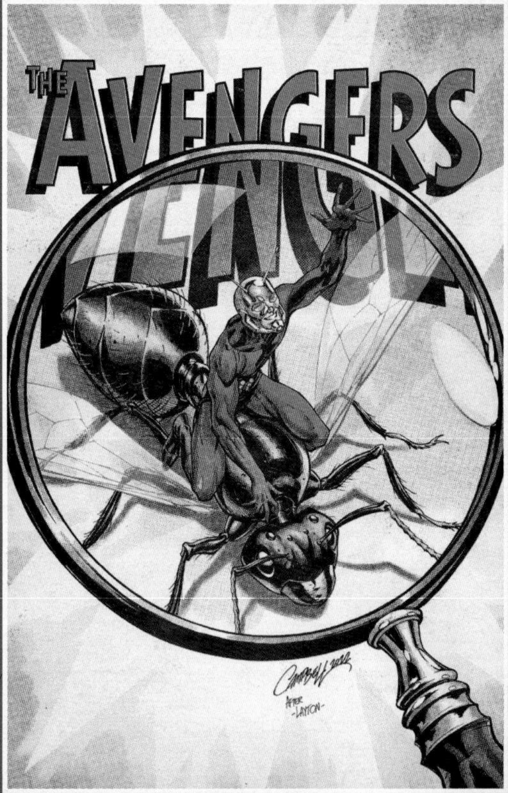
THE AVENGERS

J. SCOTT CAMPBELL & SABINE RICH
#1 RETRO VARIANT

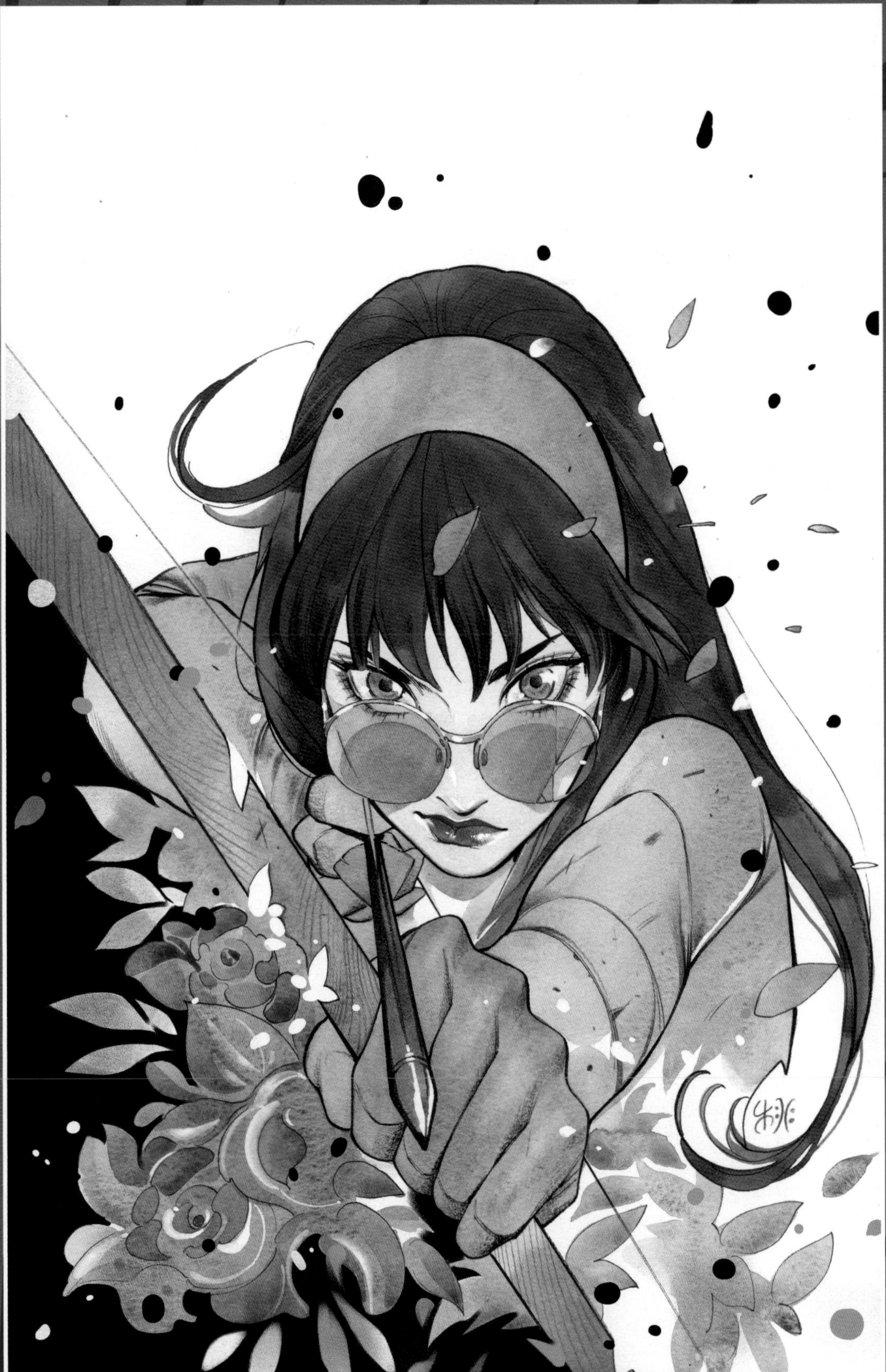

PEACH MOMOKO
#2 VARIANT

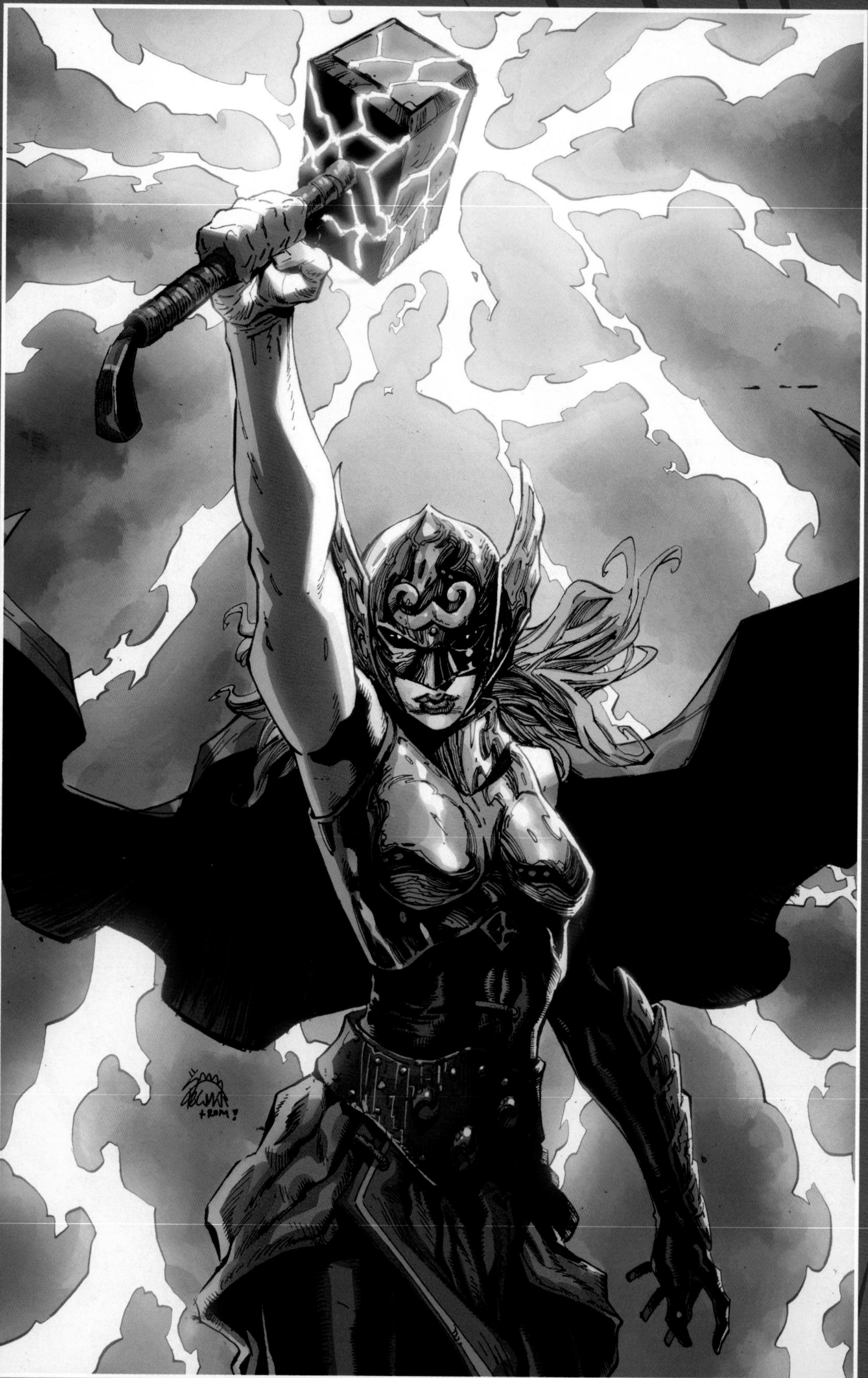

RYAN STEGMAN & **ROMULO FAJARDO JR.**
#2 VARIANT

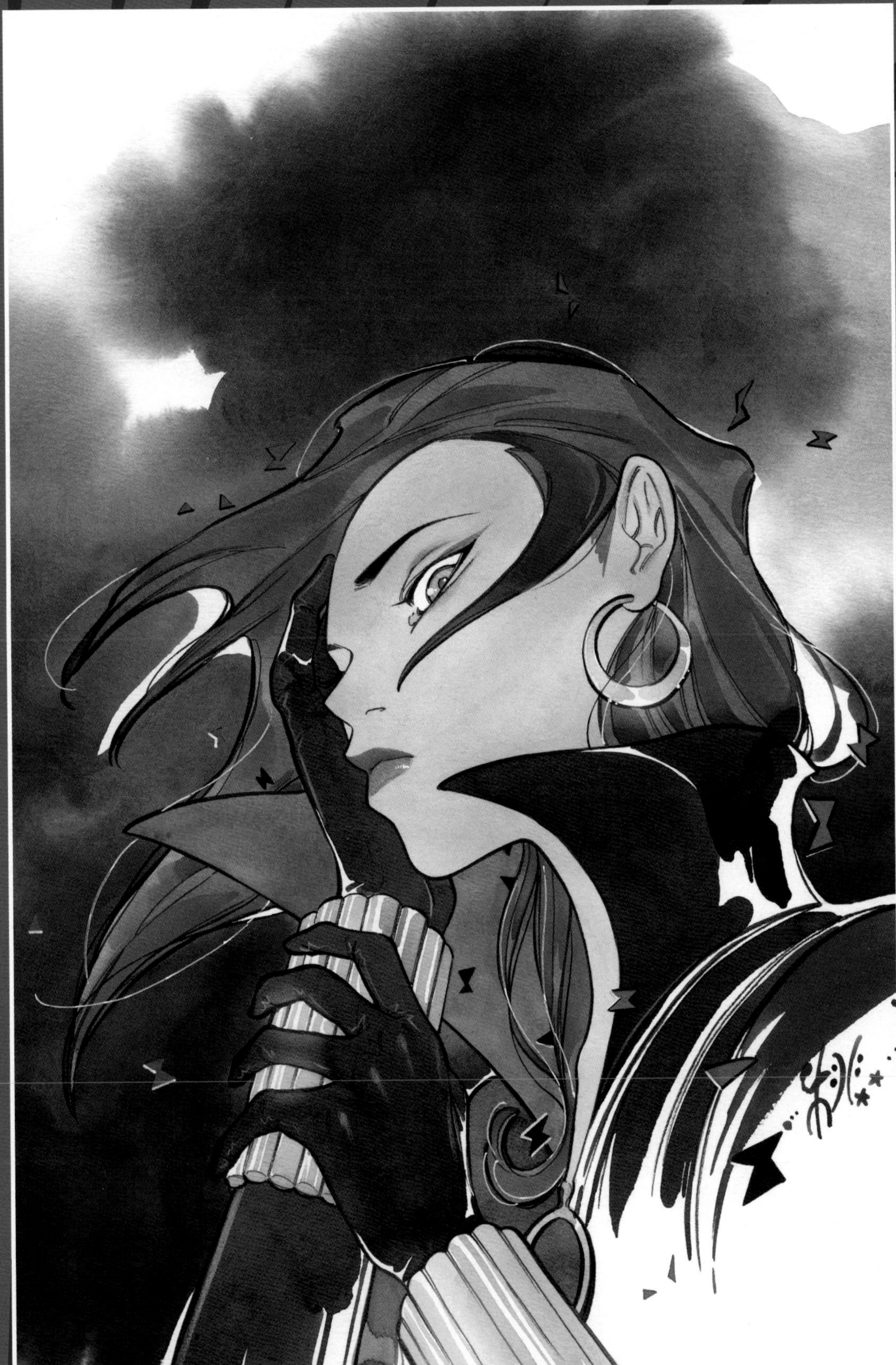

PEACH MOMOKO
#3 VARIANT

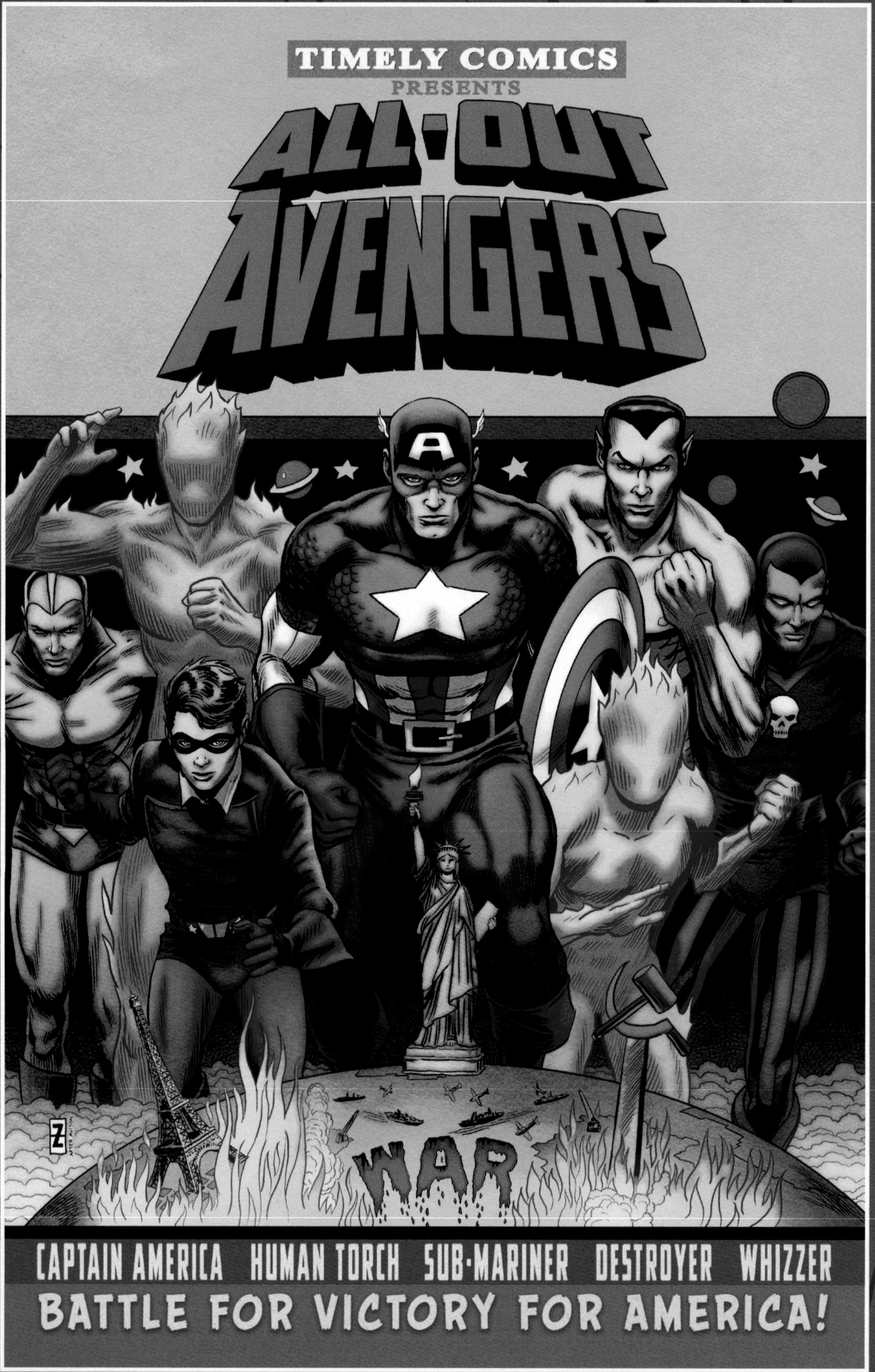
TIMELY COMICS
PRESENTS
ALL-OUT AVENGERS
WAR
CAPTAIN AMERICA HUMAN TORCH SUB-MARINER DESTROYER WHIZZER
BATTLE FOR VICTORY FOR AMERICA!

PATCH ZIRCHER & MORRY HOLLOWELL
#3 TIMELY COMICS VARIANT

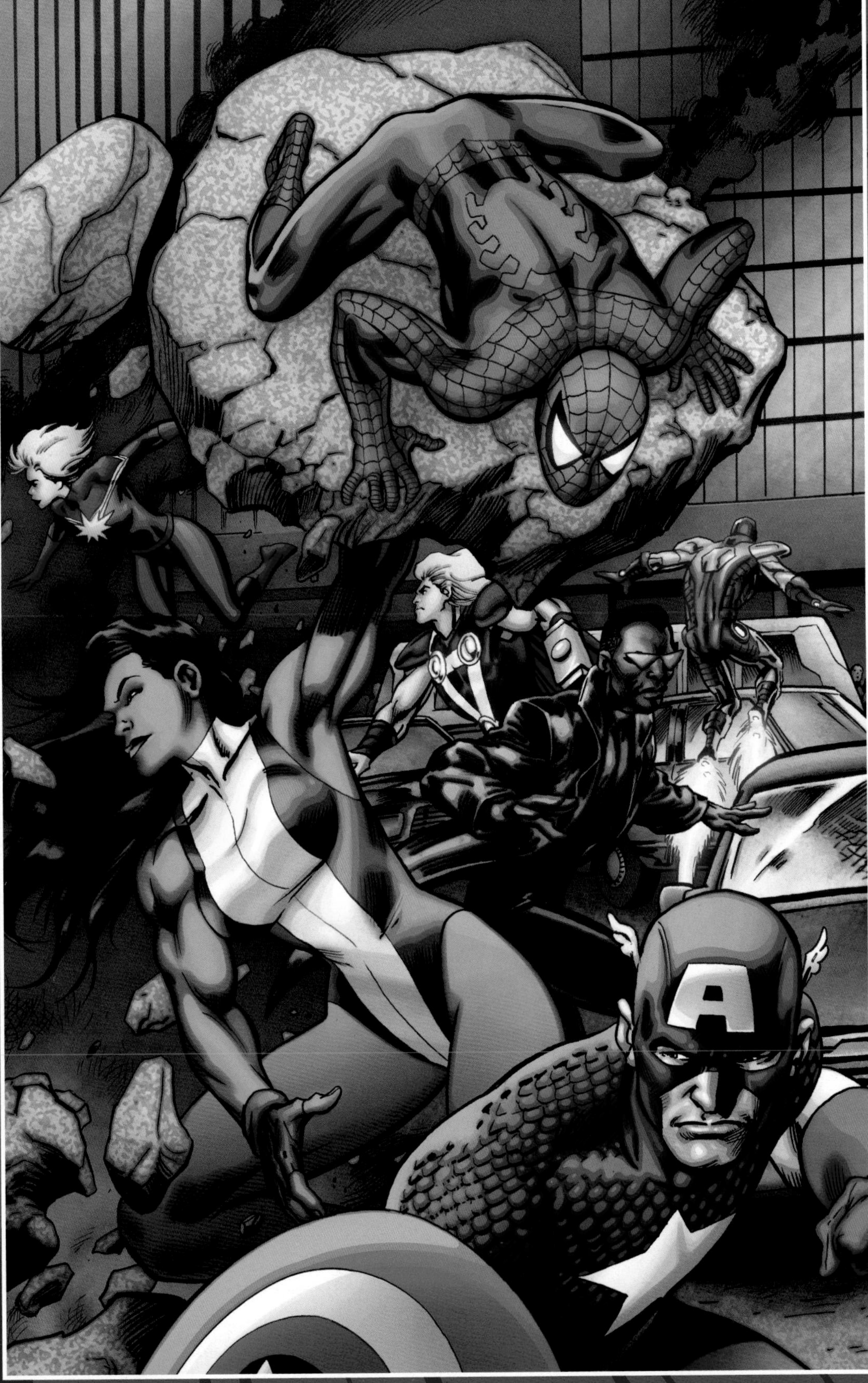

ALAN DAVIS & MORRY HOLLOWELL
#5 VARIANT

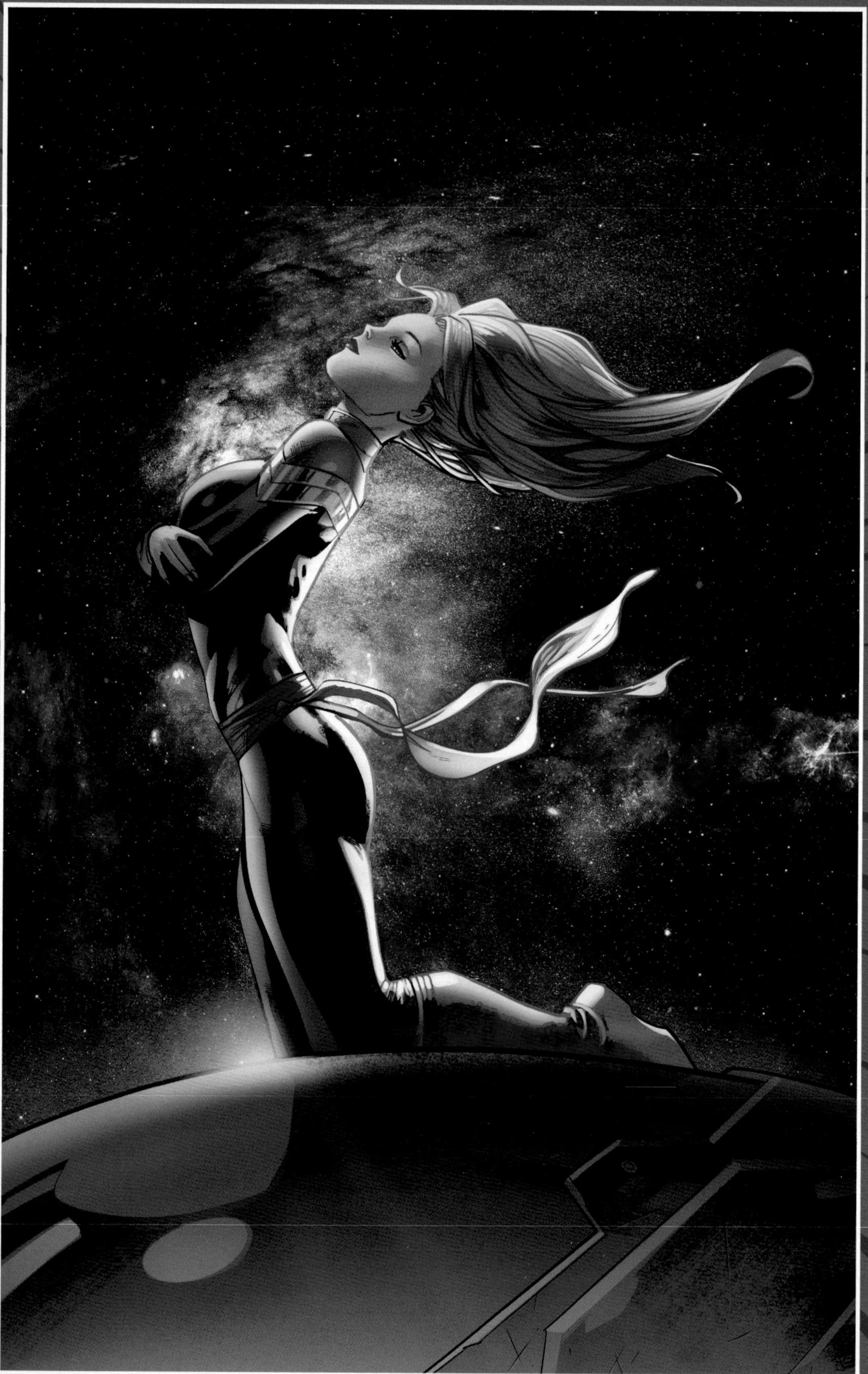

JAN BAZALDUA & **MARTE GRACIA**
#5 STORMBREAKERS VARIANT